Introduction to the Law of Treaties

A publication of the Graduate Institute of International Studies, Geneva

This translation was carried out with the financial assistance of the Fondation pour l'étude des relations internationales en Suisse (FERIS).

Introduction to the Law of Treaties

Paul Reuter

translated by José Mico
and Peter Haggenmacher

Pinter Publishers
London and New York

© Pinter Publishers 1989

English edition first published in Great Britain in 1989 by
Pinter Publishers Limited
25 Floral Street, London WC2E 9DS

This is a revised version of the second edition published in French in 1985
on behalf of the Graduate Institute of International Studies, Geneva, by
Presses Universitaires de France
108 boulevard Saint-Germain, 75006 Paris

(First edition in French published by Armand Colin, 1972)

British Library Cataloguing in Publication Data

A CIP catalogue record for this book is available from the British Library.

ISBN 0-86187-954-6

Library of Congress Cataloging-in-Publication Data

Reuter, Paul, 1911–
    [Introduction au droit des traités, English]
    Introduction to the law of treaties / Paul Reuter; translated by
José Mico.
       p.   cm. — (A Publication of the Graduate Institute of
International Studies, Geneva)
    Translation of: Introduction au droit des traités.
    ISBN 0-86187-954-6
    1. Treaties.   I. Title.   II. Series: Publications de l'Institut
universitaire des hautes études internationales, Genève.
JX4166.R4513   1989
341.3'7—dc20   69-22948
                                              CIP

Typeset by Saxon Printing Ltd, Derby
Printed and bound in Great Britain by Biddles Ltd, of Guildford and
King's Lynn

Contents

To make the text more readable, references and some additional material
have been included separately, at the end of each chapter. Each paragraph
ending with an asterisk (*) is completed by a corresponding paragraph of
notes bearing the same number.

Preface

Paul Reuter's *Introduction to the Law of Treaties,* first published in 1972 by Armand Colin in Paris, provides in-depth treatment of a standard topic of international law, as now codified and developed in the 1969 Vienna Convention on the Law of Treaties. Almost immediately the book became a classic. A second, updated French edition was published in 1985 on behalf of the Graduate Institute of International Studies, Geneva, by Presses Universitaires de France.

The Institute is proud to be able to present a new version of this classic of international law to English-speaking readers. We are confident that in its present form, the book will keep all of its old friends and win many new ones.

The preparation of the manuscript has, in many ways, been the result of a teamwork. Paul Reuter, currently a Visiting Professor at the Institute, is foremost among the members of the team since he had to accomplish the formidable task of revising and updating the French version of 1985. José Mico (Geneva) undertook to translate the book and to check the innumerable references. Peter Haggenmacher (Geneva) cooperated with him and made many valuable suggestions. Derek Bowett (Cambridge) and Nanette Pilkington (Paris) read the manuscript and presented useful suggestions for its improvement. Finally, thanks are due to Catherine Nedzynski (Geneva) who undertook the difficult task of coordinating the efforts of the team and of seeing the manuscript through.

Geneva, February 1989   *Lucius Caflisch*

Abbreviations

AF	*Annuaire français de Droit international*
AJ	*American Journal of International Law*
BYBIL	*British Year Book of International Law*
CMEA	Council for Mutual Economic Assistance
ECR	*European Court Reports*
ECSC	European Coal and Steel Community
EEC	European Economic Community
ELDO	European Launcher Development Organization
ESA	European Space Agency
ESRO	European Space Research Organization
GATT	General Agreement on Tariffs and Trade
IAEA	International Atomic Energy Agency
ICITO	Interim Committee of the International Trade Organization
ICJ	International Court of Justice
ICLQ	*The International and Comparative Law Quarterly*
ICRC	International Committee of the Red Cross
ILC	International Law Commission
ILM	*International Legal Materials*
ILO	International Labour Organisation
ILR	*International Law Reports*
IMCO	Inter-Governmental Maritime Consultative Organization
IMF	International Monetary Fund
OECD	Organization for Economic Cooperation and Development
OEEC	Organization for European Economic Cooperation
PCIJ	Permanent Court of International Justice
RCADI	*Recueil des Cours de l'Académie de Droit international*
RGDIP	*Revue générale de Droit international public*
RIAA	*Reports of International Arbitral Awards*
UNCLT	United Nations Conference on the Law of Treaties
UNCTAD	United Nations Conference on Trade and Development
UN Pub.	United Nations Publication
WHO	World Health Organization
YILC	*Yearbook of the International Law Commission*
ZaöRV	*Zeitschrift für ausländisches öffentliches Recht und Völkerrecht*

Table of cases

Chapter 1
Treaties

I Historical perspective

1 Ever since the days of antiquity, Princes and States have concluded
international treaties. In the vicissitudes of war and peace which form the
fabric of history, even semantics seem to imply that the establishment of
peace is linked to the conclusion of pacts. Yet, however interesting the fact
may be that treaties between the Egyptian pharaoh and the Hittite king were
concluded by an exchange of letters or that, closer to us, in the seventeenth
century Grotius set out the principles of treaty interpretation in terms not
unlike those of the 1969 Vienna Convention on the Law of Treaties, it is
from 1815 onwards that the development of treaties has been especially
remarkable: in a little over a century and a half, this essential instrument of
international relations has undergone a tremendous transformation. Let us
therefore begin by considering the underlying causes and main phases of this
historical evolution.(*)

1. Underlying causes

2 The fundamental cause of the development has been the increasing
solidarity between the components of international society: mechanical
solidarity between States whereby any change in one of the components
alters the balance of power within the whole system; solidarity of the general
interests of mankind, requiring problems to be tackled in common and
simultaneously; and solidarity between individuals in the development of
culture and public opinion.

3 While these aspects of solidarity are first of all apparent within the State,
they also imply going beyond the confines of the State, and international
treaties constitute the main legal mechanism which, although dependent on
national institutions for purposes of conclusion and implementation,
reaches further and transcends them. Any treaty could indeed be seen
individually as a bridge boldly built out into the void of an international
society which has yet to acquire real consistency; collectively the corpus of
concluded treaties forms the reality and substance of an international society
from which treaties in turn will increasingly derive their legal traits. In that
process, nations starting out as entities closed to one another gradually open
up and create the very environment to which they submit themselves.

4 The development of national political institutions with increasingly
distinct organs and the broader participation of private citizens in public

affairs is in many ways at the origin of an increased variety in conventional instruments. Not only does political consent to a treaty involve a greater number of organs; but the need to conclude a host of agreements on increasingly technical subjects calls for procedural simplification precisely at a time when all State activities and departments are becoming more involved in international affairs.(*)

5   Perhaps the most perceptible sign of this change has been the emergence of multilateral treaties. For a long time, a number of important settlements, such as the Treaties of Westphalia and the major eighteenth century peace treaties, did of course involve agreements between several States; at first these were made up of as many bilateral agreements as there were pairs of States concerned. In the early nineteenth century, and initially as a pure matter of form, it appeared rational to replace a whole set of bilateral treaties by a single multilateral instrument. But this was far more than a mere simplification for the sake of form or protocol. In fields such as public health, communications, maritime security, protection of maritime resources, literary, artistic and scientific property, metrological unification, and protection of certain basic human rights, multilateral treaties were called upon to serve an entirely new purpose: the defence of the common interests of mankind. The parties to such treaties are not so much setting up a compromise on diverging interests as symmetrically pooling their efforts to achieve an identical goal. The great German jurist Triepel even put forward a legal theory of this common will (*Vereinbarung*) as a central element of the theory of the law of treaties. Increasing awareness of the scale of these common interests thus provided the seed for multilateral treaties which were to multiply with the acceleration of history (Hudson in his *International Legislation*, vol. I, p. XIX, lists 157 such treaties between 1864 and 1914). Legal analysis followed suit, striving to capture the real feeling of solidarity which, in varying degrees depending on the case, prevents multilateral treaties from being viewed as merely the sum of independent bilateral agreements.(*)

6   However, the multilateral treaty drawn up at a congress or a conference is not the final and ultimate product of growing solidarity. Conferences become periodical, set up permanent secretariats, create organs which, first in minor and gradually in more important matters, enjoy a measure of legal autonomy with regard to participating States. This is how international organizations come into being on the basis of multilateral treaties, their constituent charters. In turn, as they develop they give rise to a considerable expansion of treaty-making activity: not only do international organizations, owing to their facilities, lead to a greater number of multilateral treaties, but they provide new solutions as to the form of treaties and their proper implementation. Thus the whole life of treaties between States tends from beginning to end to be entwined to some extent with the activity of the organization. Introducing a further degree of complexity in treaty-making is the fact that organizations also conclude treaties with one another and with States and even try to become parties to treaties between States.

7 Multilateral treaties and international organizations are thus the major factors in the evolution of conventional relations, and both are the result of growing global solidarity. Attention should, however, be paid to the importance of international practice, especially the inconspicuous practice of protocol and legal advisers, both domestic and international (in particular, secretariats of international organizations). They directly feel the pressure of international solidarity and try to devise the most economic and realistic responses. Initial choices are frequently guided by mere administrative convenience, and the really significant effects of certain arrangements or innovations often only become apparent later on. On the international level, the basic principles are very simple: only final consent is legally binding, but agreed formalities may act as milestones marking the procedural stages leading up to final consent. Substance prevails over form in the whole of this important field; even the actual wording matters so little that the most varied and ambiguous terms may be used, to say nothing of the considerable uncertainty of equivalent expressions in different languages (see below, No. 94). Caught as they are between the pressing needs of international relations and the rules laid down by national Constitutions, protocol and legal advisers proceed as unobtrusively as possible, seeking to secure appropriate adjustments through empirical solutions.(*)

8 In a more formal manner, and at times with considerable delay, national courts have an even more difficult role to play, for neither their position nor the training of their members gives them any familiarity with diplomatic practice, any more than with the real intentions and needs of government authorities. But in the end, after a certain amount of difficulty, and in some countries with the assistance of the Ministry for Foreign Affairs, they often do contribute to the common achievement by providing the necessary solutions to the daily confrontation between rules and the actual requirements of social conflict.

2. Contemporary developments

Historically, three periods may be distinguished: (A) from 1815 until World War I; (B) between the two World Wars; and (C) after World War II.

A. FROM 1815 UNTIL WORLD WAR I

9 Formally and generally speaking, during this period the law of treaties continued to rely on the monarchical tradition with the Head of State acting as the representative of the State in foreign relations, and all the other participants in foreign affairs, especially ministers and ambassadors, merely serving as delegates. This tradition was in some respects analogous to the one which made the king Head of State in the municipal order, but this monopoly survived longer in the sphere of external representation, while domestically it was soon eroded by the emergence of parliamentary and democratic systems. Its political justification was also more lasting, since States had an obvious interest in thus regulating their foreign relations through a single channel. Indeed, the centralization of foreign relations is still the best and only way to preserve the integration of interests at the national level alone and hence to defend the sociological basis of sovereignty. The fact that any citizen, department or ministry acquires a direct and effective capacity to take part in foreign relations marks the beginning of a federative process which will only emerge later on, eventually culminating in the demise of the sovereign State careless enough to let the threads of social solidarity stretch beyond its boundaries, thereby giving rise to the very institutions which will deprive it of its sovereignty.

10 In the early nineteenth century this stage had still not been reached. The prevalence of the Head of State in foreign affairs was still overwhelming and had lost nothing of its deep significance, as has been shown after a close scrutiny of practice by illustrious historians and jurists like Bittner, Basdevant and McNair, as well as by eminent theorists like Triepel and Anzilotti. On the other hand, these scholars have also shown how the modern multilateral treaty derives from the pragmatic innovations of practitioners. Even the collectively organized negotiations at the Congress of Vienna in 1815 were initially sanctioned by a set of bilateral treaties, as many as were required to bind each pair of States. But the real link between all these bilateral treaties was provided in the first place by a document summing up the transactions of the Congress, the Final Act of 9 June 1815. Other agreements dealing with a number of implementing measures or secondary matters were similarly recapitulated in the General Treaty of the Territorial Commission of Frankfurt of 20 July 1819 signed by the four Great Powers. Thus the idea that a treaty which is binding upon different States by the same terms constitutes a single legal instrument first appeared at the Congress of Vienna. Yet while the unicity of the legal instrument was recognized, the form was not immediately simplified; in 1815 and again in 1856 as many original copies were drawn up as there were parties, and all of them were signed by all the parties. The far simpler modern procedure based on only *one* original copy implies a very far-reaching practical innovation: the single original copy is entrusted to a particular State which not only ensures its safe-keeping but actually 'manages' the instrument. The State concerned keeps the full powers of the signatories and the instruments of ratification, denunciation, etc.; it reports to the parties all the transactions relating to the treaty; and the idea has gradually emerged that the 'depositary', as this State is called, is not acting on its own behalf but in the interests of all the parties, exercising a truly international function. It could therefore be said that any multilateral treaty, in providing for a depositary, establishes an international organ. This solution is partially apparent in one of the Acts drawn up at the Congress of Vienna, namely the Act of 8 June 1815 concerning the Federal Constitution of Germany (article XX), but less innovative methods were still used for some time: ratifications were exchanged two at a time, and copies were signed both by the State keeping the original copy signed by all parties and by the State for which the copy was intended (International Sanitary Convention of 3 February 1852).(*)

11 These secondary yet significant aspects were the first to reflect the emergence of the device of multilateral agreements, whose substance draws on a deeper reality, namely the existence of common interests. Hence the enormous expansion of all sorts of instruments covering such widely varying issues as the slave trade at the Congress of Vienna and the 'unions' concerning the telegraph (1865), postal relations, river and rail transport, public health, environmental protection (fishing), as well as freedom of religion (imposed on the new Balkan States) and protection of the wounded in wartime (1864), or codification of the law of war.

12 However, while the concept of 'interest' or of 'common interest' seems straightforward from the sociological point of view, its legal implications are vague and very slow to appear. To say that, with regard to such common interests, all States are in symmetrical positions in relation to each other is easy enough, but is only partly true; indeed to a large extent they have individual interests which make for long and arduous negotiations. Between victorious and defeated powers, between the interests of a number of States agreeing on the need to impose a particular territorial status on a given territory (neutrality, freedom of communication) and the State to which that territory belongs, any symmetry is very limited indeed. The very form of such treaties reveals that in their substance they attempt to link two sets of conflicting interests and strike a balance between them. While the number of parties makes them multilateral, by their content they are in fact bilateral, with a considerable group of States on one side and one or a few on the other. As early as the middle of the nineteenth century, these so-called 'semi-collective' treaties had begun to give rise to some well-known questions, *inter alia* as to the exact scope of the obligations resulting from the Peace Treaty of 1856 for the legal regime of the Straits: were the parties bound only as against Turkey or also as against one another? The issue was debated at the Congress of Berlin in 1878, and the difficulty of assessing the interest of a party in sanctioning a breach of a multilateral treaty has lasted to this day (see below, No. 301).

13 But perhaps, then as now, no aspect of the mechanisms leading up to multilateral treaties was more important than its preparation and adoption. The crucial question has always been which States are in charge of the preparation of a congress or a conference and how the text of a treaty is drawn up. Only the States ratifying the treaty are bound by it and States are free to ratify or not. But it is not enough not to be bound by a treaty, for the freedom preserved is largely illusory, indeed totally so in the case of treaties resolving an issue which at a given time can only be dealt with in a given way, such as a question of political or territorial status. Clearly, it is in the interest of all States that no question which might concern them should be settled without their participation, and if possible their consent; but conversely the absence of a small or even middle-ranking State has seldom been regarded as an obstacle. That is why the Great Powers — and today the main groups of Powers — have always played a leading role in the preparation and adoption of collective treaties.

14 Multilateral treaties appear to have been adopted unanimously at international congresses and conferences. But it should be observed that participants were far fewer then than today. Most of them were European States and it was only towards the end of the period that they came to number about twenty. Among these, the six Great Powers usually played a crucial role. Their desire to come to terms with one another, the pressure exerted on others too intent on furthering their own aims, the establishment of balanced solutions which were usually acceptable to smaller States, and the dominance over smaller States when major political interests were at stake all contributed to the considerable number and remarkable standard of multilateral treaties concluded during that period. It is true that the rights of smaller States were occasionally sacrificed, as in the political settlements in the Balkans, or regarding Korea at the Conferences of The Hague; that some efforts failed, for instance in the case of international justice; that the Great Powers ultimately refused to accept a number of essential obligations, as France did in the case of the Brussels Treaty of 1890 relating to the African slave trade (especially for visiting rights). Yet on the whole the general process was successful. The essential role played by some States, generally the Great Powers (and occasionally other States at humanitarian conferences), in convening, preparing, and conducting conferences must be considered on the merits of each case for each major political conference; and while it may at times appear surprising, the system can be viewed as a *de facto* international organization which in practical terms often compares rather favourably with the League of Nations or the United Nations.(*)

15 There is yet another characteristic of that period, which is so obvious that it is taken for granted: treaties began to play a major role as a source of international law. Article VII of Hague Convention (XII) for the Establishment of an International Prize Court lists them in first place among the rules to be applied by the Court. Instead of being just the source of particular obligations between States, they were to become the major source of international law with the beginning of a bold new enterprise, the codification of international law, i.e. the drawing up in written instruments of customary rules deriving from the practice of the group of countries then referred to as 'civilized nations'. Of course, codification conventions not only specify existing rules but also add new ones, and since conventions enter into force only as between the parties, formally speaking codification conventions constitute the law only of the parties; yet the codified rules tend in turn to give rise to customary rules of identical content but universal validity. Thus codification contributes at least indirectly to a substantial progress in the law.

16 Concerning humanitarian law and the law of war, the process culminated in the two Peace Conferences of The Hague. These were also able, at least on some specific points, to start laying the foundations for the peaceful settlement of international disputes.

17 Since treaties had become the main source of international law, it could have been expected that by an appropriate convention the international community would arrange for their official publication. Proposals were put forward to that effect by private scientific bodies, but were never put into practice. As in the past, therefore, private collections of treaties had to be relied upon. Apart from such collections which had existed for a long time and were restricted to the treaties of particular countries, a universal and permanent collection was to appear under the name of a well-known family of international jurists: the Martens *Recueil* thus covers the whole period to this day. Other similar attempts such as those of Descamps and Renault were interrupted by World War I.

B. BETWEEN THE TWO WORLD WARS

18 Covering every aspect of international relations, the great peace movement following World War I was to have a considerable impact on the law of treaties. It would be unfair not to mention in this respect the role of the Pan-American Union and its pre-1914 Conferences, but of course the League of Nations provided the essential form of international organization around which the development of the law of treaties was to be concentrated.

19 Trends which had already been apparent before World War I were to be largely confirmed. Monarchical institutions were declining, gradually losing their almost sacred character. At the same time, increasing international solidarity generated a need for more treaties which were often concluded quite rapidly. Treaty-making procedures were therefore simplified, no longer requiring personal representation by the Head of State who was often replaced by the Minister for Foreign Affairs or the Head of Government.

20 Initiatives or interventions by the League of Nations occurred in every field. First and foremost, despite its eventual failure, was the systematic continuation of the codification process. A Committee of Experts which was set up in 1924 and became permanent in 1929 submitted to governments a list of subjects which seemed 'ripe for codification'; among these were the 'procedure of international conferences' and the 'procedure for the conclusion and drafting of treaties'. In fact, not all States thought it possible to codify the law of treaties and a number of Great Powers such as Germany, Japan, the United Kingdom and the United States opposed the project, which was never even embarked on. Meanwhile in 1935 Harvard University published a private draft for the codification of the law of treaties which was to acquire some well-deserved authority. The topics taken into consideration by the League did not concern the law of treaties nor were they to lead to any codification, except on one minor point, the methods used and the worsening international situation hardly providing the right climate.(*)

21   A new development, however, was that the Covenant of the League of Nations, following one of President Wilson's 'Points', required member States to register all treaties with the League Secretariat, which was to ensure their publication. This is what gave birth to the *League of Nations Treaty Series*.

22   The League, and in particular its Secretariat, began to play an increasing role in the field of treaties. First of all, the organization very naturally became the depositary of many multilateral conventions, since it had international civil servants who could carry out such a function; but it was also to play a considerable part in drawing up quite a number of conventions. With its material resources, its officials and experts, the permanent international organization indeed provided an ideal framework for the preparation of international conventions. The most general and elementary pattern was for it to prepare intergovernmental conferences: it was within the organization that the usefulness of such a conference would first be recognized, that all the required preparatory measures, in particular a preliminary draft codification, would be embarked upon, that invitations would be sent out and that all the material arrangements for the conference would be made. Such conventions were said to be concluded 'under the auspices' of the organization. Accordingly, while the form of the conventions remained the same, the practical circumstances of their preparation and adoption were considerably altered owing to a broader participation of all States, however small, and the increased influence of the Secretariat.

23   But going one step further, conventions could even be prepared, discussed and finalized 'within' the organization itself. The League of Nations, just like any other international organization, included at least one organ made up of the delegations of all its member States; its structure was in fact that of a conference (and it was even called the 'conference' in some organizations); it was therefore not difficult to envisage the finalization by such an organization of a text which the States would then be called upon to adopt. This was indeed the main purpose of the International Labour Organisation which at the time was part of the League system but, on a more empirical basis and independent of any mandate of this kind, organizations were sometimes led to adopt within their framework the text of a convention, as the League Assembly did for the 1928 General Act for the Pacific Settlement of International Disputes.(*)

24   In these circumstances even the form of conventions underwent a considerable change; occasionally the signature of State representatives was no longer required, which rendered the term 'ratification' somewhat inappropriate to describe the expression of final consent to be bound by an instrument. So far-reaching did the changes entailed by the constituent charter of the International Labour Organisation appear to the French Government that it initially refused to accept them on the grounds that they were contrary to the French Constitution. Apart from such purely formal changes, the preparation and discussion of a convention resulted in a considerable change in the political climate. Indeed, *all* member States took part in the drawing up of the convention, and not only those which had the means and resources to send a delegation to a special conference: the applicable rules were those of the organization and the collective work was accomplished in a permanent framework by officials of the organization.(*)

25 Finally the interwar period was to witness a new development in the evolution of treaties which was closely linked to the emergence of the international legal personality of organizations and was hence still quite exceptional: the organization could itself be called upon to conclude some international agreements, for instance regarding material arrangements with the State where its headquarters were located or on whose territory it exercised its activities, or with States receiving specific services or financial resources. While this practice was already discernible at the time of the League of Nations, its technical and political implications were only to appear later.(*)

C. AFTER 1945

26 After World War II a dramatic expansion of international organizations took place which came to dominate in particular the whole evolution of the law of treaties. However, before dealing with the most significant aspect of the role of international organizations, it is important from the start to point out its limits. At the present stage of the development of international society, the only members of organizations are States, almost exclusively represented by their governments; they alone command the resources, manpower and whatever other means are at their disposal; they are ultimately responsible for organized human societies. Whenever major political issues are at stake, the Great Powers tend to play an essential role; and when they are prevented from discharging it by the constitutional rules of an international organization, they tend to act outside the organization, even though they may possibly use it later. To this day, some of the most important treaties are concluded, despite their importance, outside the organizational framework and bestow upon the Great Powers privileges which, natural as they may seem, are nonetheless reminiscent of nineteenth century conditions. Treaties directly or indirectly connected with nuclear weapons are a case in point, be it with respect to their drafting or their modification (Antarctic Treaty, articles 9 and 12; Nuclear Test Ban Treaty, articles II and III; Treaty on Non-Proliferation of Nuclear Weapons, article 8).(*)

27 Except in such cases, organizational action concerning the law of treaties follows the pattern set before World War II. It seems to have become more and more difficult to convene general conferences to draft treaties open to all States other than under the auspices of the world organizations most directly concerned, and a growing number of conventions are in fact elaborated within some organization. A new development due to the increase in their number and activity has been the soaring number of agreements concluded between organizations, or between organizations and States, and the practice of international secretariats is evidence of their creative role.

28 There is also a tendency for new forms of agreements to emerge, however, because the consent to be bound is given by ever less specific means. Verbal agreements leaving a written trace in the minutes of an international body, agreements deriving from implicit acquiescence or consent, and all types of informal agreements thrive in the practice of international organizations. In view of the mainly consultative or hortatory powers of the United Nations and its related bodies, it is easy to imagine that new and ill-defined situations may have to be faced. Does compliance with a non-binding United Nations recommendation by a State which has 'accepted' it give rise to a 'conventional' type of situation? When an international organization communicates texts which by its constituent instrument become binding upon non-objecting States, is it taking the initiative leading to a convention or exercising a conditional regulatory power? Many more examples could be given pointing to the extensive although still uncertain developments in the law of treaties.

29 Entrusted as it is with the preparation of many treaties, acting as a depositary of major multilateral acts, registering and publishing all international conventions, and itself already a party to a great number of agreements, the United Nations can rely on the vast experience of its Secretariat which enables it to undertake any kind of studies and publications (collections of model clauses, model treaties, etc.) and thus to have a major influence on the development of the law of treaties.

30 After the war, international organizations, especially the United Nations, resumed their codification efforts, this time successfully. But codification can occasionally be something of a misnomer: indeed in some new fields there are hardly any existing rules to codify. Such instruments as the Genocide Convention, various humanitarian conventions and conventions on space law were clearly treading new ground. Moreover the United Nations also set up a permanent and general codification machinery based on a few simple principles: the General Assembly chooses the topics to be codified; draft articles are prepared by the International Law Commission, a subsidiary body of 34 independent individuals elected for a five-year term by the Assembly; the Commission's annual work is reviewed by the General Assembly's Sixth Committee; in the course of its work, the Commission consults the governments and international organizations concerned; and the draft articles, revised in the light of government comments, are then submitted to the General Assembly which usually decides to convene a conference to draw up a treaty.(*)

31 A number of international conventions have thus been adopted following the preliminary work of the International Law Commission: the Geneva Conventions on the Law of the Sea, the Convention on Diplomatic Relations, the Convention on Consular Relations, the Convention on Special Missions, and the Convention on the Representation of States in Their Relations with International Organizations of a Universal Character. A different procedure was followed for the codification of some very specific topics such as the recasting of earlier conventions in the Single Convention on Narcotic Drugs or the codification of international trade law by a special commission. Similarly, all matters concerning outer space and the new developments of the law of the sea since 1972 were the subject of conventions prepared from the outset by government representatives.(*)

32 Moreover the United Nations undertook to codify the law of treaties itself. The subject was broached by the International Law Commission in 1950, but progress was at first rather slow, owing to the work on the law of the sea and diplomatic immunities. A far more active phase began in 1961, culminating in the 1968–1969 Vienna Conference which adopted the 1969 Vienna Convention on the Law of Treaties (hereinafter referred to as 'the 1969 Convention'). Most of the articles of the Convention were adopted unanimously or by a substantial majority. A considerable number of States have become parties to the Convention which came into force on 27 January 1980: by 30 June 1987, there were 54 States parties (with 24 reservations and declarations and 11 objections, several of which are of a general or multiple character; the Soviet Union and a group of Socialist countries acceded in 1986 and 1987 with important reservations against which objections were formulated). But the scope of the 1969 Convention goes far beyond what this numerical evidence would suggest, since most of its provisions codify rules which were already recognized, giving them a clear and precise expression. Even for such rules as are still controversial, the work of the International Law Commission and the Conference proceedings have proved invaluable. The Convention clearly marked the beginning of a new era in the law of treaties.(*)

33 The 1969 Convention did not, however, cover all the issues relating to treaties. Some of these have since been dealt with by the International Law Commission: State succession in respect of treaties is dealt with by the Vienna Convention of 23 August 1978 which has not yet come into force, and treaties concluded by international organizations are the subject of the Vienna Convention of 21 March 1986 on the Law of Treaties between States and International Organizations or between International Organizations (hereinafter referred to as 'the 1986 Convention'). By 30 June 1987, this Convention, which has also not yet come into force, had been signed by 27 States (including the United States of America, the United Kingdom, the

Federal Republic of Germany, Italy and Japan) and 10 international organizations (including the United Nations and some of its specialized agencies, and the Council of Europe). As for the relationship between the law of treaties and international responsibility, there are a few references to it in some provisions of the 1969 Vienna Convention, but the whole topic of responsibility has been tackled separately by the Commission, as has the most-favoured-nation clause. However, related topics such as the effects on treaties of war or of the use of armed force have not yet been directly dealt with.(*)

34 The law of treaties has thus been developed and made more specific. Its relationship with international organizations goes beyond occasional codifications or isolated action by one particular organization; a permanent relationship is indeed emerging through the links established between organizations and the parties or even future parties to a treaty. A great number of multilateral treaties not only lay down rules but provide for the control of such rules, sometimes by stating that they are to be made more precise, completed or adapted following an international procedure. The organization under whose auspices a convention is concluded provides the appropriate framework or has within its structure a specific organ for that purpose. There is of course nothing to prevent a multilateral treaty from establishing an autonomous organization for its own purposes, as was indeed advocated half a century ago. But it is more rational from all points of view to integrate such new bodies into an existing organization (as was done for those set up under the Convention on Narcotics or the conciliation procedure under article 66 of the 1969 and 1986 Conventions). Moreover there is a tendency to let international organizations monitor the entry into force of treaties, not only in their capacity as depositaries but by receiving information and even justifications relating to the steps taken by the parties to secure ratification. This procedure, which is sometimes referred to as the 'final phase of codification', was formally introduced in the International Labour Organisation for International Labour Conventions, and it recurs with some variations in other organizations. This provides further evidence of how the law of treaties reflects certain aspects of the legislative process.(*)

II Fundamental legal aspects

1. The domestic and the international legal order

35 Rules governing the *conclusion* of treaties are laid down partly by national constitutions — varying from one Constitution to another — partly by international customary law, recently supplemented by the 1969 Vienna Convention. As for the *application* of treaties, it sometimes seems to depend mainly on international law, for instance when a State refuses to recognize a territorial conquest made in breach of the United Nations Charter, and in other cases mainly on municipal law, as for instance when a municipal court applies an international rule relating to the uniform law for cheques. Similarly, treaties to which at least one international organization is a party bring into play both general international law and the law of the organization concerned.(*)

36 It is clear therefore from these examples that two distinct legal orders are involved; indeed it would be difficult to imagine a situation where the effect of a treaty in one legal order would have no impact on its position in the other. Thus, in the first example given above, the courts of a State refusing to recognize a territorial annexation may have to decide which law is applicable in the territory concerned: are they bound by the government's assessment or can they review it independently? In the second example, if a national court violates the Convention providing a Uniform Law for Cheques, will this entail no consequences for that State on the international level? Clearly, therefore, while a distinction can and should be made between these two aspects of the law of treaties, they cannot be entirely divorced from each other. The problem must be considered in general from a doctrinal point of view, and then more particularly with respect to the conclusion and application of treaties.

A. DOCTRINAL CONSIDERATIONS

37 It is well known that in regard to all these questions writers have developed a number of rather abstract constructions based on either dualistic or monistic tenets. Essentially, dualists regard international and municipal law as completely separate, except for the Head of State who is the only State organ entitled to represent the State both in municipal and international law. On the other hand, monists hold that municipal law is linked and subject to international law with regard to all State organs.

38 Without going any deeper into these theories and their numerous variations, it is worth observing in general terms that the appropriateness of a given theory varies according to the country concerned and to historical conditions. In fact, monism could also be characterized as a system of legal integration; international and municipal law can be said to be 'integrated' when both become one coherent and hierarchical system such as would be the case in a highly developed federal system with respect to federal and state law. Monism therefore fits cases where legal integration is matched by complete social integration, i.e. where international society is strong enough for more restricted social structures and relationships to converge and harmonize within it. But when international society is practically non-existent and States jealously close themselves to the outside world and keep their foreign relations under strict control, then hardly any international rules will penetrate the municipal shell; the fullest possible centralization of foreign affairs between the hands of the Head of State will then be in order to ensure adequate social cohesion; legal dualism is thus a fair reflection of the ideal of a State rejecting legal integration essentially because there is no social integration and no intention of bringing it about.

39 In the present state of international relations, the position is clearly an intermediate one, with considerable differences between the groups of States concerned. Some States, because of their size or political system or both, are able and anxious to ward off uncontrolled foreign influence and are quite prepared to face the consequences of a dualistic approach. Taking a more open view of international relations, other countries conclude among themselves treaties ranging over such an important part of social relations that their effects are felt by all in everyday life; they still draw back when they realize that their foreign relations are clearly leading them to a federal solution, but they have already had to accept some aspects of federalism. More than others, therefore, they are inclined to opt for compromise solutions based on practical considerations, while taking into account their constitutional and judicial traditions which give a distinctive flavour to each national view of the relationship between municipal and international law. The municipal law of treaties thus varies from country to country, but all States have to take into account the international law of treaties which is gradually evolved by practice from national attitudes and yet tends by a natural process to impose itself in turn on municipal authorities. Concerning international organizations, the same can be said of their particular rules regarding the *conclusion* of treaties: powers are distributed differently within each organization although there is a general trend towards increasing the role of the Secretary-General or Executive Director. As for the *application* of treaties (other than within the European Communities), the question of the links between general international law and the rules of each organization is only just beginning to arise (especially in the United Nations).(*)

B. CONCLUSION OF TREATIES

40 No issue has been more widely debated than the formal unconstitutionality of treaties, sometimes known as 'imperfect ratification'. What happens for instance if two States conclude a treaty and, after their representatives have declared it to be binding, one of them claims not to be bound because some of its own constitutional requirements have not been complied with? Are municipal and international validity entirely distinct and independent from each other, as the dualists would contend? Or is an internationally valid treaty necessarily valid in municipal law? Or conversely does municipal invalidity make a treaty internationally invalid, given that international law leaves the determination of the relevant procedures to the constitutional law of each country?(*)

41 It is hard to imagine, when expressions of consent are exchanged, that one party could know the other party's constitutional law better than that party's authorized representatives: hence it will normally have to accept its partner's declaration in good faith, or else no security in treaty relations would be possible. This is borne out by international practice, and article 46 of the 1969 Convention provides that a State cannot invoke the violation of a constitutional provision in such a situation 'unless that violation was manifest and concerned a rule of its internal law of fundamental importance'. A violation is manifest 'if it would be objectively evident to any State conducting itself in the matter in accordance with normal practice and in good faith'.

42 The 'normal practice' of international relations is therefore what constitutes within the limits of good faith the paramount rule in the field of treaties. This balanced rule, which incidentally shows that, far from any rigid separation, the Constitution and municipal law cooperate with international law in the conclusion of treaties, is not enough to allay all fears. Some countries have indeed laid down extremely cumbersome rules in their Constitutions, designed to prevent their representatives from concluding any treaty without the approval of Congress or Parliament. Frequent in Latin American Constitutions, those rules stem from a fear that representatives might yield to some foreign threat or enticement. Nowadays, however, international solidarity may require agreements to be rapidly concluded and implemented, and such rigid constitutional rules are therefore impracticable; although in fact they are not scrupulously observed, they do cause tiresome tensions. Similarly, without adhering to anything so strict as the *acte contraire* principle, governments are reluctant expressly to acknowledge that written agreements can be modified or even terminated by oral or tacit agreement, however frequently they might accept this in fact (see below, No. 66).

43 As for international organizations, the 1986 Convention followed the general outline of the 1969 Convention, after long waverings in the International Law Commission which had initially suggested a different solution with stricter penalties for breaches of constituent instruments. The text finally adopted by the 1986 Conference as article 46 (3) clearly reveals the intention to adopt the same solution as for treaties between States. However, the wording is different. While confirming that the general practice prevailing among States is what counts in the application of both Conventions, the 1986 Convention also provides that allowance should be made 'where appropriate' for 'the normal practice...of international organizations', thereby implying that there can be a 'normal practice' of all international organizations, which so far, owing to their different structures, only exists for very specific issues.

C. APPLICATION OF TREATIES

44 Treaties are made to be performed. The performance of treaties may require application by domestic courts, especially when rights and obligations are stipulated for individuals. Such application has raised and continues to raise a number of practical problems. It also lies behind the theoretical debates on dualism and monism. The question is: under what conditions and with what effects may a municipal court apply the rules of a treaty? Is it in the same position as when it applies municipal rules? These questions involve both general principles and practical issues and it may be convenient to deal first with the latter. Thus for instance it is well known that municipal rules on treaty publication do not always make the task of domestic courts easy. Moreover, the application of rules laid down by a treaty often requires prior regulatory, administrative or financial measures without which performance is materially impossible. In other cases, even when the question of material impossibility does not arise, it may well be that the States parties to the treaty did not intend to endow individuals with rights which could be invoked in domestic courts. With respect to the last two cases, it has been argued, somewhat ambiguously, that some treaties are not 'self-executing'.(*)

45   The basic principle here is that public international law leaves it to the constitutional law of each State to settle problems arising in the application by its courts of rules of international law, especially rules contained in a treaty. It is certainly true that a State 'may not invoke the provisions of its internal law as justification for its failure to perform the treaty' (1969 Convention, article 27); but it remains free to choose the means of implementation it sees fit according to its traditions and to the fundamental principles of its political organization. Its choice may of course have consequences in terms of international responsibility. Thus, under the local remedies rule, a State is not entitled to take up the case of its national allegedly wronged by a foreign State in breach of international law until that individual has failed to gain redress in the courts of that State. The local remedies rule will not apply, however, if those courts, under their own municipal law, are not legally entitled to redress breaches of international law.

46   But other considerations may lead to different conclusions and States have indeed adopted extremely varied solutions, all of which in their own way aim at ensuring the best possible implementation of treaty rules. In a strictly dualistic system, courts cannot apply a treaty rule until it has been 'transformed' into municipal law, usually by way of a legislative enactment. Treaties thereby take on the characteristics of municipal law and as such may be suspended or abrogated by subsequent legislation. In such a system, ultimate responsibility for the application of a treaty rests with the government and the legislature. In other States, courts apply treaty law without any previous 'transformation', and international rules prevail over municipal rules, with the possible exception of subsequent legislative enactments contrary to the treaty rule concerned. To simplify the courts' task, it is often provided that they may or must seek the advice of the Minister for Foreign Affairs in connection with the interpretation of a treaty; in other cases the Minister for Foreign Affairs himself submits his views to the court as *amicus curiae*.

47 Under international law, therefore, it is up to each State and its Constitution to ensure the correct application of treaties. But there is nothing to prevent a treaty from restricting, in a given case or in a whole series of cases, the freedom of States to do so. Thus, a treaty may specify that its provisions create rights for individuals which may be invoked before the courts. It may also provide for immediate application of its rules by municipal courts without any 'reception' or 'transformation'. It may even stipulate that its rules shall prevail in court over any municipal provision, including subsequent legislation. Of course, such obligations affect the organization of the judiciary or even the Constitution, which is why treaties of this kind — e.g. the treaties creating the European Communities — can only be concluded by observing stricter constitutional requirements.

48 If the purpose is above all to ensure uniform interpretation of multilateral conventions so as to prevent the courts of various States from destroying the unity of a treaty by diverging interpretations, it will also be necessary to provide for reference to an international body. Appeals before an international court against the decisions of municipal courts had been contemplated in the Hague Convention (XII) of 1907 on the Establishment of an International Prize Court; but adjustments had to be made to allow for the constitutional difficulties of the United States of America and, in any case, the Convention never came into force. Another solution would be to lay down an obligation for municipal courts of last resort to submit matters of interpretation and questions concerning the validity of certain unilateral decisions to an international court for a preliminary ruling. This is the solution adopted in European Community law; it is only practicable in thoroughly integrated legal systems and could prove extremely useful in a number of fields (State immunity in the Council of Europe; jurisdiction, patents, etc., in the European Communities).(*)

49 The most radical solution would of course be to ensure the supremacy of international over municipal law, especially in its most extreme form of treaties prevailing over any, even subsequent, municipal enactments; however, such a profound transformation of traditional structures is hardly within reach as yet. For, while in a federal State the relations between federal and state law in courts of member states are governed by federal law, a very different situation obtains in the international community: here, and this must be emphasized, relations between international and municipal law in municipal courts are governed by municipal law. Whenever a particular treaty prescribes the supremacy of international over municipal law in municipal courts, international law comes another step closer to the legal structure prevailing in federal entities.

Two additional points are worth making. First, these comments refer in general to any international rule irrespective of its source; some aspects, however, are specific to rules laid down by a treaty. It is especially for these, as opposed to customary rules or general principles of law, that the idea of 'transforming' a rule of international law into a rule of municipal law is relevant. Unlike treaties, custom and general principles do not derive from a juristic act. That is probably why domestic courts in the Federal Republic of Germany and in the United Kingdom apply them directly. Secondly, the application of a treaty concluded by an international organization under the 'rules of the organization' referred to in article 2 (1) (j) of the 1986 Convention theoretically raises the same problems as treaties between States. These problems, however, only materialize in practice if the organization concerned has its own court of justice and if it concludes treaties which may be applied in cases brought before such a court. So far the question only seems to have arisen in the European Communities.(*)

2. The treaty as a juristic act and as a rule

50   Treaties are binding by virtue of the will of States to be bound by them. They are juristic acts, involving the operation of human will. That is why reference may be made to a treaty mechanism or also to its operative character. The word 'treaty' thus refers both to the *act* and to its result, the *rule*. There would be no act if it were not to bring forth a rule, just as the rule can only be the result of an act. Hence it is impossible to dissociate the act from the rule, although a distinction has to be made between the two.(*)

51   On the face of it, the distinction is quite easy. Indeed, alongside its main body or substantive provisions, a treaty begins by listing the parties and their representatives and ends with their signature. Moreover, the very body of the treaty contains what, in United Nations practice in particular, are often called the 'final clauses' specifying the general conditions under which the substantive provisions will produce their effects: i.e. from when, with regard to whom, and a series of other points such as how to become a party, the manner and date of entry into force, reservations, deposit of instruments of ratification, etc. Obviously, most of the final clauses, unlike substantive rules, take effect before the treaty enters into force (article 24 (4) of the 1969 Convention), indeed as soon as the text is adopted, since their very purpose is to settle problems which arise there and then. The practical import of this distinction between the various provisions of a treaty appears for instance with regard to the identification of treaties — in situations where the rules are exceptionally dissociated from the act which has laid them down — and with regard to some basic options of the law of treaties which may vary according to whether the 'act' or the 'rule' aspect prevails.(*)

52   The identification of undertakings constituting one and the same treaty is usually quite straightforward. Generally such undertakings are assembled in a single document, except for those specifically mentioned as being dealt with in annexes which together with the preamble form the 'text' of the treaty (1969 Convention, article 31). However, the real intention of the parties is not always clearly apparent. The International Court of Justice has had to decide whether an instrument was linked to one treaty or another, or whether several agreements were part of the same transaction. For that purpose, it had to ascertain the intention of the parties by reference to the form, the final clauses and especially the object and purpose of the treaty. But even treaties with distinct though compatible final clauses may constitute a single transaction with a single object and purpose linking them all together (see below, Nos. 196 ff.).(*)

53 In dualistic systems, international rules are said to be 'transformed' in order to be applied by municipal courts. Such transformation, if it is accepted at all, only applies to the substantive rule, and not to the final clauses for which it is hardly conceivable. This would also explain why in some countries the courts do not have to consider the various issues arising out of the treaty specifically regarded as a juristic act; this can be illustrated by the courts' reluctance to ascertain the constitutionality of treaties or compliance by the other party with its own obligations when the application of a treaty is subject to reciprocity.(*)

54 A rule contained in a treaty may become applicable to a State which is not a party, for instance when a State expressly agrees to be bound by the treaty or by parts of it. Thus there are cases of State succession where the successor State, although it does not become a party, has agreed to be bound by a treaty of its predecessor; yet this kind of situation will hardly be a lasting one since the successor State has an obvious interest in enjoying all the rights corresponding to its obligations and becoming therefore a party to such treaties. If, however, one strictly follows the 1969 Convention which provides that treaties cannot create rights or obligations for third States without their consent (article 34), the rule in question is wholly or partially separated from the original treaty to become the subject of a new agreement between the initial parties and the third State. This at least is what happens if the device of *stipulation pour autrui* is rejected (see below, Nos. 168 ff.). The same mechanism is supposed to ensure the application of the rules of certain multilateral treaties by States or international organizations which are not parties thereto, for instance with regard to the Geneva Conventions of 12 August 1949 (common article 2 (3)) and 1977 Additional Protocol I) (articles 1 (2) and 96 (2)) for the States or peoples engaged in an armed conflict and with regard to a series of treaties on outer space for international organizations which were not allowed to accede (Conventions of 19 December 1967, article 6; 9 March 1972, article 22; 14 January 1975, article 7; 5 December 1979, article 16).(*)

55 In any event, determining which of the 'act' or the 'rule' aspect prevails over the other is not without consequence. With regard to treaty *interpretation*, if the rule is made strictly subject to and dependent on the act which has created it, then ascertaining the intention of the parties will be the key factor prevailing over any other consideration further removed from the circumstances under which the act was concluded (see below, No. 141). Similarly, if the act creating the treaty is essentially what counts, it becomes very difficult to lay down provisions for the resolution of conflicts between contradictory treaty rules, since all treaties proceed from sovereign and legally equal State wills; their effects are therefore merely relative, and hence there is no reason for one treaty to prevail over another. On the other hand, if it is deemed appropriate to take into account the object of the rules and their intrinsic features, an attempt might be made to establish some hierarchy between treaties (see below, No. 198). Finally the legal consequences of vitiated consent will be seen in a different light according to whether precedence is given to the act or to the rule. In the former case, there will be an extensive conception of the grounds of invalidity since consent is the sole basis of the treaty; in the latter, a more restrictive position will be taken in view of the legislative needs of international society (see below, No. 251). The distinction between the act and the rule is therefore to some extent related to another distinction, i.e. the well-known attempt to view some international treaties as contracts and others as legislation.

3. Contractual treaties and law-making treaties

56 The development of treaties during the second half of the nineteenth century (see above, No. 5) prompted several new doctrinal distinctions. Besides Triepel's theory of *Vereinbarung* as distinct from a mere *Vertrag*, the expressions 'law-making treaties' and 'contractual treaties' came into use, the former referring to the treaties which first laid down general conventional rules governing international society. This distinction refers to the substance, not to the form of treaties, although general multilateral treaties do also have some specific formal characteristics which are reminiscent of the legislative process. It is important to make clear, when speaking of treaties as either 'legislation' or 'contracts', whether they are being viewed from a legal or a sociological standpoint.

57 From a legal point of view, however popular this theory may have been, it must be recognized that the distinction between law-making and contractual treaties is neither clear nor correct. In modern law — even private law — the distinction between contract and law has lost the obvious character it seemed to have in the past. The great collective instruments of modern economic society — such as collective agreements regulating the general conditions of an industrial sector, trade union or professional regulations, and large corporations — are no longer contracts in the original sense. Major unrestricted multilateral treaties are more like the by-laws of a corporation which is entered or left regardless of other parties than a statute in the public law sense. The essential feature of legislation in the material sense is its generality. Defining such generality may be feasible in municipal law, but how is the generality of a treaty to be defined in a system like international law which has a limited number of collective entities as its subjects (some 170 States)? By the number of the parties? The permanence of the treaty (e.g. a bilateral boundary treaty)? Its abstract character (e.g. a customs arrangement)? In fact, it is very difficult to distinguish between treaties in terms of substantive criteria (see below, No. 80).

58 In any event, most treaties certainly have no homogeneous content, and rules of all kinds can be cast into the same treaty as into a mould. Even if a strict definition of contractual commitments could be given, few treaties would fit that definition throughout. The four hundred or so articles of the Treaty of Versailles (1919) included the constituent charters of several international organizations and a number of territorial settlements, and a whole series of issues were dealt with in most varied terms. If material legal distinctions were to be applied to treaties, all their provisions would in any case have to be examined separately: a superficial overview would not be enough.

59 From a sociological point of view, the contract remains an instrument ideally suited to a social environment consisting of free and abstractly equal entities. Without having to refer in this context to ideological notions such as the 'social contract' or historical conceptions such as feudalism, contracts clearly did and still do fit in well with the nature of contemporary international society made up of equal and sovereign States. It is therefore normal for all treaties — whatever their nature — to fall into a fundamentally contractual framework. But it should also be added that it is very difficult not to stray from a purely contractual line. Any attempt to find solutions to the needs of international society through the free consent of 170 States is an arduous task indeed, and the methods of concluding and revising treaties have had to take this into account. In particular, the increasing intervention of international organizations means that the contractual framework of international conventions is left open to conflicting tensions. In this context, States stress the contractual aspect of treaties which constitutes the only guarantee of their sovereignty although it is frequently distorted owing to majority constraints in conferences or organizations and to the technical peculiarities of universal conventions (see below, No. 71).

4. Treaties and general principles of international law

60 While the legal régime of treaties constitutes by itself a separate subject which is envisaged as such in this *Introduction*, it entertains close links with all the fundamental aspects of international law. It touches on the general theory of the *sources* of law and juristic acts and hence on the theory of *subjects* of international law and their *recognition*. It is characterized by the fundamentally relative effect of rules and legal situations. It must be harmonized with the theory of *responsibility* and *sanctions* which complements the theory of obligations and actually pervades the operation of the whole of the law of treaties.

61 This only illustrates how true it is to say that the most general principles in any system of knowledge are closely related. Yet in this case, there is something more: for the very core of the law of treaties involves the other basic principles of public international law. Indeed what it essentially amounts to is that consent is binding. Therefore, whenever the issue of consent appears in international law, it relates to treaties. Still today the treaty remains a universal and indispensable instrument; justice hinges on agreements, organizations are set up by treaties, and any will finds a limit to its power in the power of other equal wills. Accordingly, if international law does rest on the will of States, the law of treaties is the most constructive and rational expression of that will.

62   The law of treaties could also be seen as part of the 'constitution' of international society, although this is more a figure of speech than an appropriate legal formula. While its position, as mentioned above, is indeed central to international law, it must look beyond itself for its legal foundations; treaties are binding by virtue not of a treaty but of customary rules. In that sense, international custom is even more central than the law of treaties since it is the very pillar on which treaties rest. If one were to speak of a 'Constitution' of the international community, it would have to be a customary one. The Vienna Convention on the Law of Treaties of 23 May 1969, which entered into force on 27 January 1980, is binding as a treaty only on a certain number of States; yet not only do most of the rules it codifies continue to bind non-parties, but these rules will evolve with effects for every State and the Convention will in turn be affected by new developments: just as it originated in custom, so will it return to custom.(*)

III Definition and classification of international treaties

1. Definition

63   There is no precise nomenclature for international treaties: 'treaty', 'convention', 'agreement' or 'protocol' are all interchangeable. Furthermore the meaning of most of the terms used in the law of treaties is extremely variable, changing from country to country and from Constitution to Constitution; in international law it could even be said to vary from treaty to treaty: each treaty is, as it were, a microcosm laying down in its final clauses the law of its own existence in its own terms. The uncertainty in wording is a result of the relativity of treaties; its consequences will be discussed later in the section on the conclusion of treaties (see below, No. 94).(*)

64   Despite the terminological jumble, a definition is needed if only to delimit the scope of the rules to be discussed. The broader the definition, the fewer the rules applying to all the cases it covers. It is precisely because the rules common to *written* agreements *between States* are comparatively numerous that the Vienna Convention dealt with them alone. In order to convey the general sense of the problem, a somewhat broader definition will be presented and discussed here, although the greater part of this study is restricted to the Vienna Convention, which covers the most homogeneous and richest part of the subject. The suggested definition is as follows: 'A treaty is an expression of concurring wills attributable to two or more subjects of international law and intended to have legal effects under the rules of international law.' Each component of this definition will now be briefly reviewed in turn.(*)

A. AN EXPRESSION OF CONCURRING WILLS

65 The parties have to manifest their will by 'expressing' it. Although, as has been suggested in jest, agreements between hidden thoughts and ulterior motives may well be the only genuine treaties, law cannot take into consideration anything that remains buried away in the minds of the parties. In addition to being spelled out, their wills must concur to form the object and purpose of the agreement, both of which play so prominent a part in the whole law of treaties. That is why the debates in municipal law between supporters of the 'declared' will and 'real' will theories can be regarded as largely academic, for the expressed will is the only real will upon which the parties have been able to reach an agreement.

66 The will can be expressed in a variety of forms. While the written form is the most usual and the safest, the will can also be expressed by an oral declaration, i.e. the parties' verbal conduct. More generally *any* conduct of the parties may express a will, especially active conduct, such as performance of an obligation or departure from an earlier attitude. Does the same hold good for *passive* conduct, such as one State's silence when faced with claims resulting from another State's conduct? Such an extension of the treaty mechanism is debatable for two reasons: first, although an obligation may indeed arise in some of the cases contemplated above, it could perhaps be explained otherwise than as resulting from an agreement; second, governments are reluctant to consider themselves bound by obligations inferred from insufficiently clear or authoritative expressions of their will.

67 While the possibility of purely verbal agreements is hardly challenged in itself, construing an essentially passive conduct as an expression of will certainly is. In any event, in order to establish an obligation of this kind, it is possible to resort to other technical explanations such as unilateral acts, acquiescence, estoppel, *forclusion*, or even custom or consolidation by time. All these explanations are nothing more than expressions of recognized principles rooted in the stabilizing influence of time on legal situations and in the responsibility incurred by States owing to the positions they take or to legitimate beliefs which such positions may induce other States to hold.(*)

68 Even apart from this variety of non-contractual explanations, it may be asked to what extent an international treaty could be devoid of any form. On this basic issue, international practice is far from clear, torn as it is between two contradictory requirements: on the one hand, ensuring the observance of good faith and legal security, in line with the generally non-formalistic character of international law; and, on the other hand, bestowing a minimum of certainty if not solemnity on treaty undertakings. In order to avoid this difficulty, the 1969 Vienna Convention confined itself to written treaties, but a number of its provisions show that unwritten 'agreements' are likely to come up in close connection with written treaties (1969 Convention, articles 11, 12 (1) (b) and (c), 13 (b), 14 (1) (b) and (d), 15 (b) and (c), 24 (2), 25 (1) (b) and (2), 28, 29, 31 (2) (a) and (3) (a), 36, 37, 39, etc.). Certain reactions during the 1968–1969 Vienna Conference showed, however, that States remain reluctant to accept too liberal an approach to the form of treaty commitments.(*)

B. CONCURRING WILLS ATTRIBUTABLE TO TWO OR MORE SUBJECTS OF LAW

69 As has been stated earlier (above, No. 40), and as will be seen again (below, No. 94), the process of attribution of a will is governed in each country by international law which to a large extent, albeit not completely, refers to the legal order of each State. The point to be emphasized at this juncture is that the act must be attributable to two or more subjects of law and not to one subject alone. This matter is closely linked to the development of international organizations and has become extremely important in recent years.

70 First of all, it would seem obvious that for a treaty to have any meaning, there should be at least two parties. While this principle is sound, it is certainly liable to exceptions. If the treaty creates rights (e.g. immunities) for an international organization which is not a party to the treaty, nothing would prevent it from making its entry into force depend on a single State's consent to be bound; this may occur especially if the treaty confers some controlling power on the organization, as in the case of the International Labour Organisation. Indeed the system set up by such treaties is already fully operative as soon as one single State has become a party. In the case of the ILO, it was actually more because of a kind of legal timidity than for reasons of substance that two was chosen as the minimum number of parties required for International Labour Conventions to enter into force. This again reveals to what extent the very mechanisms of modern conventions may resemble the legislative process.(*)

71 But things can be even more intricate. A decision of government delegates amounts to a unilateral act of an international organization if they meet under its constituent charter as one of its organs; otherwise it constitutes an agreement between the States whose delegates have concurred in the decision. This is merely a logical legal consequence, and a perfect expression, of the technical device of legal personality. In fact, however, international practice abounds in borderline cases where some degree of confusion is not incompatible with a certain measure of organization. Thus the sessions of an organ within an organization may be extended in fact and thereby turn into an international conference. It has even been asked whether the positions taken by a delegate within some such organ could not constitute a treaty commitment in relation to States whose delegates had taken similar positions. Some practices owe their ambiguity to new developments in international relations calling for *ad hoc* solutions. Occasionally it is the rigidity of national constitutional rules which has to be by-passed for agreements to materialize rapidly.(*)

C. TWO OR MORE SUBJECTS OF PUBLIC INTERNATIONAL LAW

72 This condition is unquestionably fulfilled by States and also by intergovernmental organizations which are recognized to possess some treaty-making capacity. The same holds good for other entities such as the Holy See or the International Committee of the Red Cross. Doubts may arise in other marginal cases which are increasingly frequent in practice. Thus, instead of being States, the parties to an agreement may be decentralized State services or even other legal entities such as municipalities, public institutions, agencies, etc. The question is then whether those entities have the power to commit their State; and, if not, to what degree they must be deemed to have concluded some sort of international agreement more or less closely related to inter-State treaties. Another kind of agreement are those between States and entities which do not yet qualify as States (national liberation movements, or provisional governments) but which have been recognized a measure of international personality.(*)

73 Even more important and tricky is the question of whether an agreement between a State and an individual can be regarded as an international treaty. Subject to some qualifications, there is no reason to discard this possibility. In such a case the individual cannot be considered purely and simply to have become a 'subject of international law'; but he does enjoy the rights of a subject of international law *vis-à-vis* the State concerned and with respect to the matters covered by the agreement. The same situation can be brought about by an agreement between an individual and an international organization if such is their intention. Yet this kind of agreement obviously will not be governed by the legal régime of inter-State treaties except on a very limited number of points. There is considerable reluctance in particular to equate an investment agreement between a State and a foreign corporation with an international treaty. Could a contract between two individuals who in no way are subjects of international law be governed by the law of international treaties? The answer is not to be sought in some international rule, for no one may by his own authority proclaim himself a subject of international law in however restricted a field. In any event, such an agreement would not properly be ruled by international law, even if some of its provisions were to supply the 'proper law of the contract'.(*)

D. AN INTENTION TO PRODUCE LEGAL EFFECTS

74 It has been contended that agreements not having a 'normative' character because, instead of laying down specific legal obligations, they simply assert political positions, wishes or intentions, are not treaties. Such a view would lead to another instance where the act and the rule are dissociated (see above, No. 52); it would in fact amount to stating that an agreement, in order to constitute a treaty, must lay down a rule. This is untenable for a number of reasons. First of all a treaty can have legal effects other than the creation or amendment of a rule. Moreover, while the legal effects of a treaty may indeed be very limited in some cases, it is difficult to imagine a transaction having no legal effect at all: an agreement, even resulting from the mere conduct of the parties, takes its place in a whole chain of related acts and contracts; it defines interests, justifies or clarifies interpretations, and gives rise to legitimate and legally relevant expectations. Conversely, all the resources of terminology are put to use by governments in order to avoid acknowledging that they are concluding a treaty, at least as far as their national Constitution is concerned, even though they may acknowledge that they are internationally bound, and above all in order to claim that the other parties are. The more solemn the form of an agreement, the more obvious the wish becomes to have it match a reality which is both 'legal' and 'political'. Ambiguity starts when States make it clear that they intend to stay free from any commitment, for instance by exchanging documents deemed to be non-papers or when their representatives conclude 'gentlemen's agreements' which in the past at least, however fictitiously, were supposed to carry no more than a personal commitment. There is considerable uncertainty as to the import of documents such as joint 'press communiqués' or concerted governmental action before or following discussion within an organization. While some formal treaties may have very limited legal effects, other apparently insignificant documents may turn out to be by their wording, their context or their consequences fraught with substance and obligations. The real import of documents has to be established in each case by reference to their nature after inspection of all the relevant evidence.(*)

E. LEGAL EFFECTS UNDER PUBLIC INTERNATIONAL LAW

75 States are free to conclude agreements under a given municipal law instead of international law. Obviously such agreements will not be treaties but contracts. There may of course be municipal rules governing a State's contracts, either in general or depending upon their subject-matter, preventing it from contracting under a foreign law. International law itself could rule out such a course of action in case of an agreement bearing on an essentially international matter. The problem which arises in practice may be to establish whether a given agreement, relating for instance to a loan, constitutes a treaty under international law or a contract under municipal law if the parties have left the point unspecified. The issue might be settled by reference to the object of the contract and the circumstances of its conclusion.(*)

2. Classification of treaties

76 Certain distinctions, like the one between law-making and contractual treaties, have already been shown to be rather inaccurate and irrelevant. For its part, the 1969 Convention takes a cautious approach, avoiding any systematic classification of treaties and restricting itself to a few distinctions of limited scope. Treaties present a great variety of different aspects according to whether one considers their elaboration, interpretation, modification, effects, violation and so forth, all of which call for a specific analysis. Without attempting a general classification, some important distinctions should at least be briefly outlined.(*)

77 The most obvious means of classifying treaties is first to take into account the nature and the number of the parties. As for their nature, treaties which are binding only upon States form the largest and best-established category. Then come treaties between a State and an international organization, between several international organizations or between several States and one or several international organizations. The crucial difference between States and international organizations is that the latter are defined and contained by their constituent instruments. During discussions at the International Law Commission and in the Commission's final draft, the socialist countries were at pains constantly to restate this limitation, recognizing nonetheless that the law of treaties was bound to be the same for both. The Convention of 21 March 1986 deleted some of these references which were not deemed essential. Except for a number of specific provisions due to the structure of organizations, the régime of treaties where the parties include one or several organizations entirely conforms to the régime of inter-State treaties. The same can be said of entities assimilated to States or international organizations (Holy See, International Committee of the Red Cross). While the case of individuals should be set apart (see above, No. 73), both the 1969 and 1986 Conventions allow for a possible extension of their provisions to agreements which are binding on subjects of international law other than States or organizations.(*)

78 The number of parties is traditionally regarded as an important though superficial criterion for classifying treaties. It has indeed some almost mechanical consequences such as negotiation by conference as the parties become more numerous; and it is certainly useful to distinguish between bilateral and multilateral treaties. However, just counting the parties is not enough; it is more essential to know whether a given number of parties at any given time is immutable or whether and to what degree the treaty is open to others and what are the real reasons for limiting their number — but this cannot be answered without considering the substantive features of the treaty (see below, No. 80).

79   The form of a treaty would seem to be another important criterion. Attention has already been drawn to the distinction between written and unwritten treaties (see above, No. 66). Other formal criteria, in particular classification according to the degree of solemnity, may be constitutionally relevant in municipal law, but are much less so in international law (however, see above, No. 74), which leaves the parties to each treaty free to agree on a given form in which to express their consent or even to provide for several alternative forms in which to do so (see below, No. 93).

80   The substantive features of treaties ought to have pride of place in the classifications of treaties. Yet they will hardly result in clear-cut and generally acceptable categories. Suffice it to recall the example of law-making and contractual treaties (see above, No. 57). Such distinctions are bound to remain somewhat theoretical: seldom will they have any bearing on international practice. Obviously, the object and purpose of a treaty are crucial for its legal régime, as the 1969 and 1986 Conventions state time and again (articles 18, 20 (2), 41, 58, 60 (3) (b)). But a general classification by object and purpose is an impossible task: indeed, in many cases it will prove difficult even to define the object and purpose of a treaty (see below, No. 127, the problem of reservations).

81   In a number of well-identified cases the specific features of a treaty are characteristic enough to be generally recognized as typical; thus constitutive instruments of international organizations are governed by their own principles, in particular with respect to reservations and interpretation. Certain general types of treaties may emerge in the practice of a given period, like treaties of establishment or navigation, treaties concerning double taxation, headquarters agreements of international organizations, treaties laying down rules of private international law or uniform law, etc. There is certainly no theory of 'nominate treaties' in international law comparable to what certain legal systems call 'nominate contracts'; yet international judicial authorities, when called upon to interpret a treaty, do turn to other treaties of the same group and period, examining their terminology and provisions in order to solve various difficulties (see below, No. 148).(*)

82   One of the most interesting and arduous points raised by the classification of treaties based on their substantive features pertains to the degree of interdependence between the various obligations stipulated in one and the same treaty. In some cases they are indeed utterly indivisible. Two situations should be distinguished, depending on whether the indivisibility relates to the provisions of a treaty or to its parties. The provisions of a treaty may be so closely connected that none of them can be severed from the rest through the operation either of reservations or of some legitimate ground for non-application (1969 and 1986 Conventions, article 44): instead, the treaty can only be accepted and applied as a whole. Or the nature of the treaty may be such as to preclude breaking it down into a set of bilateral relationships: any non-performance by one of the parties would seriously affect all the others. Thus, to take a typical example, in the case of a disarmament treaty, surely 'a material breach of its provisions by one party radically changes the position of every party with respect to the further performance of its obligations under the treaty' (1969 and 1986 Conventions, article 60 (2) (c)). The specific features of treaty obligations lend themselves to an analysis based on various other considerations such as substance or mutual interdependence. This is particularly useful when the breach of a treaty raises issues of State responsibility (see below, No. 296).(*)

IV Work on international treaties

1. Codification

83 The official process of codification which has been going on since 1950 in the United Nations, culminating in the Vienna Convention on the Law of Treaties of 23 May 1969, overshadows all previous endeavours in the field. The law of treaties has been renewed not just because of the final outcome of this work but by the wealth of information submitted to, and discussed by, the International Law Commission and the 1968–1969 Vienna Conference. It is only fair, however, to recall that this achievement was preceded, accompanied and followed by many others. No doubt, little is to be gathered from the attempts initiated by the League of Nations between 1924 and 1929 which quickly ran aground. However, the law of treaties was also tackled on a regional level in the draft submitted to the 1928 Havana Conference of American States, while the problem of reservations was considered by the Interamerican Legal Committee in 1955 and 1959 as well as by the Council of Europe (especially with regard to its own treaty practice). The codification of the law of treaties has now come to an end with the Vienna Convention on the Law of Treaties between States and International Organizations or between International Organizations of 21 March 1986, which followed the Vienna Convention on the Succession of States in Respect of Treaties of 23 August 1978. This does not, however, preclude research projects from going on within the United Nations for instance on the drawing up of multilateral treaties (see above, No. 33).(*)

84 Apart from this official process of codification, a number of earlier, no less remarkable endeavours undertaken privately by independent bodies or universities also deserve to be mentioned. First there is the research done by the Institute of International Law. Even before World War I, the Institute had dealt with the question of publication of treaties (1885, 1891 and 1892); it went on in parallel with the International Law Commission with treaty interpretation (1956), modification and termination of collective treaties (1963, 1967), most-favoured-nation clauses in multilateral treaties (1969), intertemporal law (1973, 1975), international texts devoid of legal import (1979, 1983) and instruments of normative import (1985), and the effect of war on treaties (1985). Also the International Law Association has dealt with State succession (1966, 1968). Yet the most remarkable work prior to the International Law Commission remains Harvard University's research and draft on the law of treaties (1935).

2. Research

A. OBJECT AND NATURE OF CURRENT RESEARCH

85   The International Law Commission's codification work prompted a renewal of scientific research on the law of treaties, as shown by the great number of studies based on its discussions and the material involved. Efforts to analyse the Vienna Convention and to supplement it are noticeable in two main directions: judicial practice relating to treaties in municipal law, and theoretical studies. Clearly, although to varying degrees, national practice turned out not to be as well known as had been thought. Despite a regular flow of valuable publications on the subject, it was found in general that only a small proportion of instruments were accessible and that on many points a genuine and, as it were, statistical knowledge of the content of treaties was lacking. On the other hand, owing to its empirical bias, the 1969 Vienna Convention fails to decide any of the issues calling for a somewhat more abstract analysis, such as the place of the law of treaties within a wider theory of juristic acts and all the problems raised by unwritten agreements, whether connected or not to the activities of international organizations. On all these topics, recent studies have shown what directions are being followed.(*)

86   Questions concerning international treaties are also being reconsidered not from a legal point of view, but in the light of political science and international relations. Owing to computer technology, earlier studies based on history and diplomacy are now being supplemented by a quantitative analysis of the mass of contemporary agreements. Yet whether one refers to the broad survey carried out by the Council of Europe or to the work of American or European universities, one is struck both by the variety and scope of the prospects and by the relative uncertainty of the immediate objectives to be pursued. In its initial stages, this type of research highlighted the gaps in the publication of treaties on the national and international level; while it does afford summary quantitative evidence of the density of the treaty network between States, it will hardly yield as yet any more detailed results.(*)

B. RESEARCH POINTERS

The following references are intended to assist academic study of the law of treaties with respect to bibliographical research and treaty texts.

(a) Bibliographies

87 Bibliographical references have been published in the documents of the Vienna Conferences on the Law of Treaties, especially in documents A/CONF. 39/4 and A/CONF. 129/6. Periodical bibliographies are published by the *Annuaire français de droit international* (Tables décennales 1955–1964, 1965–1974, 1975–1984), by the *United Nations Juridical Yearbook*, the *New Publications in the Dag Hammarskjöld Library*, or in the bibliography periodical *Public International Law* (Heidelberg). Detailed indications are given in the classical works of international law: Ch. Rousseau, *Principes généraux du droit international public* (Paris, Pedone, 1944) and *Droit international public*, vol. I (Paris, Sirey, 1970), L. Oppenheim, *International Law*, 8th edn., H. Lauterpacht, ed., vol. I (London, Longmans, Green and Co., 1955), and Lord McNair, *The Law of Treaties*, 2nd edn. (Oxford, Clarendon Press, 1961), as well as in: United Nations, *Laws and Practices Concerning the Conclusion of Treaties* (UN Pub., Sales No. 1952. V. 4, p. 141); G. Haraszti, *Some Fundamental Problems of the Law of Treaties* (Budapest, Akadémiai Kiadó, 1973); A. Maresca, *Il diritto dei trattati* (Milan, Giuffrè, 1971); G.E. do Nascimento e Silva, *Conferência de Viena sôbre o direito dos tratados* (Brasilia, Ministério das Relações Exteriores, 1971); S. Bastid, *Les traités dans la vie internationale* (Paris, Economica, 1985).

(b) Treaty series

88 There are few general works giving substantial information on the different treaty series apart from P. Guggenheim, *Traité de droit international public*, 2nd edn. (Geneva, Georg, 1967), vol. 1, p. 122. The excellent memorandum by the United Nations Secretariat, *Ways and Means of Making the Evidence of Customary International Law More Readily Available* (UN Pub., Sales No. 1949. V. 6), as well as D.P. Myers, *Manual for Collections of Treaties and Collections Relating to Treaties* (Cambridge, Mass., Harvard University Press, 1922), updated in United Nations, *List of Treaty Collections*, ST/LEG/5, 1956 (UN Pub., Sales No. 1956. V. 2), remain the basic guides in this difficult field. See also C. Parry, 'Where to look for your treaties', *International Journal for Law Libraries*, Feb. 1980, No. 1, and A. Sprudzs, 'Status of multilateral treaties: researcher's mystery, mess or muddle?', *AJ*, vol. 56 (1972), p. 365; to the collections mentioned, add in particular C. Parry, ed., *Consolidated Treaty Series (1648–1919)* (Dobbs Ferry, Oceana, 1969–). For research on recent treaties likely to be registered with the League of Nations or the United Nations, refer to League of Nations, *Treaty Series, Publications of Treaties and International Engagements Registered with the Secretariat of the League*, 205 vols., 1920–

1943 (9 general indexes) and to United Nations, *Treaty Series, Treaties and International Agreements Registered or Filed and Recorded with the Secretariat of the United Nations*, 1193 vols. until 1986 (14 cumulative indexes until vol. 900). For multilateral treaties, see M.J. Bowman and D.J. Harris, *Multilateral Treaties. Index and Current Status* (London, Butterworths, 1984) and, for unpublished French treaties, R. Pinto and H. Rollet, *Recueil général des traités de la France publiés et non publiés* (Documentation française).

Notes

1*　For the historical aspects of the law of treaties, apart from the works listed below (No. 10*), see the major pre-1970 works such as Lord McNair, *The Law of Treaties*, 2nd edn., (Oxford, Clarendon Press, 1961) and P. Guggenheim, *Traité de droit international public*, 2nd edn. (Geneva, Georg, 1967), vol. 1, pp. 114 ff. See also a number of more specific studies such as J. Mervyn Jones, *Full Powers and Ratification* (Cambridge, Cambridge University Press, 1946) and K. Marek, 'Contribution à l'histoire du traité multilatéral', *Festschrift für Rudolf Bindschedler* (Bern, Stämpfli, 1980), p. 17.

4*　Whether it is real or imaginary, there is nothing new about the attraction for all ministers and senior State officials to intervene in foreign affairs. The texts establishing the exclusive powers of the French Ministry for Foreign Affairs in matters of external relations go back to the order of 22 Messidor, Year VII (1799) and the decree of 29 December 1810. More recent circular letters (26 March 1962, 2672/SG), as well as letters from the President of the Republic to the Prime Minister and from the Prime Minister to other Ministers, restate the same principles while leaving some room — exactly how much remains unclear — for the 'development of international relations'. Concerning the United States and the United Kingdom, see D.P. O'Connell, *International Law*, 2nd edn. (London, Stevens, 1970), vol. I, p. 214.

5*　Initially the *Vereinbarungstheorie* was part of a general conception of juristic acts. In Triepel's view, it was the cornerstone of the whole of public international law as distinct from municipal law, and it was as such that the theory was criticized. This is its most original aspect and it could be revived with regard to several issues concerning the essential characteristics of treaties such as separability *vel non* of treaty provisions (see below, No. 241).

7*　Domestic practice relating to treaties has been divided by legal writers according to whether it stems from protocol or from legal advisers. For a strong criticism of the former, see Judge Basdevant's Dissenting Opinion in the *Ambatielos, Preliminary Objection* case (*ICJ Reports 1952*, pp. 69–70). In any event there is no more convincing example of the influence of the latter than those taken from French practice or international organizations. In French practice, since the abolition of the formality of treaty promulgation, treaties have been published uniformly by way of presidential decree; the courts regard this as an indispensable prerequisite for the treaty to be applied and the *Conseil d'Etat* considers it so essential a formality that it could even replace an omitted ratification (*Société Navigator, Recueil des arrêts du Conseil d'Etat*, 1965, p. 422). Moreover the Constitution does not specify which is the authority that has to approve the 'agreements' mentioned by it; practice alone has determined that in general such approval is given by the government and notified by the Minister for Foreign Affairs. For international organizations, see J. Groux and Ph. Manin, *Les Communautés européennes dans l'ordre international* (Brussels, Perspectives européennes, 1984), pp. 57 ff.

10* L. Bittner, *Die Lehre von den völkerrechtlichen Vertragsurkunden* (Stuttgart, Deutsche Verlagsanstalt, 1924); J. Basdevant, 'La conclusion et la rédaction des traités et des instruments diplomatiques autres que les traités', *RCADI*, vol. 15 (1926-V), p. 535; H. Triepel, *Völkerrecht und Landesrecht* (Leipzig, Hirschfeld, 1899); D. Anzilotti, *Corso di diritto internazionale*, 3rd edn., (Rome, Athenaeum, 1928).

14* M. Sibert, 'Quelques aspects de l'organisation et de la technique des conférences internationales', *RCADI*, vol. 48 (1934-II), p. 387; S. Hoffmann, *Organisations internationales et pouvoirs politiques des Etats* (Paris, Armand Colin, 1954).

20* For the Reports of the Committee of Experts in charge of the preparatory codification work, see League of Nations documents C. 196 M. 70 and A. 15 (S. Rosenne, ed., *League of Nations Conference for the Codification of International Law* (Dobbs Ferry, Oceana, 1975)). The Harvard Law School's Draft Convention on the Law of Treaties was published in *AJ*, Supplement to vol. 29 (1935), p. 657.

23* The case of the General Act for the Pacific Settlement of International Disputes adopted on 26 September 1928 by a vote of the Assembly of the League of Nations is the most characteristic because the text was signed only by the President of the Assembly and the Secretary-General, for the sole purpose of authentication; the adoption of the text of a treaty 'within' an international body does not necessarily rule out the eventuality that the States will be called upon to sign it later, usually within a rather short time-limit.

24* More significant even than the General Act for the Pacific Settlement of International Disputes is the example of International Labour Conventions. These are adopted by a majority vote of the International Labour Conference and submitted by governments to the domestic authority competent to give effect to their provisions, whereupon the Ministries for Foreign Affairs inform the Organisation of the acceptance by that authority, notification taking the place of deposit or ratification. For the constitutional conflicts arising from this procedure, see Ch. Rousseau, *Principes généraux du droit international public* (Paris, Pedone, 1944), vol. 1, para. 94.

25* *Modi vivendi* of 19 July 1921 between Switzerland and the League of Nations and 20 September 1926 between Switzerland and the ILO. However, such agreements were rare: see B. Kasme, *La capacité de l'ONU de conclure des traités* (Paris, Librairie générale de droit et de jurisprudence), p. 8. Moreover the legal personality of the League appeared doubtful (see the observations of Judges Spender and Fitzmaurice in *South West Africa, Preliminary Objections, ICJ Reports 1962*, p. 475, as well as the Court's Judgment on the second phase, *ICJ Reports 1966*, p. 30). But by 1960, according to an estimate by O. Schachter, there were about one thousand treaties between organizations and States and some two hundred between international organizations (*AJ*, vol. 54 (1960), p. 201).

26* In fact, apart from the legal expression the concept of the 'Great Powers' finds in permanent membership of the Security Council, there is a more realistic and restricted definition based solely on full nuclear capacity. In the law of treaties, this is the only field in which prerogatives of the Great Powers have been effective; but they are increasingly challenged, as became apparent during the preparation of the treaty concerning the neutralization of the sea-bed. Any negotiated or spontaneous agreement between the Soviet Union and the United States weighs very heavily indeed on the preparation of a treaty, but it is no longer enough to impose a solution even with respect to security issues as has been seen in relation to aircraft hijacking.

30–33* Although the ILC is not the only United Nations organ involved in codification (see the general table in the excellent survey of international law by the UN Secretary General (A/CN.4/245) reprinted in *YILC 1971*, vol. II (part 2), p. 1), it does remain the principal one and is indeed the only one to deal with the law of treaties. In this regard, see H.W. Briggs, *International Law Commission* (Ithaca, Cornell University Press, 1965), and Sir Ian Sinclair, *The International Law Commission* (Cambridge, Grotius Publications, 1987). On the Vienna Convention, see the bibliographical note and introduction by P. Reuter, *La Convention de Vienne du 23 mai 1969 sur le droit des traités* (Paris, Armand Colin, 1970); for a historical study on the elaboration of the Convention article by article, the fundamental work is S. Rosenne, *The Law of Treaties. A Guide to the Legislative History of the Vienna Convention* (Leyden, Sijthoff, 1970). See also: R.G. Wetzel and D. Rauschning, *The Vienna Convention on the Law of Treaties — Travaux préparatoires* (Frankfurt, Metzner, 1978); E. de La Guardia and M. Delpech, *El Derecho de los Tratados y la Convención de Vienna* (Buenos Aires, La Ley, 1970); T. Elias, *The Modern Law of Treaties* (Dobbs Ferry, Oceana, 1974); Sir Ian Sinclair, *The Vienna Convention on the Law of Treaties*, 2nd edn, (Manchester, Manchester University Press, 1984).

34* The theory of 'linked' organs contrasts with the theory of 'subsidiary' organs whose legal source is a unilateral act of the organization; but it remains to be clearly delineated out of confused and hesitant practice. It should be elaborated in parallel with another theory concerning the possibility to confer by convention non-statutory powers on an organ of an organization. The question incidentally arose at the International Court of Justice in the *South West Africa* cases; see W. Riphagen, 'Over concentratie en delegatie bij internationale instellingen', *Varia Juris Gentium. Liber Amicorum Presented to Jean Pierre Adrien François* (Leyden, Sijthoff, 1959), p. 229. As for measures, partly dating back to the period of the League of Nations, which confer some supervisory powers on organizations, especially with regard to ratification of, and accession to, treaties concluded under their auspices, their tendency is to bring about important transformations in treaty mechanisms. UNITAR, *Wider Acceptance of Multilateral Treaties* (Unitar Series No. 2, 1969); R. Ago, 'The final stage of the codification of international law' (A/CN.4/205 Rev. 1), *YILC 1968*, vol. II, p. 171, and 'La codification du droit international et le problème de sa réalisation', *Recueil d'études de droit international en hommage à Paul Guggenheim*, (Geneva, Faculté de droit, 1968), p. 93; F.M. Hondius, 'La préparation et la gestion des traités conclus dans le cadre du Conseil de l'Europe', *Annuaire de l'Université de Clermont-Ferrand*, vol. 95 (1979), p. 283; V. Coussirat-Coustère, *La contribution des organisations internationales au contrôle des obligations conventionnelles des Etats* (Thesis, Paris II, 1979).

35* As proposed by the ILC, the expression 'rules of the organization' used in article 2 (1) (j) of the 1986 Vienna Convention stands for the legal framework of an organization and is defined non-exhaustively as meaning 'in particular, the constituent instruments, decisions and resolutions adopted in accordance with them, and established practice of the organization'.

39* This is essentially a relativist view based on the consideration that relations between international and municipal law are determined by factors of political sociology and by the extent of social integration; but legal rules of course do not necessarily keep pace with the social integration reached at a given time in a given country; they can also be in advance of it or lagging behind. For international organizations, see below, No. 229. For the European Communities, see J. Groux and Ph. Manin, *Les Communautés européennes dans l'ordre international*, pp. 116 ff.

40* The solution chosen by the 1968-9 Vienna Conference does seem to be confirmed by international practice (H. Blix, *Treaty-Making Power* (London, Stevens, 1960)) and constitutes a reasonable compromise between extreme theoretical positions (R.D. Kearney, 'International limitations on external commitments, Article 46 of the Treaties Convention', *The International Lawyer*, vol. 4 (1969), p. 1). For a similar study of municipal law, see S. Rosenne, 'Problems of treaty-making competence', *Essays in Honor of Haim H. Cohn*, (New York, 1971), p. 115. The 1969 Vienna Convention did not, however, determine whether a treaty which does not specify the point has to be considered as final upon signature or upon ratification. In fact, legislative assemblies in many countries claim more powers than they could in practice be granted. Some Constitutions even go so far as to require approval by Parliament or Congress for every single treaty (which explains the reservations to the 1969 Convention by Costa Rica and Guatemala). Since this requirement is impracticable, the only solution in terms of constitutional law is to define treaties more strictly on the constitutional level than on the international level. Even so, some uncertainty may arise for third States. The emergence of entities such as the European Communities has brought about two developments. First, national Constitutions have been supplemented by stricter rules for treaties which were felt to entail a transfer of sovereignty, either because the Constitution had to be amended or because other conditions had to be fulfilled to allow ratification (referendum, qualified majority) (P. Reuter, *Droit international public*, 6th edn. (Paris, PUF, 1983), p. 129). Thus the Single European Act of 17 and 28 February 1986, which was declared unconstitutional by the Irish Supreme Court (despite its moderation), could only be ratified by Ireland following the referendum of 26 May 1987. The second development concerns the new problems raised for third States by the treaties concluded by the Communities themselves (see below, Nos. 44*, 45* and 176* to 180*).

44* On these questions in general, see: the bibliography in P. Reuter, *Droit international public*, p. 87; M. Waelbroeck, *Traités internationaux et juridictions internes* (Paris, Pedone, 1969); *L'application du droit international par le juge français* (Paris, Armand Colin, 1972); and references below at No. 85*. For the uncertainty of the term 'self-executing' used mainly in United States practice, see S. Riesenfeld, 'The doctrine of self-executing treaties and *U.S.* v. *Postal*: win at any price?', *AJ*, vol. 74 (1980), p. 292, and J.J. Paust, 'Self-executing treaties', *AJ*, vol. 82 (1988), p. 760.

48–49* Conventional régimes instituting a special kind of relationship between international and municipal law have long been used in international law (*Polish Postal Service in Danzig, Advisory Opinion, PCIJ, Series B, No. 11*, p. 17). It is, however, within the European Communities that the most significant evolution has taken place in domestic courts regarding the relation between Community and municipal law. Not only do the treaties instituting the Communities give an important place to preliminary rulings (Art. 177 EEC), but the Court of Justice of the European Communities, extending the principle of immediacy of Community law, requires national courts, acting in fact as Community courts, to give absolute priority to Community law over municipal law, including subsequent legislation (see in particular the *Simmenthal* case 106/77 of 9 March 1978, *ECR 1978*, p. 629). In France, the *Cour de cassation*, unlike the *Conseil d'Etat*, gives priority to community law over subsequent municipal law (see the official study 'Droit communautaire et droit français', *Notes et études documentaires*, Nos. 4678 to 4681). In the United Kingdom, the courts have made the most of the European Communities Act (1972); see case-law reviews, in *European Law Review* (especially 1976, p. 388, and 1986, p. 287), and *Revue trimestrielle de droit européen* (especially vol. 22 (1986), p. 435). See also: G. Olmi, 'Les rapports entre droit communautaire et droit national dans les arrêts des juridictions supérieures des Etats membres', *Revue du Marché commun*, vol. 24 (1981), pp. 178, 242, 379; H.G. Schermers, *Judicial Protection in the European Communities* (Deventer, Kluwer, 1976).

50* While all modern authors consider treaties in the context both of the sources of international law and juristic acts, many of them fail to distinguish between the two aspects. However, see: P. Chailley, *La nature juridique des traités internationaux selon le droit contemporain* (Paris, Sirey, 1932), paras. 42 and 110; P. Reuter, 'The operational and normative aspects of treaties', *Israel Law Review*, vol. 20 (1985), p. 123.

For the translation of 'acte juridique' it was decided to use the expression 'juristic act' following T. E. Holland, *The Elements of Jurisprudence*, 12th edn. (Oxford, Clarendon Press, 1916), pp. 117–118 and G.W. Paton, *A Text-Book of Jurisprudence*, 3rd edn. (Oxford, Clarendon Press, 1964), p. 279, para. 69.

51* United Nations Secretariat, *Handbook of Final Clauses*, ST/LEG/6, 1957; H. Blix and J.H. Emerson, eds, *The Treaty Maker's Handbook* (Stockholm, Almqvist and Wiksell, 1973).

52* *Ambatielos, Preliminary Objection, ICJ Reports 1952*, p. 28, and *Interpretation of the Agreement of 25 March 1951 between the WHO and Egypt, ICJ Reports 1980*, p. 73. P. Reuter, 'Traités et transactions. Réflexions sur l'identification de certains engagements conventionnels', *International Law at the Time of its Codification. Essays in Honour of Roberto Ago* (Milan, Giuffrè, 1987), vol. I, p. 299.

53* No country has of course ever been able to go to the logical end of the dualistic theory and isolate treaty rules from certain specific factors determining their application by judicial authorities (state of peace or war, reciprocity, etc.). See P. Lagarde, 'La condition de réciprocité dans l'application des traités internationaux: son appréciation par le juge interne', *Revue critique de droit international privé*, vol. 64 (1975), p. 25, as well as chronicles and articles in *Revue du droit public*, 1981, p. 1707, *Journal du droit international*, vol. 109 (1982), p. 439, and *RGDIP*, vol. 87 (1983), p. 780. Thorough studies have been devoted to this aspect in Italian law in keeping with the prevailing doctrine of 'transformation': G. Morelli, *Nozioni di diritto internazionale*, 7th edn. (Padua, CEDAM, 1967), p. 76.

54* Whether a State could by its own free will be bound by treaties concluded by another State without itself becoming a party to such treaties was considered on several occasions by the ILC which gave a negative answer both for a technical reason — a State represented by another *ipso facto* becomes a party to the Convention in question — and for a political reason, i.e. exacerbated hostility towards anything that might justify colonialism (*YILC 1964*, vol. I, 732nd, 733rd and 750th meetings). Similar problems arise in connection with the status of non-self-governing territories in relation to treaties applying to such territories, especially constituent charters granting the parties — and only the parties — the status of 'members of the organization'; for here too the application of a given legal régime may to some degree be dissociated from the status of 'party'; see R. Kovar, 'La participation des territoires non autonomes aux organisations internationales', *AF*, vol. 15 (1969), p. 522. Also to be noted is the curious formula used in conventions concluded under the auspices of IMCO, for instance in Article XIII of the International Convention Relating to Intervention on the High Seas in Cases of Oil Pollution Casualties which provides for extension of the Convention to territories under the administration of the United Nations or of a State Party.

62* This is no more than a doctrinal perception of the 'international community'. While it clearly covers a social reality, it does not at present seem to constitute a legal reality. Some views, however, even in official circles, tend to endow the international community with the features bestowed in municipal law upon *de facto* associations without legal status, by granting it certain powers and a representation which would be either Great Powers acting in concert or the organs of the United Nations, whose powers therefore would no longer be clearly defined (see the statement by the Netherlands representative at the International Court of Justice in *Legal Consequences for States of the Continued Presence of South Africa in Namibia (South West Africa) notwithstanding Security Council Resolution 276 (1970)* (hereinafter referred to as the *Namibia* case) (*ICJ Pleadings*, vol. II, p. 122). Such speculations are reminiscent of the theory of 'quasi-universal treaties' (see below, No. 166). The customary character of certain provisions of the Vienna Convention is apparent in decisions of the International Court referring thereto (*Namibia, ICJ Reports 1971*, p. 47; *Fisheries Jurisdiction (United Kingdom* v. *Iceland) (Jurisdiction of the Court)*, *ICJ Reports 1973*, pp. 14 and 18; *Aegean Sea Continental Shelf, ICJ Reports 1978*, p. 39; *Interpretation of the Agreement of 25 March 1951 between the WHO and Egypt, ICJ Reports 1980*, pp. 92 and 94). The Court also refers to codification conventions which are not yet in force: the 1978 Convention on Succession of States in Respect of Treaties (*Continental Shelf (Tunisia/Libya), ICJ Reports 1982*, p. 66) or the draft articles on treaties concluded by international organizations (*ICJ Reports 1980*, pp. 92 and 94). See the studies by P. Ziccardi in *Comunicazioni e Studi*, vol. 14 (1975), p. 1043; S. Rosenne in *Homenaje al profesor Miaja de la Muela* (Madrid, Tecnos, 1979), vol. I, p. 441; and E.W. Vierdag, *AJ*, vol. 78 (1982), p. 778. See also Sir Ian Sinclair, 'The impact of the unratified codification convention', *Realism in Law-Making. Essays on International Law in Honour of Willem Riphagen* (Dordrecht, Kluwer, 1986), p. 211, and L.B. Sohn, 'Unratified treaties as a source of customary international law', ibid., p. 231.

63* Yet in spite of the equivalence of these terms as evidenced by their use in the most basic treaties (art. 7 Hague Convention (XII): 'Convention'; League of Nations Covenant: 'Treaty' (Preamble), 'international obligations' (Art. 1, para. 2), 'understandings *inter se*' (Art. 20); Art. 38 PCIJ Statute: 'international conventions': United Nations Charter: 'treaties' (preamble), 'regional arrangements' (Chapter VIII), 'conventions' (Art. 62, para. 3)), the differences in terminology may sometimes have legal connotations; thus 'agreement' is less formal than 'treaty' and the same may be true of 'convention', at least with regard to its derivative 'conventional'. The term 'treaty' is defined differently in the 1969 and 1986 Vienna Conventions to allow for their distinct field of application but its meaning remains otherwise unaffected.

64*   As far as possible, the 1969 Convention endeavoured to lay down general rules uniformly covering all the agreements falling within its field of application; when it proved necessary to formulate specific rules for multilateral treaties or a special kind of multilateral treaty, this was only done incidentally and undogmatically (e.g. arts. 20 (2), 40, 41, 55, 58, 60, 59 (4), 70 (2)). See J. Dehaussy, 'Le problème de la classification des traités et le projet établi par la Commission du droit international des Nations Unies', *En hommage à Paul Guggenheim*, p. 305; M. Virally, 'Sur la classification des traités', *Comunicazioni e Studi*, vol. 13 (1969), p. 16.

67*   In a number of major international cases — *Legal Status of Eastern Greenland (PCIJ, Series A/B, No. 53), Fisheries (ICJ Reports 1951*, p. 139), *Temple of Preah Vihear, Merits (ICJ Reports 1962*, p. 6) — the Court refrained from too rigid a construction, whereas widely differing theories are put forward by legal writers, especially concerning territorial situations (P. Reuter, *Droit international public*, pp. 97 and 108). But even apart from the finer theoretical differences characterizing the various explanations (G. Sperduti, 'Prescrizione, consuetudine e acquiescenza in diritto internazionale', *Rivista di diritto internazionale*, vol. 44 (1961), p. 3), intellectual constructions do not equally fit the circumstances of each case, as is fully realized by agents and counsel and even more so by international tribunals. This is probably why reliance is placed in some cases on sources of law by resorting either to local custom or tacit agreement or even to some unilateral act, while in other cases it is placed on prescription or consolidation of a title, and in others still on estoppel or acquiescence. While the circumstances of each case are thus taken into account, some theoretical explanations would seem to be more appropriate than others, as being more consistent with the features of international law; thus estoppel may be somewhat narrower than acquiescence (compare J. Barale, 'L'acquiescement dans la jurisprudence internationale', *AF*, vol. 11 (1965), p. 389, and Ch. Dominicé, 'A propos du principe de l'*estoppel* en droit des gens', *En hommage à Paul Guggenheim*, p. 327), while the concept of consolidation of a title is preferable to that of prescription (Ch. De Visscher, *Les effectivités du droit international public* (Paris, Pedone, 1967), p. 159). As for the different doctrinal attempts to endow General Assembly resolutions with a force denied them by the Charter, they are bound to remain very fragile, however ingenious they may be, since they are not recognized by the Great Powers.

67*-68*   The draft articles prepared by the ILC already included many provisions relating to non-formal agreements, most of which became part of the 1969 Convention (e.g. art. 12 (c) which became art. 15 (c) in the Convention, see commentary *YILC 1966*, vol. II, p. 199, para. 4). But article 38 of the ILC draft — which followed the reasoning of the arbitrators in the *Case concerning the Interpretation of the Air Transport Services Agreement between the United States of America and France signed at Paris on 27 March 1946, RIAA*, vol. 16, p. 11 ('A treaty may be modified by subsequent practice in the application of the treaty establishing the agreement of the parties to modify its provisions') — met with fierce resistance at the Vienna Conference (*Official Records of the United Nations Conference on the Law of Treaties, First Session, Summary records of the plenary meetings and of the meetings of the Committee of the Whole* (UN Pub., Sales No. E.68.V. 7) 37th and

38th meetings of the Committee of the Whole), and despite eloquent statements denying *inter alia* the relevance of the *acte contraire* principle in international law, it was rejected by 53 votes to 15 with 26 abstentions; however, this rejection is inconsistent with other provisions of the Convention.

70* The Secretary-General of the United Nations has consistently maintained that the Organization was a party to the Convention on the Privileges and Immunities of the United Nations of 13 February 1946 (*ICJ Pleadings, Reparations for Injuries Suffered in the Service of the United Nations*, p. 71; *YILC 1967*, vol. II, p. 221; *Official Records of the General Assembly*, 22nd session, annexes, docs. A/6965, (para. 14, and A/C.6/385, p. 4). It is very doubtful whether the formula is technically correct: it would be better to say that the Organization in this case as in many others is not a third party (see below, No. 121). For a discussion of the question concerning the 1946 treaty, see K. Zemanek, *Agreements of International Organizations* (Vienna, Springer, 1971), p. 185.

71* The problem of the legal nature of certain acts of 'State representatives in the Council' has become a classical problem in the European Community; G. van der Meersch, *Droit communautaire* (Bruxelles, Larcier, 1969), para. 1173. For the problem of decisions based on EEC Article 235, see case 38/69, *ECR 1970*, p. 47 ('an act which has the characteristics of a Community decision because of its objective as well as of the institutional framework within which it has been drawn up, cannot be described as an "international agreement" '). On the other hand, the legal nature of mandates and trusteeship agreements remains controversial; see: ICJ decisions on South West Africa; P. Leroy, 'La nature juridique des accords de tutelle', *RGDIP*, vol. 69 (1965), p. 977; M. Virally, 'Sur la notion d'accord', *Festschrift für Rudolf Bindschedler*, p. 159. As for regarding occasional votes — let alone abstentions — within an organ of an organization as acts binding upon a State under the law of treaties, this is clearly an exaggeration, rightly rejected by G.I. Tunkin, *Droit international public* (Paris, Pedone, 1965), p. 104.

72* There are no difficulties concerning international agreements negotiated and concluded by technical agents in fields where this is the usual practice, e.g. postal and military agreements (Ch. Rousseau, *Principes généraux du droit international public*, p. 255). Inasmuch as agreements are concluded between administrative authorities of different States, domestic courts may refuse to consider them as treaties in municipal law and to enforce them as such (Consorts Châtelain, 18 June 1965, *Recueil du Conseil d'Etat*, 1965, p. 366); G. Burdeau, 'Les accords conclus entre autorités administratives ou organismes publics de pays différents', *Mélanges offerts à Paul Reuter. Le droit international: unité et diversité* (Paris, Pedone, 1982), p. 103. In French practice, departments of specialized ministries may conclude 'administrative' agreements to the same extent as they can commit the State on the municipal level. See: O.J. Lissitzyn, 'Territorial entities other than independent States in the law of treaties', *RCADI*, vol. 125 (1968-III) p. 1; L. Di Marzo, *Component Units of Federal States and International Agreements* (Leyden, Sijthoff, 1980); Y. Lejeune, *Le statut international des collectivités fédérées à la lumière de l'expérience suisse* (Paris, Librairie générale de droit et de jurisprudence, 1984).

73* On the extension of the theory of treaties to agreements with an entity recognized by some States as endowed with international personality, see: for the Order of Malta, D.P. O'Connell, *International Law*, p. 85, and Kiichiro Nakahara, 'The Sovereign Order of Malta today: an inquiry into its treaty making', Hogaku

Shimpo (*Chuo Law Review*, vol. 76, No. 10 (1970), p. 23); for the ICRC, P. Reuter, 'La personnalité juridique internationale du CICR', *Studies and Essays in Honour of Jean Pictet* (Geneva, ICRC, 1984) p. 723. See also for the internationalization of an agreement between an international organization and an individual, *YILC 1967*, vol. II, p. 207. On the other hand, the idea of two individuals concluding an agreement in a legal no man's land unconnected to any State order continues to be rejected by all those for whom law is linked to the State. But the main question relates to State commitments concerning foreign investment. For a synthetic study and references, see: P. Weil, 'Problèmes relatifs aux contrats passés entre un Etat et un particulier', *RCADI*, vol. 128 (1969-III), p. 25; J.-F. Lalive, 'Contrats entre Etats ou entreprises étatiques et personnes privées. Développements récents', *RCADI*, vol. 181 (1983-III), p. 9; P. Mayer, 'La neutralisation du pouvoir normatif de l'Etat en matière de contrats d'Etat', *Journal du droit international*, vol. 113 (1986), p. 5; N. David, 'Les clauses de stabilité dans les contrats pétroliers. Questions d'un praticien', ibid., p. 79.

74* The proposed analysis fully allows for the position of the United States of America concerning certain acts like the Yalta agreements; see: D.P. O'Connell, *International Law*, p. 200; K. Marek, 'Retour sur Yalta', *RGDIP*, vol. 86 (1982), p. 457. For a different analysis, see: M. Virally's provisional report 'La distinction entre textes internationaux de portée juridique et textes internationaux dépourvus de portée juridique', *Annuaire de l'Institut de Droit international*, vol. 60-I (1983), p. 146; K. Widdows, 'What is an agreement in international law', *BYBIL*, vol. 50 (1979), p. 117; J.A. Barberis, 'Le concept de "traité international" et ses limites', *AF*, vol. 30 (1984), p. 239; P.M. Eisenmann, 'Le "gentlemen's agreement" comme source du droit international', *Journal du droit international*, vol. 106 (1979), p. 925; and the articles by Sperduti, Treves and Villani in the *Italian Yearbook of International Law*, vol. 2 (1976), pp. 33 ff. On the divergent characterizations of the Helsinki Act, see: the study in *AF*, vol. 21 (1975), p. 1012; N.A. Ouchakov, 'Le développement des principes fondamentaux du droit international dans l'Acte final sur la sécurité et la coopération en Europe', *Essays in International Law in Honour of Judge Manfred Lachs* (The Hague, Nijhoff, 1984), p. 217; answer of the Council of Ministers of the European Communities to written question 1120/84, *Official Journal of the European Communities* C 62/42 of 11 March 1985.

The inconsistent position of international organizations about what they regard as an international agreement is often due to incidental factors; J. Gold, 'On the difficulties of defining international agreements', *Essays in Honour of Dr C.D. Deshmukh*, p. 25. But for State Constitutions, it is sometimes possible to adopt a more formalistic conception of treaties between States than that of the organizations concerned, as was done for the European Monetary System by the decision of the French Conseil Constitutionnel of 21 December 1978 (*Journal du droit international*, vol. 106 (1971), p. 79) or for the revision of the IMF Statutes by a majority deliberation (Conseil constitutionnel, 9 April 1978; *Journal du droit international*, vol. 105 (1978), p. 577).

The legal nature of certain acts which take a conventional form and include as parties both States and individuals may give rise to diverging interpretations according to whether the individuals are in a position equivalent to that of the States; French case-law, relying perhaps on the particular legal situation of 'non-State persons' (*personnes non étatiques*) who are parties to such an agreement has assimilated the agreement to a treaty (Cass. civ., 5 October 1965, *RGDIP*, vol. 70 (1966), p. 501).

75*   Arbitral award of 10 June 1955 between the United Kingdom and Greece in the *Diverted Cargoes* case, *RIAA*, vol. 12, p. 65. J. Verhoeven, 'Traités ou contrats entre Etats? Sur les conflits de lois en droit des gens', *Journal du droit international*, vol. 111 (1984), p. 4.

76*   See references, above, No. 64 and the Report by S. Rosenne, 'Terminaison des traités', *Annuaire de l'Institut de Droit international*, vol. 52-I (1967), p. 96, para. 19.

77*   On multilateral treaties, see: the study by J. Monnier, *Annuaire suisse de Droit international*, vol. 31 (1975), p. 31; H. Blix and K. Skubiszewski, 'Les techniques d'élaboration des grandes conventions multilatérales et des normes quasi-législatives internationales', *Annuaire de l'Institut de Droit international*, vol. 57-II (1972). On treaties concluded by international organizations, see: S. Rosenne, 'United Nations treaty practice', *RCADI*, vol. 86 (1954-II), p. 275; K. Zemanek, *Agreements of International Organizations and the Vienna Convention on the Law of Treaties* (Vienna, Springer, 1971). For a historical review of the work of the ILC and the General Assembly (including the 11 reports by Special Rapporteur P. Reuter), see the Report of the Commission to the General Assembly on the work of the thirty-fourth session, *YILC 1982*, vol. II (part 2), p. 9. The documents of the Vienna Conference (18 February–21 March 1986) appeared under reference A/CONF./129/.

81*   The specificities of international organizations' constituent charters have invited studies either in works devoted to international organizations or elsewhere: Ch. De Visscher, *Problèmes d'interprétation judiciaire en droit international public* (Paris, Pedone, 1963), p. 140; D. Simon, *L'interprétation judiciaire des traités d'organisations internationales* (Paris, Pedone, 1981); S. Rosenne, 'Is the constitution of an international organization an international treaty?', *Comunicazioni e Studi*, vol. 12 (1966), p. 21; R. Zacklin, *The Amendment of the Constitutive Instruments of the United Nations and Specialized Agencies* (Leyden, Sijthoff, 1968). But groups of treaties covering the same subject have seldom been considered as such, although the ICJ did so for instance in the following cases: *Rights of Nationals of the United States of America in Morocco* (*ICJ Reports 1952*, p. 176), *Constitution of the Maritime Safety Committee of IMCO* (*ICJ Reports 1960*, p. 150), and *Interpretation of the Agreement of 25 March 1951 between the WHO and Egypt* (*ICJ Reports 1980*, p. 73) (see above, No. 52).

82*   Sir Gerald Fitzmaurice was the first to undertake a really detailed study of this aspect of the problem in his Third Report on the Law of Treaties (*YILC 1958*, vol. II, p. 20); for Article 60, which took this into account, see below, No. 299).

83*   See above, Nos. 20* and 33*. For the Havana Convention, Carnegie, *International Conferences of American States* (New York, 1931), and the classical works of Latin American legal writers: H. Accioly, *Traité de droit international public* (Paris, Sirey, 1941), vol. II, p. 415; D. Antokoletz, *Tratado de derecho internacional publico* (Buenos Aires, La Facultad, 1944), vol. III, p. 89; A.S. de Bustamante y Sirven, *Droit international public* (Paris, Sirey, 1936-1939), vol. III, p. 343; L.M. Moreno Quintana, *Tratado de derecho internacional* (Buenos Aires, Librería del Colegio, 1950), vol. I, p. 525; see also the publications of the Consejo interamericano de jurisconsultos, especially for 1955 and 1959. For the Council of Europe, see H. Golsong, 'Quelques remarques à propos de l'élaboration de la nature juridique des traités conclus au sein du Conseil de l'Europe', *Mélanges offerts à Polys Modinos* (Paris, Pedone, 1968), p. 51.

85* Add to the references listed above at Nos. 43* and 44*: A. Cassese, 'Modern constitutions and international law', *RCADI*, vol. 192 (1985-III), p. 331; J. Dhommeaux, 'La conclusion des engagements internationaux en droit français', *AF*, vol. 21 (1975), p. 815; L. Saïdj, *Le Parlement et les traités* (Paris, Librairie générale de droit et de jurisprudence, 1979); G. Bacot, 'Remarques sur le rôle du référendum dans la ratification des traités', *RGDIP*, vol. 82 (1978), p. 1024; P. Rambaud, 'Le Parlement et les engagements internationaux de la France sous la Vème République', *RGDIP*, vol. 81 (1977), p. 617; D. Lasok, 'Les traités internationaux dans le système juridique anglais', *RGDIP*, vol. 70 (1966), p. 961; A.M. Jacemy-Millette, *Introduction and Application of International Treaties in Canada* (Ottawa, University of Ottawa Press, 1975); J.F. Triska and R.M. Slusser, *The Theory, Law, and Policy of Soviet Treaties* (Stanford, Stanford University Press, 1962); J. Viret, 'La loi du 6 juillet 1978 sur la procédure de conclusion, d'exécution et de dénonciation des traités internationaux de l'Union soviétique', *Annuaire de l'URSS* (1979–1980), p. 9; Hungda Chiu, *The People's Republic of China and the Law of Treaties* (Cambridge, Mass., Harvard University Press, 1972); L.J. Adams, *Theory, Law and Policy of Contemporary Japanese Treaties* (Leyden, Sijthoff, 1974); M.J. Glennon and Th. Franck, *United States Foreign Relations Law: Documents and Sources* (Dobbs Ferry, Oceana, 1980); Ch. Rousseau, 'Etats-Unis — Régime constitutionnel de la dénonciation des traités internationaux', *RGDIP*, vol. 84 (1980), p. 613; *Evolution constitutionnelle en Belgique et relations internationales. Hommage à Paul De Visscher* (Paris, Pedone, 1984); G. Burdeau, 'Les engagements internationaux de la France et les exigences de l'Etat de droit', *AF*, vol. 32 (1986), p. 837.

86* Elementary applications of statistical methods are far from new. On the ratification of treaties published in the League and United Nations Series, see H. Blix, 'The requirement of ratification', *BYBIL*, vol. 30 (1953), p. 352, and M. Frankowska, 'De la prétendue présomption en faveur de la ratification', *RGDIP*, vol. 73 (1969), p. 62. For agreements concluded by exchange of notes, see J.L. Weinstein, 'Exchanges of notes', *BYBIL*, vol. 29 (1952), p. 205. For research using computer technology, see: *Proceedings of the American Society of International Law*, 1965, p. 93; *The Texas International Law Forum*, 1966, No. 2, p. 167; *AJ*, vol. 61 (1967), p. 61; *Fifth Maxwell Institute on the United Nations* (Oud Wassenaar, The Hague, 25–30 August 1968, mimeo); *International Studies Quarterly*, vol. 12 (1968), p. 174; and P.H. Rohn, University of Washington, Seattle, Washington, *UN Treaty Series Project* (vol. I, 503), *World Treaty Index*, 2nd edn. (Oxford, Clio Press, 1983) and *Treaty Profiles* (Santa Barbara, Clio Press, 1976). This statistical research, generally based on the League of Nations and United Nations Treaty Series, shows that 25 per cent of treaties have been registered by neither. Other attempts have been made from a political science viewpoint to measure by quantitative methods the density of treaty relations between specific countries (P.H. Rohn, 'Canada in the U.N. Treaty Series: a global perspective', *Canadian Yearbook of International Law*, vol. 4 (1966), p. 102) or the formal aspects of treaty technique, (J.K. Gamble, 'Multilateral treaties: the significance of the name of the instrument', *California Western International Law Journal*, vol. 10 (1980), p. 1, and 'Reservations to multilateral treaties: a macroscopic view of State practice', *AJ*, vol. 74 (1980), p. 372).

Chapter 2
Conclusion, entry into force and participation

I General considerations

1. The concept of conclusion

89 'Conclusion' may have quite a number of meanings, the narrowest of which should be considered first: a treaty is 'concluded' once the States have expressed their definitive intention to be bound. Whenever this intention derives merely from an oral declaration, an act or particular conduct, the difficulty may be to show that there really is an intention to be bound. Frequently this type of commitment is therefore not regarded as a treaty (see above, Nos. 28 and 66) and examples of verbal agreements do often remain controversial. Moreover, the difficulty in proving the existence of a commitment may also cause problems in the determination of its date. But apart from these important restrictions, there is nothing else to be said in this case about the form of conclusion, precisely because there is no form at all. Things change however with 'written' treaties, which after all represent the most common type of conventional commitments in international law. Here indeed the States' intentions combining to form a treaty are expressed in written documents specifically devised for that purpose, which accordingly may be called instrumental acts or simply 'instruments' (articles 2 (1) (a), 13, 16, 31 (2) (b), 77 (d) and (f), and 79 (1) (b) of the 1969 Convention).(*)

90 A single treaty can be made up of a varying number of instruments, following a procedure which may vary in length and complexity. Often it is not until the very last stage that States express their intention to be bound definitively. In that case, the term 'conclusion' is understood in its strictest meaning, implying that a treaty is 'concluded' once the States have definitively expressed their consent. But in a more general sense, which is the one used in this chapter, 'conclusion' refers to the whole set of procedures involving various instruments, whereby international treaties come into existence.

A treaty enters into force when it acquires full legal effectiveness as a source of obligations. The concept appears simple enough; yet identifying entry into force, especially in time, is a complex operation because it has to take into account all the acts making up the 'conclusion' — in its wider sense — of the treaty.

Finally several ancillary formalities linked to conclusion such as deposit, notification, corrections, registration and publication have to be considered.

Unless otherwise stated, comments in this chapter concerning States and their Constitutions also apply to international organizations and their rules.

2. A complex process

91   There are three reasons why concluding a treaty is a long and complex process: they concern the object of the treaty, the nature of the parties and the number of parties.

A. THE OBJECT OF THE TREATY

The object of a treaty may be quite simple, for instance extending the duration of an expiring treaty. Usually, however, treaties deal with complex matters requiring a rather long text which has to reconcile conflicting interests and which invariably involves negotiations culminating in the drawing up of a text.

B. THE NATURE OF THE PARTIES

The parties, either States or international organizations, are corporate entities with different constitutional structures. They can only act through organs, i.e. through individuals duly authorized to bind them. In any case, even to take part in negotiations, these individuals have to establish their competence to perform any act which might bind the State. They do so normally by submitting instruments called 'full powers'. But nowadays the State's intention often cannot be expressed without several organs giving their consent, either because the supreme organ needs time to reflect upon the matter before making a definitive commitment on behalf of the State or because elected assemblies have to share in bringing to perfection the State's determination to be bound. Thus, once the text has been drawn up, instead of expressing in a single act the willingness to be bound, it becomes possible to divide the procedure into two acts: one merely stating the intention to continue the process of conclusion, and the other expressing the intention to be definitively bound.

C. THE NUMBER OF PARTIES

When a treaty is intended to bind more than two States, and especially when it is meant to bind States which cannot yet be precisely identified at the time negotiations begin, either because the treaty comes into force for fewer States or because it is open to other States than had taken part in the negotiations, a number of changes can be observed which have already been mentioned (see above, Nos. 13, 22 and 25); they concern collective negotiations, the character of the instruments, the date and mechanisms of entry into force.

3. Phases and procedural techniques

92   The genesis of a treaty can therefore be broken down into several phases: drawing up the text, authenticating it as drafted, undertaking to carry on with the procedure on that basis, expressing final consent and becoming finally bound. Some of these phases may of course prove superfluous: States, as has already been pointed out, may accept to be bound immediately without giving themselves more time, or one of the phases may be dispensed with owing to the circumstances under which a given treaty has been drawn up. Thus, when a bilateral treaty is drawn up in two identical copies, it may not be felt necessary to authenticate a common text first.

93   At each stage, a number of procedural techniques come into play: international conferences with all their technical arrangements; initialling; signature; exchange, deposit or communication of certain instruments; and various notifications.

These techniques have no magical power of their own. Their legal effect essentially depends on the meaning given to them by the parties. This meaning in turn is established by usage and by the conduct of the parties in each particular case.

A possible difficulty is that one and the same procedural device may have a very different import depending on the treaty or even on the parties concerned. For instance, the simplest of them — signature — may amount to mere authentication, or it may express authentication and willingness to pursue the procedure, or again authentication with the intention to be finally bound, or even just the intention to be finally bound. Understandably enough, the simpler the procedure, the greater the potential significance of a single formality.

4. International law and municipal law: problems of terminology and substance

94   There necessarily have to be at least some international rules governing the conclusion of treaties: in their absence, treaty-making would be utterly impossible. But there are also relevant rules belonging to each State's constitutional law (in the widest sense). This familiar situation, which has already been touched upon (see above, No. 40), raises a number of problems not the least of which concerns terminology.

National legal orders are free to define the terms they use as they please, and indeed they do so. But international law also has to make use of certain terms and accordingly to define them. The same term may therefore have different meanings in international law and in the constitutional law of a given country (1969 Convention, article 2 (2)). This can be somewhat confusing and the ideal solution would be to set up a specifically international terminology. While this line has been pursued (for instance by introducing new and neutral terms on the international level such as 'acceptance'), it cannot ensure a lasting separation of both terminologies, for eventually municipal rules may use the same terms and distort their meaning. This is indeed what actually happens and is bound to happen since there can be no impenetrable barrier between municipal and international law: the requirements of international relations give rise to a common practice which calls for mutual adjustments in both legal orders.

95 To overcome these terminological obstacles, there is one last solution, which was skilfully adopted by the 1969 Convention so as largely to dispose of the problem of terms and definitions. Comparing for instance articles 2(1)(b), 11 and 14, it becomes clear that the Convention nowhere defines the terms 'ratification', 'acceptance' or 'approval', but simply states that all of them are 'means of expressing consent to be bound by a treaty'. All that matters under the Convention is that States agree to consider these terms as expressing the consent to be bound; that they so agree may be apparent from the provisions of the treaty itself, from the attitude of the negotiating States or from any unilateral statement during negotiations in relation to full powers or signature. The international rule is thus cleared of terminological constraints so that any terms could actually be used, provided their meaning is clear. A number of apparently intricate rules are thus brought down to one essential rule: *Everything depends on the States' intentions so long as they are sufficiently clear in the light of ordinary practice.*(*)

96 This basic principle can be made more precise by rules clarifying the practice or laying down presumptions concerning States' intentions. Thus article 7 (2) of the 1969 Convention provides that for some acts, certain State representatives, by virtue of their functions, are not required to produce full powers. It was not possible to lay down a similar rule for international organizations in view of the considerable differences in structure and capacity between organizations. While other more debatable rules may be contemplated (see below, No. 105), they do not alter the fundamental fact that the principle of consent is paramount in the law of treaties and that the intention of the parties completely commands treaty-making patterns. Form and terminology are only relevant in so far as they may clarify such intentions at the various stages of treaty-making: full powers, negotiation, adoption and authentication of the text, willingness to continue the procedure, and expression of the consent to be bound.

97 Practice thus appears as the supreme and ultimate guide in the interpretation of their intentions; at the same time, it reveals how easily and smoothly international treaty-making procedures are adjusted and arranged for. The day-to-day reality of diplomatic relations generates a whole system of identification, recognition and perception, of traditions and habits, of courtesies and precautions; nobody could be deceived by unauthorized officials, bogus documents or worthless commitments. Governments are kept continuously informed of one another's intentions through the customary channels of representatives sent out to, and received from, other States. Article 46 of the 1969 Convention should be read in the light of this basic observation (see above, No. 40), and after some waverings similar considerations were to prevail in the 1986 Convention for international organizations. Even when a State is confronted by a serious crisis such as secession or civil war, possible difficulties are quickly solved by recognition or non-recognition. Real problems only arise for States whose extreme constitutional rigidity makes them averse to the flexibility required by modern international relations or for those resisting the federal trends characterizing the international community as a whole and, even more clearly, certain regional systems.(*)

II A review of treaty-making procedures

1. Description

98 Treaty-making procedures will be described here from the point of view of international law alone, disregarding therefore the rules and terminology prevailing in the various national Constitutions. Accordingly, four models of treaties will be presented, taking into account three main variables: the number of parties, the length of the procedure and the number of instruments involved.

The number of parties is the most important factor, since it is with multilateral as opposed to bilateral treaties that collective procedures emerge which attempt to reconcile the contractual aspects of treaties with their law-making finality. The distinction between short and long procedures is mainly due to constitutional considerations: the conclusion procedure is inevitably more prolonged if several organs have to concur under municipal law before the State's consent to be bound becomes final. Somewhat less essential, the third factor concerns the number of instruments making up the treaty: while the overwhelming majority of treaties involve a single instrument (of which there may be several identical copies), they may also consist of two instruments, i.e. an exchange of letters, following a commercial practice originating in private business life and currently gaining ground among States.

These three factors combine to a certain extent, giving rise to four main categories of treaties which will be briefly reviewed below.

A. BILATERAL TREATIES CONCLUDED BY LONG PROCEDURES

99 In this type of treaty, negotiation, adoption and authentication of the text are all quite straightforward. The negotiators may or may not be provided with full powers, according to whether these appear necessary: Heads of State or of Government and Ministers for Foreign Affairs do not need them (1969 Convention, article 7) since they are the ones to issue full powers to representatives. The negotiations are concluded by authentication which is mostly brought about by signature. If for some reason (several versions in different languages, preparation of neat final copies, special signing ceremonies) authentication is distinguished from signature, it is usually done by initialling. The text is then signed by representatives duly authorized to do so by full powers or by their status. Full powers, if required, are submitted to the other party. In addition to authentication, signature also expresses willingness to continue the procedure. The parties then review the proposed undertaking and seek whatever constitutional authorization may be required to perfect their commitment. The treaty becomes binding on them as soon as their final consent has been mutually expressed and exchanged. The actual form in which that consent is given may vary: it is generally the subject of special instruments often, but not invariably, called instruments of ratification, approval or acceptance. The use of one term rather than another is irrelevant in international law. The more formal procedure is to exchange the instruments and to keep a record of the transaction, but nowadays notification is usually deemed sufficient. Each State keeps one of the copies of the treaty together with all the annexed documents which establish the reality and validity of the other party's undertaking (full powers, instrument of ratification, approval or acceptance). In theory one of the States could conceivably act as a depositary of a single copy, but in practice this method is only followed in the case of multilateral treaties.(*)

B. BILATERAL TREATIES CONCLUDED BY SHORT PROCEDURES

100 The main difference with the previous category is that signature in this case expresses final consent. Mere initialling instead of signature may have the same effect if the States so agree (1969 Convention, article 12 (2) (a)). Signature *ad referendum* only becomes effective upon confirmation, although usually with retroactive effect (article 12 (2) (b); *YILC 1966*, vol. II, p. 196).

C. BILATERAL TREATIES CONCLUDED BY EXCHANGE OF LETTERS

101 This procedure very often amounts to a variation of the preceding one. Its basic characteristic is that the signatures do not appear in one but in two separate documents. The agreement therefore lies in the confrontation of both instruments, each State being in possession of the one signed by the representative of the other. In practice, the second letter generally, if not invariably, reproduces the text of the first one, to which it is an answer.(*)

D. MULTILATERAL TREATIES CONCLUDED BY LONG OR SHORT PROCEDURES

102 In the case of multilateral treaties, there are very important features concerning the conference machinery and the final consent to be bound; equally significant are the way they enter into force and the procedure of deposit (see below, Nos. 108 and 113). These specific features may, however, be more or less pronounced according to the treaty concerned. Indeed, strictly speaking, three parties are enough for a treaty to be multilateral; but recourse to conferences and to new ways of expressing final consent is only meaningful with a greater number of parties and 'open' treaties. Thus the treaties establishing the European Communities (and even the agreements to increase the number of member States) followed procedures closer to those of bilateral than of multilateral treaties (see above, No. 78, and below, No. 104).

(a) The international conference

103 As soon as the object of the proposed treaty becomes complex, even bilateral negotiations require some kind of organization (venue, working groups, drafting and translation problems). With a greater number of participants, these problems are further complicated by political questions which emphasize the importance of international conferences. These questions mainly concern participation in the conference, its precise object and the voting procedure, and are so important that they have to be settled before negotiations actually begin in the conference itself. Practically speaking, until World War II, the initiative of convening a conference was taken by States; the Great Powers, or other States in consultation with them, settled these matters all the more smoothly as there were only a small number of so-called 'civilized States' and the rule of unanimity was normally complied with, at least when negotiations drew to a close. Nowadays, international organizations have developed to such an extent that they are able to accomplish all the preliminary work, often including a draft convention and provisional rules of procedure which are submitted to the first meeting of the conference. The latter thus tends to become an organized entity whose links with the organization get closer and closer. It functions according to its own will and its work is concluded by a Final Act recording the adopted texts, which become treaties, declarations and resolutions, emanating either from the conference as such or from the participating States in more or less close connection with the treaties which have been drawn up.(*)

104 Inasmuch as these diplomatic meetings have come to resemble parliamentary assemblies, they have led to a change in the methods of adopting and authenticating treaties. It is difficult to determine exactly at what stage multilateral treaty-making methods depart from bilateral ones. The only criterion which the International Law Commission was able to mention in this respect was the number of States involved: the fact that it becomes physically impossible for all the participants to sit around the same table is of some importance. Parliamentary methods for drafting the text of a multilateral treaty are implied in the term 'conference' and merely involve the use of well-known techniques (rules of procedure, officers, committees, plenaries, drafting committees, etc.). While the Vienna Convention fails to define the term 'conference', it does take into account, in its stand on the crucial and repeatedly mentioned issue of voting procedures, the fact that a text is adopted in a conference (see above, No. 14).

105 Traditionally, up to the time of the League of Nations, decisions taken by international conferences had to be unanimous. The practice of voting by a two-thirds majority was, however, resorted to in the International Labour Organisation, and after 1945 it became the rule for conferences held under the auspices of the United Nations. For treaties drawn up by the General Assembly, even a simple majority is sufficient and the same rule applies to the assemblies of a number of specialized agencies. Article 9 of the 1969 Convention, and in slightly different terms article 9 of the 1986 Convention, have introduced a residual rule for conferences held outside the framework of an international organization, to the effect that texts are adopted by a two-thirds majority unless a different rule is previously agreed upon by the same majority. International organizations taking part in a conference have the same voting rights as States unless the States have decided otherwise. At the 1986 Vienna Conference, international organizations only enjoyed limited rights (they had no vote; their proposals were put to the vote only if requested by a State; and entry into force was based on the number of States parties alone). In future, States are likely to determine on an *ad hoc* basis the conditions and effects of participation by one or more international organizations in unrestricted multilateral treaties. There should therefore not be too much optimism about the effect of article 9 of the 1986 Convention. Yet, more generally speaking, the adoption of majority voting in universal conferences has profoundly altered the treaty-making policies of States and especially of the Great Powers. Indeed the majority rule enables developing countries, and in general countries relying on their number rather than on their individual weight, to further their interests. Such attempts are often frustrated, for treaties adopted by international conferences are not ratified by States whose views have been ignored, and do not always come into effect as between the others. Moreover, States whose suggestions have been rejected and which nevertheless ratify the treaty formulate reservations, occasionally disregarding the relevant rules (see below, Nos. 129 ff.). In some cases, which have so far been exceptional, the Great Powers have drawn up the text of political treaties between themselves, later opening them to accession by other States (e.g. the 1963 Moscow Nuclear Test Ban Treaty; see below, No. 125). Another solution at major conferences is to avoid putting questions to the vote — and thereby to avoid objections being made known — until the final stage, while instead trying by informal negotiation in restricted groups to reach a compromise between the main Powers or groups of States concerned. This method was widely used during the lengthy Third Conference on the Law of the Sea (lasting from 1973 to 1982 with a total of 11 sessions, five of which were in two parts); it was also included in the Rules of Procedure of the 1986 Vienna Conference (Rule 63). In a less systematic way, it has now become possible to avoid voting on a step- by-step basis by resorting to 'consensus' decisions: unofficial negotiations between dynamic and influential representatives lead to the drawing-up of a text which is then put forward by the chairman who observes without a formal vote that the text is unopposed and therefore adopted: those who oppose the text, but feel too isolated or too weak, are reluctant to stand in the way of such a 'consensus'.(*)

106 With regard to authentication also, new solutions have emerged for multilateral treaties adopted by a conference or an international organization. The Final Act of a conference authenticates all the texts it covers. If the text of a treaty is adopted within an international organization, the relevant method is determined by the rules of procedure of the organ concerned, e.g. authentication by resolution, or by signature of the assembly president, or of a senior official of the organization (1969 and 1986 Conventions, article 10).

(b) Final expression of the consent to be bound

107 Consent to be bound by a treaty can take different and more or less expeditious forms whereby the distinction between short and long procedures again becomes relevant. It cannot, however, be as clear-cut for multilateral treaties as it is for bilateral ones. Indeed, as with bilateral treaties, although less frequently, there is nothing to prevent a State or international organization from finally committing itself by a simple expression of its consent such as signature (1969 Convention, article 12), while other States or organizations bind themselves only by ratification (*YILC 1966*, vol. II, p. 196). Moreover, there is a simple but delayed procedure for expressing consent to be bound by an unrestricted multilateral treaty: instead of going through preliminary stages like signature, consent is expressed in a single act by accession (occasionally called adhesion, acceptance or even approval, although the latter usually refers to an act subsequent to signature). Negotiations are indeed normally followed by signature, and unrestricted multilateral treaties may be signed during a period following the Final Act of the conference; yet after a reasonable period of time it is normally assumed that States or organizations which have failed to sign will choose to express their consent definitively by a single act: it no longer serves any purpose to do so in two stages since they have all the time they need to make their decisions and meet whatever complex constitutional requirements may exist.(*)

2. Entry into force

A. MANNER AND DATE

108 Under article 24 of the 1969 and 1986 Conventions, the manner and date of a treaty's entry into force are normally determined by specific treaty provisions or by an agreement between the negotiating States and international organizations. Failing this, the treaty comes into force as soon as the consent of all the negotiating States and organizations has been established. While bilateral treaties enter into force upon a twofold consent as expressed by an exchange of instruments or notification, things are less simple with multilateral treaties: here entry into force depends either on the consent of all the negotiating States or organizations, or just some of them, or of a given number of States or organizations regardless of whether they have taken part in the negotiations. Unless otherwise stated, restricted treaties normally require the consent of all the negotiating States or organizations and therefore enter into force once the last consent has been given. Unrestricted treaties generally come into force when the number of consents is deemed sufficiently representative by whatever criteria may be chosen; failing such a provision, however, ratification by all the negotiating States or organizations would again seem to be required. As for States or organizations acceding to a treaty already in force, it is of course the date of accession that determines its entry into force for them.

B. EFFECTS

109   The fact that a treaty is in force does not imply that its provisions are already operative, for all or some of them may be subject to some time-limit or condition. Conversely, a treaty may have certain effects even before it comes into force; these may arise from some obligations of conduct prior to entry into force, from certain immediately operative clauses, or from provisional application of the treaty.(*)

(a) Obligations of conduct prior to entry into force

110   The negotiating States or international organizations owe each other a duty of loyalty in their conduct with respect to the proposed treaty. They should not embark on a treaty commitment and at the same time defeat its purpose. Such a course of action, while it could not amount to a breach of any conventional undertaking since there is no such undertaking as yet, would indeed entail its author's international responsibility. Yet the exact content of this obligation of conduct, as established by international custom on the basis of good faith, is not easy to determine. In its initial draft article 15 the International Law Commission had defined it by reference to the obligation as from the beginning of the negotiations not to frustrate the object and purpose of the treaty. In 1969, these obligations were slightly reduced by the Vienna Conference which maintained them only in the case of a State having signed the treaty subject to subsequent final consent, until it has made its intention clear not to become a party, and for a State which 'has expressed its consent to be bound by the treaty, pending the entry into force of the treaty and provided that such entry into force is not unduly delayed' (1969 Convention, article 18).(*)

(b) Immediate effect of certain clauses

111   Clauses bearing on the conclusion of the treaty apply before it becomes operative, since their very purpose is to bring it into force (1969 and

1986 Conventions, article 24 (4)). These clauses do not concern the substantive rules of the treaty but its genesis as a juristic act, following the distinction made above at No. 50. These are also the clauses providing for the immediate application of certain rules to the period directly preceding entry into force. In particular in treaties creating international organiza-tions, a clause normally provides for the immediate setting up of a commission to prepare the constitution and operation of the organization. The legal basis of such clauses lies in the consent implicit in the very adoption of the text of the treaty.(*)

(c) Provisional application prior to entry into force

112 States or international organizations are free during negotiations to provide in the treaty itself or in an annexed agreement that the treaty applies provisionally, in full or in part, before properly entering into force. In principle such an undertaking by definition can only be precarious, and in the absence of a contrary provision it may be denounced if the final agreement is unduly delayed or if a State (or international organization) notifies the other States (or organizations) to which the treaty is provi-sionally applicable of its intention not to become a party (1969 and 1986 Conventions, article 25).(*)

3. Ancillary procedures

A. APPOINTMENT OF A DEPOSITARY

113 The appointment of a depositary answers the practical needs arising from multilateral treaties. Initially, the functions of the depositary were carried out by States, and later on also by international organizations. The device of multiple depositaries first appeared — for political reasons — in connection with the 1963 Moscow Test Ban Treaty and was again resorted to thereafter for conventions on the non-proliferation of nuclear weapons, outer space, hijacking, etc. The aim of this device, which was adopted under Soviet pressure, was to avoid certain entities (like the German Democratic Republic, North Korea, North Vietnam) being denied accession to a treaty by a depositary which failed to recognize their right to participate, yet without compelling that depositary to accept their participation. This is why several depositaries are selected: it is enough for such entities' claim to be recognized by one of them, whatever the opposition of the others. This device, which was adopted as a general possibility in the 1969 Convention (article 76), could cause practical difficulties and should only be regarded as an expedient. The provision was retained by the 1986 Conference, although it had fallen into disuse by then, after the 'normalization' of the situations concerned.(*)

114 The functions of the depositary cover the management of the instruments relating to the treaty and all the acts required by its continued existence. One might ask whether this amounts to a merely executive, almost mechanical, task or whether the depositary enjoys some degree of power to resolve the legal problems which inevitably arise with respect to the validity of the acts received, the powers of those sending communications, the admissibility of reservations, the number of parties whose consent has been received for the purpose of entry into force, etc. In fact the decisions to be taken concern all the parties to the treaty and must therefore be taken by each of them individually. This still leaves some room for the depositary to express a provisional opinion before submitting the matter to the parties. Yet, ever since 1945 the activities of depositaries have raised highly political issues which, for treaties deposited with the United Nations, have considerably affected and burdened the Secretariat. The tendency has therefore been to restrict their functions as far as possible to a purely mechanical role, thus increasingly turning their duty of impartiality into an absence of responsibility. The essential functions of the depositary have thus been reduced to nearly automatic ones as reflected in article 77 of the 1969 Convention and article 78 of the 1986 Convention, and practice is following this lead. The list of functions set out in these articles is supplemented by other provisions regarding the correction of errors (1969 Convention, article 79 (2), and 1986 Convention, article 80 (2)) and the registration of treaties (articles 80 (2) and 81 (2) respectively).(*)

B. NOTIFICATIONS AND COMMUNICATIONS

115   The conclusion of treaties involves a great variety of notifications and communications. Notification is increasingly resorted to as early as the stage of expressing final consent. Thus in the case of bilateral treaties, instead of exchanging instruments to that effect, the parties are generally content to notify them. Similarly, multilateral treaties may provide that deposit is replaced by mere notification. Consent to be bound is therefore established either upon exchange of the instruments between the contracting parties or their deposit with the depositary, or upon their notification to the parties or to the depositary (1969 and 1986 Conventions, article 16). However, all the other acts and instruments relating to the life of a treaty also call for notifications and communications. In the case of multilateral treaties, these are made through the depositaries. Such formalities raise a number of issues, the most interesting of which concerns the time elapsing between the dispatch of the communication and its receipt by the final addressee (which may on occasion take up to several weeks). These are practical details which it is in the parties' interest to settle carefully beforehand. Generally speaking, the depositary is not regarded as their representative and a communication cannot therefore be deemed to have been received until the depositary has forwarded it to the recipient. For that matter articles 16 and 24 of the 1969 and 1986 Conventions have to be construed in the light of the principles laid down in the previous paragraph. In any event, difficulties are likely to arise if all these points are not carefully dealt with in the treaty or otherwise at the time of its conclusion.(*)

C. REGISTRATION AND PUBLICATION

116 Article 18 of the League of Nations Covenant laid down the obligation to register and publish international treaties, and the same rule is stipulated in similar terms by Article 102 of the United Nations Charter. The Covenant deprived non-registered treaties of any legal force whereas the Charter simply denies the right to invoke such treaties before organs of the United Nations. The precise effects of non-registration have given rise to several discussions before the International Court of Justice, from which, however, no definite conclusions may be drawn. For its part, the General Assembly has drawn up detailed regulations for the implementation of Article 102, although their legal validity has been challenged by some authors. Practice on this point has expanded significantly and, among many other issues, it has provided an opportunity to define exactly what is to be considered as a treaty within the meaning of those regulations. However that may be, it is currently an established fact that a considerable proportion of international treaties are not registered (see No.86*). Moreover, to avoid the constraints or inconveniences of publication, States and even international organizations have narrowed down the concept of treaties far more than would seem appropriate. Both the 1969 Convention (article 80 (1)) and the 1986 Convention (article 81 (1)) have attempted in provisions of debatable effectiveness to extend the obligation to register to non-member States and international organizations. Some international organizations have provided for a similar obligation to register certain categories of treaties in their specific field of activity (Arab League, Pan-American Union, ICAO, IAEA, etc.).(*)

III Participation

117 The question of participation in treaties — essentially multilateral treaties — has arisen since 1945 for a number of reasons such as increasing international solidarity, the growing number of international organizations, decolonization, and East–West antagonism. The need to participate in more treaties has been felt by a growing number of States and intergovernmental organizations. This has led to the convening of international 'conferences' (see above, No. 104) where decisions, owing to extensive participation, are taken by majority votes which are bound to displease some participants. These therefore claim, as an ultimate consequence of their participation in the treaty, the right to exclude from their final consent such provisions as do not suit them. This they do by means of 'reservations' to the treaty. As will be seen, the legal expression of all these needs involves a variety of elements, some traditional, others more recent, concerning either States or entities other than States. The two main questions, however, concern (1) the general capacity to conclude treaties and (2) reservations. They relate to different moments in time; the first, involving as it does a distinction between States and non-State entities, highlights the political tensions in contemporary international society, whereas the second is more of a technical nature.

1. General capacity to conclude treaties

A. STATES

118 Any State has the capacity to conclude treaties. Calling this a right seems to miss the crucial point: in fact it would be closer to the truth to call it a definition. An entity lacking the general capacity to conclude treaties could not take part in the ordinary course of international relations and would not therefore qualify as a State. On the other hand, any State may renounce this capacity, either completely and irrevocably, thereby ceasing to be a State, or provisionally, or partially, as in the case of protectorates and federal unions ranging from confederacies to federal States. Despite the occasional complexity of these federal entities, owing to specific provisions as well as to delegated powers or representation, the constant trend in their external relations has been towards simplification. Such entities, themselves based on treaties, were to be taken into account by third parties only inasmuch as they were recognized by them, as indeed was usually the case.

119 In pure theory, however, federal unions had to be set apart. According to dualistic thinking, it was up to the domestic constitutional law of federal States to grant powers for the conduct of foreign relations, possibly maintaining some limited 'provincial' or 'cantonal' capacity. Conversely, if the union was not strictly speaking a federal State, it did not really have a 'constitutional law', its structure being governed by a particular treaty law; third States therefore, unless they had recognized the situation, could invoke the *pacta tertiis* principle and claim that restrictions to treaty-making capacity were irrelevant with regard to them: if any such restrictions failed to be observed, this would amount to a case of conflicting treaties (see below, Nos. 175 and 195).

120 By 1962, when the International Law Commission, with Sir Humphrey Waldock as new Special Rapporteur, set out to reassess its earlier work on the law of treaties, western countries outside and within the United Nations had adopted a position of non-recognition both regarding so-called divided States (Germany, Korea, Viet Nam) and the Communist Government controlling mainland China. Decolonization was well under way but not completed and the full impact of the host of new States had not yet been felt within the United Nations. In order to introduce changes with regard to this situation, a number of theories were put forward concerning the capacity to conclude treaties and the right to participate in multilateral treaties. These theories were discussed within the United Nations but the final text of the 1969 Vienna Convention only faintly bears their mark. Since then, the specific political problems have by and large been resolved as contemplated by these theories, which have therefore become of less immediate political concern although they still influence the practice of political organs in the United Nations. A short critical review may therefore be useful.(*)

121 Two different aspects of the capacity of States to conclude treaties have to be distinguished. First there is an original and general capacity to conclude treaties which is inherent in statehood, and therefore is sometimes said to be inalienable. Secondly, it has been maintained that if the interests of a given State are affected by a treaty, either universal, regional or local, this State is entitled to participate in it. Before dealing with these two problems, it should immediately be noted that, while the moral and political concerns from which they spring are readily apparent, it is *a priori* difficult to subject them to effective legal rules in the absence of a firmly structured international organization, for States by their sovereignty are free to dispose of their rights and to decide with whom they wish to enter into agreement.

(a) Renunciation of the right to conclude treaties

122 This issue seems to originate in the existence of colonial protectorates. In spite of their own individual traits, protectorates share some common features, especially the fact that the conduct of external relations is delegated, usually by way of a treaty. It has been argued that treaties establishing a protectorate are null and void because they are either unequal (see below, No. 272) or procured by coercion (No. 270) or even contrary to a peremptory rule (No. 279) precluding States from renouncing their treaty-making capacity. In this context, only the last argument calls for comment and further specification, however valid or invalid it may be on political or moral grounds. Obviously there always have been federal systems whereby States surrender all or part of their treaty-making capacity by transferring it to a joint authority. If therefore certain types of renunciation are to be reproved, others must still be seen as perfectly legitimate. Possible criteria could be based on the concept of 'reciprocity' or better still 'mutual benefit'; or the theory of the 'fundamental rights of States' could be further elaborated. But it has to be recognized that practice does not provide the elements necessary for such an elaboration. This is clearly no easy task and the application of the relevant criteria would require the intervention of a common authority with very strong political backing of a kind not yet in existence.(*)

123 It is in this spirit that article 6 of the 1969 Convention, providing that '[e]very State possesses capacity to conclude treaties', should be under-stood, a provision so obvious that it was not repeated in the 1986 Convention. This rather terse statement is all that remains of a more ambitious draft article which initially also covered federal unions and international organizations. The draft article was quite logical but appeared injudicious to the International Law Commission and even more so to the Conference since it might have jeopardized the status of such entities as the

Gulf Emirates, Quebec and the Republics of the USSR other than Byelorussia and the Ukraine. In any event, article 6 does not so much lay down a rule as describe one of the essential attributes of statehood, i.e. the capacity to conclude treaties. Even if States are no longer the only subjects of international law, they do remain its original subjects: as such, they enjoy a full legal personality the essential manifestation of which in international law is the capacity to conclude treaties.

(b) Access of all States to certain treaties

124 Accepting in principle that States have a right to share in the negotiation and conclusion of certain treaties amounts to a far-reaching change in the law of treaties. In the Commission's discussions in 1962 and 1965, only 'general multilateral treaties' were taken into account, i.e. treaties covering general rules of international law or questions of general interest to all States. But similar considerations should apply on a regional or local level. Thus, for instance, it was suggested that a treaty dealing with the use of an international waterway or its waters should entitle all riparian States to take part in its negotiation and conclusion, whereas treaties concluded in disregard of this right of participation in favour of interested States should be considered illicit and invalid. This radically novel approach to the legislative function in international relations would require an authority to apply and sanction the rules. Such a system would also imply a change in the conditions for international recognition. There currently exists a rather cautious and flexible relationship between treaty-making and recognition. As a rule, participation in general multilateral treaties does not amount to recognition by the other States parties of a non-recognized situation. With restricted treaties, everything depends on the status of the organs responsible for concluding treaties, as well as on the form and specific object of the treaty; there are plenty of cases where the refusal to admit a State to a multilateral treaty spells out a refusal to accept its territorial status. Predicating rights and prohibitions in treaty-making on the sole interest at stake would in fact amount to setting up a new international community.(*)

125 The 1968–1969 Vienna Conference did not establish such a system. It simply stated the wish to open the 1969 Convention to all States while reserving the right for the United Nations General Assembly to invite any State which was not a member of the United Nations or of specialized agencies or a party to the Statute of the International Court of Justice to accede to the Convention. Moreover, by a Declaration on Universal Participation in the Vienna Convention on the Law of Treaties, the Conference called on the General Assembly to ensure the widest possible participation in the Convention, but this call was not answered until 1974 (see above, No. 120*). While the expression 'any State' is now used for the conferences organized by the United Nations and held under its auspices, this does not imply recognition of a general right of participation for all States. The expression 'any State' is confined to the law of the Organization and can be restricted by that very law; in addition, there is no United Nations monopoly in drawing up and concluding general multilateral treaties. It is quite possible for negotiations to take place within a group of States and to result in treaties of a universal character or covering questions of universal interest, yet without being open to all States. Whatever the objections against such an approach for the sake of justice or mere political propriety, it is not prohibited by any rule of general international law and it has often been resorted to in the field of disarmament or territorial settlements in order to allow for an unequal distribution of political responsibilities among States.(*)

B. OTHER ENTITIES

126   As has already been stated (see above, No. 72), entities other than States can be parties to agreements governed by public international law. But they radically differ from States for they never possess a full and unqualified capacity to be parties to any kind of treaty. They only enjoy this right inasmuch as it is conferred on them by their particular status and to the extent it is recognized by the other parties to the agreement. This even applies to entities set up to hold power in a State not yet in being but *in fieri* such as national committees, movements of national liberation or a revolutionary power in conflict with a government. Agreements concluded with such entities by a State may constitute treaties with regard to that State. The (very limited) participation of some movements of national liberation in United Nations conferences and their outcome has been closely defined (General Assembly resolution 3280 (XXIX) of 10 December 1974); this is also true for Namibia whose status under General Assembly resolutions, although only binding upon the States having recognized it, has earned it full access to international conferences (General Assembly resolution 37/233C of 20 December 1982) as well as to the Convention on the Law of the Sea of 10 December 1982 (article 305 (1) (b)) and the 1986 Vienna Convention (article 82). The general régime of international organizations, as derived from the latter Convention, follows the same principles. Treaty-making capacity varies from one organization to another and is governed by the rules of each organization (article 6), i.e. in particular by 'the constituent instruments, decisions and resolutions adopted in accordance with them, and established practice of the organization' (article 2 (1) (j)). As for the right to take part in unrestricted multilateral treaties, it only exists under the terms of the treaty, if it exists at all, and then only for organizations expressly mentioned. Despite considerable political and doctrinal support, such access is still very limited. Thus the United Nations was not granted access to the Geneva Conventions with respect to peace-keeping forces. The only agreements to allow for that possibility are those on commodities, environmental protection and nuclear safety, and above all the 1982 Law of the Sea Convention (Annex IX); in all those cases, it is restricted to organizations enjoying powers transferred to them by their member States, essentially in fact the European Communities. As the Communities do not exactly fit the mould of international organizations, such precedents carry little weight. In the end, the 1986 Convention itself is the only example of an unrestricted multilateral treaty open to all international organizations, *viz.* to 'international organizations invited to participate in the... Conference' (article 82), for signature and acts of formal confirmation and to any other organization having the capacity to conclude treaties whose instrument of accession 'shall contain a declaration that it has the capacity to conclude treaties' (article 84).(*)

2. Reservations

A. GENERAL BACKGROUND

127 Under article 2 (1) (d) of the 1986 Convention, which restates the terms of article 2 (1) (d) of the 1969 Convention (except for the reference to international organizations and formal confirmation), reservation 'means a unilateral statement, however phrased or named, made by a State or by an international organization when signing, ratifying, formally confirming, accepting, approving or acceding to a treaty, whereby it purports to exclude or to modify the legal effect of certain provisions of the treaty in their application to that State or to that organization'.

Formally speaking, reservations generally appear as an incident in the conclusion of a treaty, although some treaties provide for the possibility to make specific reservations 'at any time' in the event of given circumstances modifying the scope of the undertakings. Reservations essentially spell out a condition: the State consents to be bound provided certain legal effects of the treaty do not apply to it, either by exclusion or modification of a rule or by its interpretation or application. Often States express their intention ambiguously, usually for domestic political considerations, in particular by means of 'interpretative declarations' which would be meaningless if they were not in fact reservations. The question of reservations is fraught with difficulties as shown by important international judicial decisions. However, the following brief presentation will only deal with the basic import of reservations as revealed by their contemporary evolution governed by the problems of participation in treaties, especially in treaties of a universal character.

128 Indeed, while they are technically possible in bilateral treaties, reservations in that case have no practical meaning nor any genuine function to fulfil since they in fact amount to reopening negotiations which have just ended. Their full meaning becomes apparent in multilateral conventions in close connection with the rule governing the adoption of a treaty text. If, as was normally the case before 1914, the text has to be adopted unanimously, any State could be sure that no provision it found unacceptable could be invoked against it without its consent. The negotiating States either had to draw up provisions acceptable to all or, if this proved impossible, unanimously decide what provisions could be set aside or modified for States which could only accept restricted commitments. The only admissible reservations were those unanimously accepted and generally provided for in advance in the treaty. The decision of the negotiators would therefore depend on the need they felt for universal participation and on the price they were prepared to pay for it.

129   The practice of adopting the text of relatively unrestricted multilateral treaties by a two-thirds majority has brought about at least a formal shift in the problem since there is now a minority which is no longer sure that its point of view will be taken into consideration. It cannot prevent a given regulation from being carried in spite of its dissent: its only option is not to take part in the treaty, but this may not be enough to safeguard its interests. The possibility of reservations can of course be provided for ahead of time in order to accommodate the minority view. Yet recourse to such a solution currently depends on the decision of a majority: hence the need felt by some for greater flexibility in matters of reservations than prevailed in the past.

130   Since each treaty is entirely free to provide for its own rules on reservations, this is in fact a mere question of treaty-making policy. Difficulties arise when a treaty fails to deal with the issue. This happens often enough, especially in difficult situations where the subject is avoided during negotiations for fear of lengthy discussions or of an uncertain outcome. The 1969 and 1986 Conventions both provide a striking example of this since they both fail to deal with the issue of reservations in their final provisions! The Convention on the Prevention and Punishment of the Crime of Genocide which was also silent on that point prompted a well-known Advisory Opinion of the International Court of Justice (*ICJ Reports 1951*, p. 15) which had to choose between two opposite theories. One was the traditional theory favouring the integrity of the Convention, and thus subjecting the admissibility of reservations to the consent of all contracting States. The Court found for the other theory which gave precedence to universality in the case of largely unrestricted treaties and accepted the possibility of reservations on the sole condition that they did not jeopardize the object and purpose of the treaty. According to the Court, however, each contracting State was entitled to appraise the validity of a reservation individually and from its own standpoint, and the reserving State therefore became a party to the treaty in relation to the States accepting its reservation but not in relation to the others. As a result of this radically relativistic position, each treaty found itself broken down into a set of distinct conventional relationships not only with different contents but linking States some of which would not recognize all the others as parties to the treaty. (*)

131   This Opinion, favouring what was then a minority group within the United Nations, namely the Soviet Union and its allies, followed a trend which had emerged in particular in the inter-American system where a similar solution was used, preceded by a notification procedure informing States of their mutual reactions before a final decision was taken. Some controversy ensued. The International Law Commission was critical of the Court's Opinion and at the time maintained the principle of treaty integrity. International organizations, especially the United Nations and IMCO, were confronted with the issue on several occasions: international secretariats serving as depositaries asked to be relieved of all responsibility in this field, and this solution was indeed accepted by the General Assembly (resolution 598/VI of 12 January 1952). Finally, once the unanimity rule is no longer upheld for the acceptance of reservations, the problem arises of how the effects of the opposite principle can be mitigated so as to lessen the total relativism of conventional obligations which it entails. In its draft articles on the law of treaties, the International Law Commission relied to a great extent on the 1951 Advisory Opinion. At the Vienna Conference, the basic aspects of the problem were again rehearsed and a formula of limited freedom was put forward whereby a reservation would only be consistent with a treaty if it was recognized as such by a qualified majority of States parties, in principle a two-thirds majority. But in the end a very liberal current prevailed, fostering maximum participation in treaties and protecting minorities against majority oppression, so much so that on two points at least the final text was even less restrictive than the Commission's draft.(*)

B. THE 1969 CONVENTION, SUBSEQUENT PRACTICE, AND THE 1986 CONVENTION

132 Without settling all the points concerning reservations, the 1969 Vienna Convention includes fairly detailed provisions on the subject (articles 19 to 24). Practice since then has largely confirmed the trends apparent in the Convention. This is at least what appears from the Arbitral Award of 30 June 1977 in the *Case concerning the Delimitation of the Continental Shelf between the United Kingdom and France* as well as from decisions concerning the American and European Conventions on Human Rights, and from State conduct. When it considered the question of reservations in connection with international organizations, the International Law Commission spent a long time seeking a solution acceptable to all its members and finally adopted draft articles assimilating international organizations to States in that respect. The Commission's point of view was endorsed by the 1986 Conference which simplified the proposed wording. The practice of international organizations concerning reservations is still quite limited; it mainly concerns the European Communities, the only original aspect being the case of so-called 'mixed' treaties, i.e. treaties to which both a Community and its member States are parties: in such cases the need for coherence between Community and State obligations also restricts their freedom to make reservations (see below, No. 177). The system of reservations deriving from the Vienna Conventions of 1969 and 1986 is therefore common to States and international organizations; as it stands at present, it may be outlined as follows:

1. The right to make reservations as laid down in the Vienna Conventions remains the dominant feature for general multilateral treaties in

the absence of specific provisions to the contrary. But the majorities in the United Nations system have shifted and may try to increase their influence by severely curtailing the right to make reservations in universal treaties, for instance by providing that they must be approved by a two-thirds majority of the contracting parties or by expressly ruling them out (1982 Convention on the Law of the Sea, article 309).

2. As a rule, States use reservations quite sparingly and objections even more so. Often the political context is what accounts for their restraint. Unfortunately, faced with the divisions of contemporary international society, they tend to refrain from becoming parties to treaties of universal scope, preferring to wait for the written texts to be clarified by custom.

3. Apart from the crucial problem of the right to make reservations, there are a great number of difficult technical questions relating to the application of reservations which deserve attention, yet cannot be discussed in this *Introduction*: extension of reservations to other sources of law (customary rules, unilateral acts of international organizations); reservations and reciprocity; and lawfulness and scope of reservations in specific types of treaties (constituent instruments of international organizations; codification treaties; treaties directly establishing individual rights especially in the field of human rights; treaties applied under the supervision of international organizations, etc.).

The following section therefore includes no more than a brief overview of the provisions of the 1969 and 1986 Conventions dealing with the right to make reservations, the mechanisms of acceptance and objection, and the general effects and regime of reservations.(*)

(a) The right to make reservations

133   The right to make reservations as recognized by the Vienna Conventions has a residual character: any treaty may restrict it, in particular by prohibiting reservations or certain types of reservations. If the treaty allows only specified reservations, any other reservation is excluded (article 19 (b)). If the treaty is silent, the only prohibited reservations are those which would be incompatible with its 'object and purpose', a concept again used by the Vienna Conventions although its interpretation remains as uncertain as when it first appeared in the Court's Advisory Opinion of 1951. But the system of reservations in the Vienna Conventions is based on the principle that each State appraises for itself whether or not a reservation is compatible with the object and purpose of a treaty. This appraisal, which is implemented through a mechanism of acceptance or objection, is left to the discretion of the States and hence to decisions which are likely at the very least to be influenced by considerations of national policy. Article 20 seems to provide an example of what the object and purpose of a treaty might be (but not without some ambiguity since it implies that a reservation running counter to the object and purpose of a treaty may be authorized if it is accepted by all the parties); this is the case where 'it appears from the limited number of the negotiating States and negotiating organizations or, as the case may be, of the negotiating organizations and [from] the object and purpose of a treaty that the application of the treaty in its entirety between all the parties is an essential condition of the consent of each one to be bound by the treaty'.(*)

(b) Acceptance and objection

134 When a reservation is made, the other States or organizations are faced with a choice. If the reservation is expressly authorized by the treaty, the mechanism of acceptance or objection does not come into operation, except for a possible controversy about whether the reservation as formulated is actually covered by the authorization. If the reservation is not expressly authorized, the other States or organizations may accept it, object or remain silent. Under article 20 (5) of the Vienna Conventions, a reservation is considered to have been accepted by such States as have failed to object by the end of a twelve-month period after they have been notified of the reservation or by the date on which they express their consent to be bound by the treaty, whichever is later. Acceptance of a reservation by a State which has agreed to be bound by a treaty has an important effect: the reserving State becomes a party to the treaty 'in relation to' the accepting State from the time of acceptance if the treaty is in force for both of them, or else from the time of its coming into force. One State or organization accepting the reservation is enough for its author to become a party to the treaty. This provision highlights the extremely liberal spirit of the Vienna Conventions: acceptance of a reservation by only one State or organization, even through its silence, is enough for the author of the reservation to enjoy all the rights flowing from its status as a party. It would indeed be quite extraordinary in a community of some 170 States and over 200 international organizations not to find at least one party to 'accept' a reservation of any kind. In this respect and to that extent, the obligation to comply with the object and purpose of a treaty is likely to be of little practical significance.

As a matter of principle, an objection to a reservation should prevent the reserving State or organization from becoming a party to the treaty in relation to the objecting State or organization; otherwise objection would have practically the same effect as acceptance. Nevertheless, in order for the objection to have that preventive effect, article 21 (3) requires the objecting State or organization to oppose the entry into force of the treaty between itself and the reserving party. In the 1977 Arbitral Award — while France had refused to sign the 1969 Convention and while, at the time the objections concerned were being formulated, the International Law Commission had put forward a draft provision under which an objection to a reservation precluded the setting up of treaty relations — the Tribunal found that a simple objection did not have such an effect between the reserving and objecting parties. In fact, following the Vienna system, acceptance of a reservation renders the provisions concerned applicable as modified by the reservation, whereas the same provisions are made inoperative by objection but only to the extent of the reservation: whatever subtle distinction a court might possibly draw between a partly applicable and a partly inapplicable provision, the difference would surely be a small one. It can therefore be said that the present tendency is to consider that a simple objection does not amount to a refusal to regard a State as a party to a treaty, its import being at the most similar to that of an interpretative declaration.

(c) General effects and régime of reservations

135   After examining the specific effect of reservations and objections, some attention should now be devoted to their general effect on the whole set of rules contained in a treaty. This effect quite simply amounts to breaking the treaty down into a series of different treaties: the treaty is binding in its entirety as between mhe States which have made no reservations; the parts of the treaty unaffected by reservation A apply as between the reserving States or organizations and those regarding them as parties; the same goes for the parts of the treaty unaffected by reservation B, etc. For the system to work, the provisions of a treaty must be separable to the extent implied by the reservations, following the rule that reservations have to be compatible with the object of the treaty (see above, No. 133); the general problem of the separability of treaty provisions therefore arises here as it does elsewhere (see below, No. 204). To further the unity of the treaty régime, article 22 of the 1969 and 1986 Conventions allows reservations or objections to reservations to be unilaterally withdrawn at any time, unless otherwise provided in the treaty, as if they were appended to, rather than part of, the treaty. However, in the case of succession of a newly independent State to a multilateral treaty, the reservation made by the predecessor State is maintained, unless the newly independent State expresses a contrary intention or formulates a reservation relating to the same subject-matter as the former reservation (Convention on Succession of States in Respect of Treaties, article 20).

Both the 1969 and 1986 Vienna Conventions prescribe whatever notifications, communications and confirmations are needed to protect the parties' rights; the more important ones have to be made in writing.

Notes

89*   Art. 2 (1) (a) of the 1969 Convention defines the term 'treaty' '[f]or the purposes of the ... Convention' only, as does the corresponding provision of the 1986 Convention. The concept of 'instrument' is used in this definition as well as in later provisions (for instance arts. 11, 13, 16, 67 and 77) but without being defined. For models of usual instruments, see *Satow's Guide to Diplomatic Practice*, 5th edn., (London, Longman, 1979) and H. Blix and J.H. Emerson, eds, *The Treaty Maker's Handbook*. The position presented here focuses on the concept of instrument: an instrument is necessarily a written document, but in this author's view only those documents whose specific object is to incorporate an agreement should be regarded as instruments. This definition excludes written documents mentioning an agreement incidentally and in a non-specific way, e.g. the general minutes of a discussion which may include statements constituting a verbal agreement. Neither in the *Dictionnaire de la terminologie du droit international* (Paris, Sirey, 1960) nor in his course on the conclusion of treaties (*RCADI*, vol. 15 (1926-V), pp. 554 and 601) did Basdevant develop a legal theory of international instruments. The ILC has remained rather vague, stating for instance that 'very many single instruments in daily use such as the "agreed minute" or a "memorandum of understanding" could not appropriately be called *formal* instruments but they are undoubtedly international agreements subject to the law of treaties' (*YILC 1966*, vol. II, p. 188); see also *Aegean Sea Continental Shelf, ICJ Reports 1978*, p. 39.

95*   The wording of art. 11 of the 1969 Convention, which added to all the known means 'any other means if so agreed', is quite convincing as to the informal character of the procedure (*Official Records UNCLT, I, Summary Records...*, Committee of the Whole, 15th meeting, pp. 83 – 84, paras. 43 – 48).

97*   The flexibility of French practice adapting itself to the requirements of international relations by interpreting obscure texts while safeguarding the traditional role of the Head of State is quite remarkable. There is now in the 1958 Constitution a distinction according to whether or not the Head of State is involved in negotiations by powers he has issued. If French representatives have powers issued in his name, he has to ratify treaties by 'letters patent of ratification'; in case of accession, if full powers have been delivered, practice has developed 'letters patent of accession'. When the Head of State is not concerned, treaties may just be 'approved'; according to practice, approval emanates from the French Government and is notified by the Minister for Foreign Affairs; in case of accession, a declaration of accession signed by the Minister for Foreign Affairs is enough. If the final formulation of the treaty provides that it will be open to acceptance, the notification sent by the Minister for Foreign Affairs states that the letter of approval serves as 'acceptance within the meaning of the treaty'. In any case, whether the treaty is ratified or approved, it must be published in a decree of the President of the Republic, and the *Conseil d'Etat* has regarded this as a formality having the same effect as ratification under the 1946 Constitution (*Société Navigator, Recueil des arrêts du Conseil d'Etat*, 13 July 1965, p. 422). The same flexibility prevails in the practice of international organizations, and the 1986 Vienna Conference eventually took this into account by assimilating international organizations to States for the purposes of art. 46 (see above, No. 43). See P. Reuter, 'Quelques réflexions sur la notion de "pratique" internationale, spécialement en matière d'organisations internationales', *Studi in onore di Giuseppe Sperduti* (Milan, Giuffrè, 1984), p. 189.

99*   In international organizations, representatives very often do not have actual 'full powers' and article 7 (3) of the 1986 Convention allows for this by using terms slightly different from those referring to States in paragraph 1 (b). Rule 3 of the Rules of Procedure of the 1986 Conference provided that the representatives of international organizations invited to participate should produce 'corresponding documents', 'with a statement on behalf of the organization confirming that such document is issued in accordance with the internal rules and practices of the organization concerned'. According to the Report of the Credentials Committee (A/CONF. 129/10), 14 international organizations had submitted such 'corresponding documents' in the form of 'letters or notes verbales' with the appropriate declaration, three in the same form without declarations and two by cable without declarations (P. Reuter, 'La Conférence de Vienne sur les traités des organisations internationales et la sécurité des engagements conventionnels', *Du droit international au droit de l'intégration. Liber Amicorum Pierre Pescatore* (Baden-Baden, Nomos, 1987), p. 545). The mention of the term 'formal confirmation' to designate for international organizations the operation corresponding to the ratification by States does not imply any real difference, its only object being to express a difference in dignity between organizations and States according to the wishes expressed by the Soviet delegation.

101*   In some cases, letters are exchanged in the special form of an 'instrument' as defined above at No. 89*; in others, the existence of a treaty may be inferred from a whole exchange of correspondence (P.C. Szasz, *The Law and Practices of the IAEA* (Vienna, IAEA, 1970), p. 154, shows that agreements spontaneously deriving from an exchange of letters include explicit elements of consent and are not registered). For statistical studies, see J.L. Weinstein, 'Exchanges of notes', *BYBIL*, vol. 29 (1952), p. 205; out of a total 4 831 treaties published between 1920 and 1946, 1 078 (or 25 per cent) were exchanges of notes; their share goes up to 27 per cent for the first 1 000 treaties registered with the United Nations; according to *Satow's Guide to Diplomatic Practice*, 5th edn., p. 248, they represent 54 per cent of the treaties published by the United Kingdom from 1971 to 1974. At the same time, there is a decline in ratification clauses even in treaties concluded otherwise than by exchange of letters; according to a somewhat fragmentary enquiry (*AF*, vol. 13 (1967), p. 544), more than half of all treaties enter into force by signature alone. Of course if a treaty by exchange of letters forms an ancillary part of a broader set of agreements constituting a whole, the agreement by exchange of letters only enters into force with the whole set of agreements to which it belongs (see for instance the agreement by exchange of letters between Germany and France concerning the Saar included in the European Coal and Steel Community Treaty of 18 April 1951). M. Virally, 'Résolution et accord international', *Essays in Honour of Judge Manfred Lachs*, p. 299.

103*   Many studies have considered negotiations from a political science point of view and most of them cover all relevant aspects, e.g.: G. Geamănu, 'Théorie et pratique des négociations en droit international', *RCADI*, vol. 166 (1980-I), p. 365; M. Merle *et al.*, *La négociation* (*Pouvoirs*, No. 15, 1980); A. Plantey, *La négociation internationale: principes et méthodes* (Paris, CNRS, 1980); V.D. Pastuhov, *A Guide to the Practice of International Conferences* (Washington, Carnegie, 1945); J. Kaufmann, *Conference Diplomacy* (Leyden, Sijthoff, 1968). Interestingly enough, since 1945 there has been a tendency to institutionalize international conferences and to turn them into 'entities'. This tendency is particularly noticeable with respect to the immunities régime they may give rise to, not just for government delegations but for the conference itself and its agents. This was apparent during the discussion on the Convention on Special Missions at the General Assembly and also at the ILC during the discussion concerning the draft articles on the legal position of representatives of States to international organizations and other 'paradiplomats' (*YILC 1969*, vol. II, p. 1). Thus during the discussions in 1968, international conferences were described as 'temporary organizations', and '*ad hoc* organs responsible for settling specific questions' (*YILC 1968*, vol. I, 944th meeting, p. 9 (para. 21) and p. 12 (para. 64)). The adoption of art. 9 (2) by the Vienna Conference is also in line with this tendency.

105*   It should be noted that when the United Nations General Assembly itself adopts the text of a treaty it does so by a *simple majority*, which is the opposite of a consensus approach. The Law of the Sea Conference not only made frequent use of consensus which had already been widely resorted to in international meetings (H. Cassan, 'Le consensus dans la pratique des Nations Unies', *AF*, vol. 20 (1974), p. 456), but also of new methods for the drafting, discussion and collective negotiation of a text, concessions being brought together in a series of package deals, with a correlative prohibition of reservations to the Convention. The bibliography on the methods of the conference is already considerable (see the data collected by P.M. Eisemann, in 'La Convention des Nations Unies sur le droit de la mer', *Notes et Etudes documentaires*, Nos. 4703 and 4704, p. 198; of particular note are: D. Vignes, 'Organisation et règlement intérieur de la IIIᵉ Conférence sur le droit de la mer', *Revue du droit public*, vol. 91 (1975), p. 337; R.Y. Jennings, 'Law-making and package deal', *Mélanges offerts à Paul Reuter*, p. 347; G. de Lacharrière, 'La réforme du droit de la mer et le rôle de la Conférence des Nations Unies', *RGDIP*, vol. 84 (1980), p. 216.

107* Ever since the League of Nations, this has not prevented some States from communicating their accession 'subject to ratification'; but it is then without legal effect and the Secretary-General of the United Nations regards such a communication simply as a declaration of intention (ST/LEG/7, para. 48). A State like France, whose constitutional law mentions neither 'accession' nor 'acceptance' but only 'approval', will 'approve' a treaty under municipal law and notify that this amounts for instance to 'acceptance' within the meaning of the treaty.

109* Technically speaking, certain multilateral treaties could create obligations following a single State's consent to be bound, as did the General Convention on the Privileges and Immunities of the United Nations of 1946. The essential reason for this is that the Convention gives rise to obligations with regard to entities which are not parties and sets up a machinery to sanction them, although the situation has often been viewed as if the United Nations was in any case a party to the Convention (see above, No. 70*). As for the 1947 Convention on the Privileges and Immunities of Specialized Agencies, it would seem to have effects only once at least two consents have been given, one of which may stem from an entity which is not fully a party.

110* *Certain German Interests in Polish Upper Silesia, Merits, PCIJ Series A, No. 7*, p. 30; Ph. Cahier, 'L'obligation de ne pas priver un traité de son objet et de son but avant son entrée en vigueur', *Mélanges Fernand Dehousse* (Paris, Nathan, 1979), vol. I, p. 31. These obligations are connected to the broader problem of the content of the principle of good faith in treaty-making; J.-P. Cot, 'La bonne foi et la conclusion des traités', *Belgian Review of International Law*, vol. 4 (1968), p. 140, and *Lake Lanoux*, *RIAA*, vol. 12, p. 281. In the *North Sea Continental Shelf* cases, the ICJ firmly defined the content of the obligation to negotiate in good faith; the parties 'are under an obligation so to conduct themselves that the negotiations are meaningful, which will not be the case when either of them insists upon its own position without contemplating any modification of it' (*ICJ Reports 1969*, p. 47); it did so again in *Fisheries Jurisdiction, Merits* (*ICJ Reports 1974*, p. 3) and in the *Interpretation of the Agreement of 25 March 1951 between the WHO and Egypt* (*ICJ Reports 1980*, p. 73); see also T. Gebrehana, *Duty to Negotiate: An Element of International Law* (Uppsala, Swedish Institute of International Law, 1978).

111* Such interim committees occasionally survive although the proposed organization fails to be created. This happened in the case of the Interim Committee of the International Trade Organization (ICITO) which took over the operation of

GATT. The Convention on the Law of the Sea entrusted some extremely important functions to a Preparatory Commission, in particular for the management of privileges immediately conferred upon 'pioneer investors' (Final Act, Annex I, resolution II).

112* In the case of a transnational contract to which the general principles of law were applicable, article 25 of the 1969 Convention was elaborated upon in this direction by an arbitral tribunal (Kuwait v. Aminoil, paras. 532 – 4, *ILM*, 1982, p. 976).

113* On Finland's initiative, this practice was enshrined in art. 76 of the 1969 Convention despite some objections by the Expert Consultant (*Official Records UNCLT, I, Summary Records...*, Committee of the Whole, 77th meeting, p. 457, paras. 2–3); at the Secretary-General's request, it was stipulated that the chief administrative officer of an organization could be the depositary, without considering how such a provision could take legal effect with regard to an organization not party to the Vienna Convention. As for the relationship between access to a treaty and recognition of a State or government, see below, No. 124*.

114* The 1968–1969 Conference restricted still further the scope of the depositary's role as compared with the ILC draft. Under draft article 72 (d), the depositary was to examine the conformity of a signature, instrument, or reservation with the treaty provisions and the projected Convention, whereas under article 77 (d) of the Convention the depositary merely examines whether the signature, instrument, notification or communication is 'in due and proper form', if necessary bringing the matter to the attention of the State in question. The depositary may on occasion exercise other functions under a convention as does the Secretary-General of the Council of Europe under the European Convention of Human Rights (see the study by P.H. Imbert, *RGDIP*, vol. 87 (1983), p. 580). On the practice of the United Nations Secretary-General concerning the date of entry into force, see the same author's article in *AF*, vol. 26 (1980), p. 524.

115* The Vienna Conventions of 1969 (art. 77 (g)) and 1986 (art. 78 (g)) added to the functions of the depositary that of registering treaties. In order to confer upon the depositary a power not granted by the treaties concerned, the Conventions curiously provided that authority to do so derived from its actual designation (1969 Convention, art. 80 (2); 1986 Convention, art. 81 (2)). It was quite rightly pointed out that because of the relative effect of treaties, so strictly adhered to by the Conventions, these provisions could not achieve such a purpose.

116* P. Guggenheim, *Traité de droit international public*, 2nd edn., vol. I, p. 177; M. Brandon, 'The validity of non-registered treaties', *BYBIL*, vol. 29 (1952), p. 186, and 'Analysis of the terms "treaty" and "international agreement" ', *AJ*, vol. 47 (1953), p. 49; A. Broches and S. Boskey, 'Theory and practice of treaties registration with particular references to agreements of the International Bank', *Netherlands International Law Review*, vol. 4 (1957), pp. 159 and 277; and W.K. Geck, 'Registrierung von Verträgen', *Wörterbuch des Völkerrechts*, 2nd edn., (Berlin, de Gruyter, 1962), vol. III, p. 96, and 'Die Registrierung und Veröffentlichung völkerrechtlicher Verträge', *ZaöRV*, vol. 22 (1962), p. 113. For the practice of publication and its effects in France, see above, No. 88, as well as R. Pinto, 'Le juge devant les traités non publiés de la France', *Mélanges offerts à Marcel Waline. Le juge et le droit public* (Paris, Librairie générale de droit et de jurisprudence, 1974), vol. I,

p. 233. The French Minister for Foreign Affairs has confirmed that many treaties have never been published (Question écrite No. 22893, *Journal officiel de l'Assemblée nationale*, 1975, p. 8353). On the retroactivity of the effects of publication, see Cour de Cassation, Première Chambre civile, 30 November 1976 (note by D. Ruzié in *Journal du droit international*, vol. 104 (1977), p. 83).

120* The debate on participation in treaties started in 1962 with two draft articles, one of which initially contemplated the treaty-making capacity of States, members of a federal union and international organizations (which were left aside in 1965), while the other dealt with the parties to a treaty and stipulated that any State could become a party to a 'general multilateral treaty', i.e. a 'multilateral treaty relating to general rules of international law or covering questions of general interest for all States'. The Commission adopted the latter provision in 1962 but deleted it in 1965. At its second session in 1969, the Vienna Conference left out the provision concerning members of a federal union. It rejected an amendment again providing for the access of 'any State' to general multilateral treaties, and this caused the Soviet Union to refuse to sign the Convention. The 1969 Convention (arts. 81 and 83) retained the traditional (so-called 'Vienna') formula opening participation to States which are members of the United Nations, of specialized agencies or of the IAEA, parties to the ICJ Statute or invited by the General Assembly. The conflict between supporters of the 'all States' formula and the 'Vienna' formula for conventions concluded under the auspices of the United Nations was still going on in 1973 (I.I. Lukashuk, 'Parties to treaties: the right of participation', *RCADI*, vol. 135 (1972-I), p. 231). By resolution 3233 (XXIX) of 12 November 1974, the General Assembly invited 'all States' to become parties to the 1969 Convention on the Law of Treaties. But while the convening of the Third United Nations Conference on the Law of the Sea (resolution 3067/XXVIII) of 16 November 1973) still gave rise to some difficulties, the nine-year Conference was always very liberal in that respect and the Convention of 10 December 1982 spelt out the issue in new terms with new formulations, extending participation to certain organizations and to entities resulting from decolonization. See S. Rosenne, 'La participation à la Convention des Nations Unies sur le droit de la mer', in D. Bardonnet and M. Virally, eds, *Le nouveau droit international de la mer* (Paris, Pedone, 1983), p. 287.

122* The ILC and the Vienna Conference closely considered the issue of federal unions; see the statements by Jiménez de Aréchaga and Verdross on whether the rights of a member state of a federal union are determined by international law or by municipal law (*YILC 1965*, vol. I, 810th meeting, p. 245 (paras. 29–30) and p. 246 (para. 45); P. Reuter, 'Confédération et fédération: "vetera et nova" ', *Mélanges offerts à Charles Rousseau. La communauté internationale* (Paris, Pedone, 1974), p. 199; *Official Records UNCLT, I, Summary Records...*, Committee of the Whole, 11th, 12th and 28th meetings, and *Official Records UNCLT, II, Summary Records...*, Plenary, 7th and 8th meetings. For a recent updating of the whole question, see special issue No. 1 of the *Belgian Review of International Law*, vol. 17 (1983): 'Les Etats fédéraux dans les relations internationales'; and references mentioned above at No. 72*. For the 'fundamental rights' of States, see *Preparatory Study concerning a Draft Declaration on the Rights and Duties of States* (A/CN.4/2)(UN Pub., No.1949.V.4), and R. Geiger, *Die völkerrechtliche Beschränkung der Vertragsschlussfähigkeit von Staaten* (Berlin, Duncker und Humblot, 1979).

124* See ILC discussion, *YILC 1962*, vol. I, 660th, 666th and 667th meetings; and *Official Records UNCLT, I, Summary Records...*, Committee of the Whole,

88th – 91th meetings and 105th meeting (paras. 2–15) and Plenary 34th–37th meetings. The problem of participation in treaties of a universal character was also examined (more serenely) at the time of the reopening of participation in treaties concluded under the auspices of the League of Nations (General Assembly resolution 1903 (XVIII)), *YILC 1963*, vol. II, p. 217; see M. Hardy, 'The United Nations and general multilateral treaties concluded under the auspices of the League of Nations', *BYBIL*, vol. 39 (1963), p. 425; as well as the studies in *YILC 1965*, vol. I, p. 113, and *AJ*, vol. 58 (1964), p. 170. On the links between participation and recognition, see: M. Lachs, 792nd ILC meeting, *YILC 1965*, vol. I, p. 117; B.R. Bot, *Nonrecognition and Treaty Relations* (Leyden, Sijthoff, 1968); H. Alexy, 'Indirekte Anerkennung von Staaten', *ZaöRV*, vol. 26 (1966), p. 495; and J. Verhoeven, *La reconnaissance internationale dans la pratique contemporaine* (Paris, Pedone, 1975), pp. 390 and 428. The Vienna Convention on the Succession of States in Respect of Treaties of 23 August 1978 provides for the faculty to participate in certain multilateral treaties, especially by way of a relatively open system (art. 17), in favour of newly independent States which may participate as of right; the same rule applies in a wider manner to the other cases of State succession (see below, Nos. 170 ff.).

125*   The privilege of the Nuclear Powers in the elaboration of a text open to all States for signature was most apparent in the Nuclear Test Ban Treaty of 25 July 1963; the 1959 Antarctic Treaty was also drawn up by a limited number of States and is widely open to other States although it confers particular rights to States having established their interest in scientific research in Antarctica. See the Report of the Secretary-General to the UN General Assembly of 31 October 1984, A/39/583, Parts I and II, on the question of Antarctica.

126*   The Convention on the Law of the Sea went somewhat further in respect of a number of national liberation movements; without allowing their accession as had been requested, the Convention accepts in resolution IV that they may sign the Final Act of the Conference; contrary to well-established practice, they thereby acquire the right to take part as observers in the work of the Authority (art. 156) and the Preparatory Commission (Final Act, Annex I, resolution I, para. 2) as well as to receive from the depositary the documents and invitations mentioned in art. 319. These privileges, however, are not conferred on national liberation movements in general but only on those already admitted by name by the General Assembly to take part in the Conference as observers. See S. Rosenne's article referred to at No. 119*. As for Namibia, it was admitted by article 305 (1) (b) to sign the Convention, interestingly enough in its capacity as 'Namibia represented by the United Nations Council for Namibia', which raises the question of the representation of a territory by an international organization; see the Secretary-General's study on that subject, *YILC 1974*, vol. II (part 2), p. 8.

There is no doubt that an organization's 'capacity' essentially depends on the rules of each organization; but some authors hold that there is a general rule of international law conferring on any intergovernmental organization the right to conclude the treaties necessary to discharge its functions. This is echoed in the tenth preambular paragraph of the 1986 Convention which reads as follows: 'Noting that international organizations possess the capacity to conclude treaties which is necessary for the exercise of their functions and the fulfilment of their purposes'. But this text, which was drafted by an unofficial committee, should be read in the light of art. 2 (1) (j) which regards established practice as a source of the 'rules of the organization'; it has always been admitted that practice can evolve (*YILC 1982*, vol. II (part 2), p. 24 (para. 6 of commentary to draft article 6)). See also P. Reuter, 'Quelques réflexions sur la notion de "pratique" internationale spécialement en matière d'organisations internationales'. *Studi in onore di Giuseppe Sperduti*, p. 187. Yet even a very extensive capacity would merely be one of the conditions for participation; it would never actually confer a right.

130*   For the historical background, see the Report of the Committee of Experts for the Progressive Codification of International Law adopted by the Council of the League of Nations in 1927 (C. 212.1927. V) and the Report of the Secretary-General to the Fifth Session of the General Assembly (A/1372); see the general bibliography in J.M. Ruda, 'Reservations to treaties', *RCADI*, vol. 146 (1975-III), p. 95. See also: D.W. Bowett, 'Reservations to non-restricted treaties', *BYBIL*, vol. 48 (1976–1977), p. 67; P.H. Imbert, *Les réserves aux traités multilatéraux* (Paris, Pedone, 1979) and 'La question des réserves dans la décision arbitrale du 30 juin 1977', *AF*, vol. 24 (1978), p. 29; Sir I. Sinclair, *The Vienna Convention on the Law of Treaties*, pp. 51–83; J.F. Flauss, 'Note sur le retrait par la France des réserves aux traités internationaux', *AF*, vol. 32 (1986), p. 857.

131*   The two changes made to the ILC draft concern arts. 19 (b), 20 (4) (b), and 21 (3). The Commission suggested that the mere mention of authorized reservations should exclude the possibility of other reservations and that an objection to a reservation should be presumed to prevent the reserving State from being considered as a party in its relations with the objecting State. While both the 1969 and 1986 Conventions are silent on the question of reservations to their own provisions, several States did make reservations, some of which prompted objections by other States (see above, No. 32).

132*   Reservations to certain Conventions (e.g. Single Convention on Narcotic Drugs of 30 March 1961 (art. 50); International Convention on the Elimination of All Forms of Racial Discrimination of 21 February 1965 (art. 20 (2)); Convention on Psychotropic Substances of 21 February 1971 (art. 32)) have to be accepted by a two-thirds majority. See A. Cassese, 'A new reservations clause (Article 20 of the United Nations Convention on the Elimination of All Forms of Racial Discrimination)', *En hommage à Paul Guggenheim*, p. 266.

133*   National constitutional practice regarding reservations and objections varies from country to country; see for instance R. Szafarz, 'Reservations and objections in the treaty practice of Poland', *Polish Yearbook of International Law*, vol. 6 (1974), p. 245. In France, the Government does not submit reservations to Parliament with the request for authorization to ratify or accede; see the general study of J. Dhommeaux, *AF*, vol. 21 (1975), p. 815, and 'Question écrite 14593', *Journal officiel de l'Assemblée nationale*, 28 December 1974, p. 372. For particular aspects, see: D.M. McRae, 'The legal effect of interpretative declarations', *BYBIL*, vol. 49 (1978), p. 155; F. Majoros, 'Le régime de réciprocité de la Convention de Vienne et les réserves dans les Conventions de La Haye', *Journal du droit international*, vol. 101 (1974), p. 73. For the relationship between a customary rule and reservations to a treaty, see below, No. 216. For the interpretation of reservations to human rights conventions, see the advisory opinions of the Inter-American Court of Human Rights (OC/2 1982 and OC/3 1983), and the *Temeltasch* case settled by the European Commission of Human Rights and the Committee of Ministers as well as the commentary by Ph. Imbert, *RGDIP*, vol. 87 (1983), p. 580; G. Cohen Jonathan and J.P. Jacqué, *AF*, vol. 28 (1982), p. 524.

Chapter 3
The effects of treaties

136   The effect of a treaty is essentially to create legal rules, to generate rights and obligations. Any treaty 'is binding upon the parties to it and must be performed by them in good faith' (1969 and 1986 Conventions, article 26).

For its effects to be determined, the treaty must first be viewed in isolation, irrespective of any other legal rules which may be applicable in a given situation (without prejudice to problems of interpretation; see below, No. 145) first with regard to parties (Section I) and then to non-parties (Section II), whereupon it will be considered in relation to other rules which may have to combine with it, giving rise to some specific issues (Section III). (*)

I Effects with regard to the parties

137   It has been noted (see above, No. 50) that a treaty, by its very nature, closely links a juristic act and a rule laid down by means of that act. The effects of the treaty relate to the authors of the act: from their will do they proceed and they are nothing apart from that will. That very generally is the basic principle. It makes it possible to formulate from the outset a problem arising even before the treaty is being performed, namely how to determine the intention of the parties. This is the issue of treaty interpretation, which is the subject of Sub-Section 1. Apart from interpretation, several aspects regarding the scope and extent of the undertaking concern the 'application' of a treaty. The application of treaties in the municipal order has already been dealt with (see above, No. 44); their application in space and time remains to be considered in Sub-Section 2.(*)

1. Interpretation

138   States or international organizations which are parties to a treaty have to apply the treaty and therefore to interpret it. In the case of States, the organs having concluded the treaty are the most qualified to do so, but their courts also have to interpret an increasing number of treaties. If the parties to a treaty agree on a common interpretation either by a formal treaty or otherwise, this interpretation acquires an authentic character and prevails over any other. But other entities beside the parties also interpret the treaty, for instance an arbitral tribunal or an international organization which, although not a party, has to apply a treaty or control its application, in particular when the treaty concerned is its constituent charter.(*)

139   The fact that different entities are called upon to interpret the treaty does not in principle affect the manner in which interpretation must be performed. What does change from one situation to another is the extent of the interpreter's powers, and also the effects of his interpretation. While the right of the governments parties to interpret a treaty is unchallenged, the same cannot be said of municipal courts whose powers, laid down by their national Constitution, vary considerably from State to State and occasionally from court to court within the same country. In international organizations, it is generally accepted that each organ, within its functions, is called upon to interpret the treaties which concern it although the interpretations of some, especially judicial, organs may in some cases be binding on the other organs as well.

140   We shall not go into the constitutional issues of which some aspects have already been mentioned (see above, No. 44) but will simply present the basic rules of treaty interpretation. Interpretation is governed by legal rules, for disputes concerning treaty interpretation are the very type of legal disputes which can be settled by judicial means (Article 36 of the Statutes of the Permanent Court of International Justice and of the International Court of Justice). These rules are necessarily applicable by all entities called upon to interpret a treaty. There has, however, been much discussion about the method of interpretation, the most difficult issue being the distinction between what can be the subject of specific *rules* of interpretation and what in a concrete case should be left to the interpreter's *art*.

141   Yet there is one fundamental observation which makes such a distinction possible. The purpose of interpretation is to ascertain the intention of the parties from a text. The problem is quite different in the case of agreements not recorded in an instrument, whether verbal or implicit, where the existence and the content of a spontaneous will emerge simultaneously, without any recourse to a formal document specially designed for that purpose. If, on the contrary, there is such a document, the intention has become a text by means of a very specific operation. Interpretation is the reverse operation, going backwards from the text to the initial intention. Drafting methods and rules of interpretation are therefore two aspects of the same problem viewed from two opposite angles: both deal with an intention embodied in a text.(*)

142   The primacy of the text, especially in international law, is the cardinal rule for any interpretation. It may be that in other legal systems, where the legislative and judicial processes are fully regulated by the authority of the State and not by the free consent of the parties, the courts are deemed competent to make a text say what it does not say or even the opposite of what it says. But such interpretations, which are sometimes described as teleological, are indissociable from the fact that recourse to the courts is mandatory, that the court is obliged to hand down a decision, and that it is moreover controlled by an effective legislature whose action may if necessary check its bolder undertakings. When an international judge or arbitrator departs from a text, it is because he is satisfied that another text or practice, i.e. another source of law, should prevail.(*)

143 In the interpretation of international law, because of the submission to the *expression* of the parties' intention, it is essential to identify exactly how and when that intention was expressed and to give precedence to its most immediate manifestation. In this respect the draft provisions drawn up by the International Law Commission, and barely modified by the Vienna Conferences, are one of the most remarkable achievements of the 1969 Convention (articles 31 and 32).(*)

144 According to article 31 of the 1969 and 1986 Conventions, interpretation must be based simultaneously on the 'context' (paragraph 2) and on other elements (paragraph 3) which appear to carry less weight. The 'context' covers the text itself (including the preamble and annexes) and any agreement relating to the treaty which has been reached between all the parties in connection with its conclusion, as well as 'any instrument which was made by one or more parties in connexion with the conclusion of the treaty and accepted by the other parties as an instrument related to the treaty'. The other elements to be 'taken into account' are 'any subsequent agreement between the parties' regarding interpretation or application of the treaty, 'any subsequent practice in the application of the treaty which establishes the agreement of the parties regarding its interpretation' and 'any relevant rules of international law applicable in the relations between the parties'.

These carefully and subtly graduated elements constitute, primarily and simultaneously, the basic guidelines of interpretation. As for the terms used in these agreements, they are to be interpreted in good faith following their ordinary meaning and in the light of the object and purpose of the treaty. The ordinary meaning of the terms may only be departed from if the parties' intention to do so can be established.(*)

145 It is from these elements, since they primarily incorporate the parties' intention, that the meaning of the treaty should normally be derived. Recourse to supplementary means of interpretation (article 32) — including preparatory work or deductions to reconstitute the parties' intention especially by reference to the circumstances of the conclusion of the treaty — is only admissible at a later stage, either to confirm the results of the interpretation or to avoid reaching ambiguous or manifestly absurd or unreasonable results on the sole basis of the primary elements.

146 When articles 31 and 32 were considered, one point which gave rise to serious discussion was whether preparatory work should only play a secondary role. This solution was favoured for two reasons. As a matter of law, all the factors listed in article 31 constitute an authentic expression of the parties' intentions, whereas the intentions recorded in the preparatory work are not final. As a matter of fact, recourse to preparatory work means treading uncertain ground: its content is not precisely defined nor rigorously certified, and it reveals the shortcomings or possible blunders of the negotiators as well as their reluctance to confront the true difficulties. Moreover, preparatory work is not always published, and even when it is there could be some misgivings about invoking it against States, ever more numerous on account of the modern methods of accession, which did not take part in the negotiations. (*)

147 Nevertheless, the International Law Commission's commentary shows how important preparatory work is in practice and the judicial decisions it mentions reveal that it does help to clarify points which would otherwise have remained obscure. In the end, the provisions of both Conventions are very moderate and it would be inappropriate to challenge them on doctrinal grounds alone. There may be slight variations in the positions of the authors, and while these nuances may be linked to doctrinal preference, they do not really coincide with any of the world's main legal systems. The transition from an intention to its written expression has given rise to identical problems and to similar solutions all over the world.

148 It would be equally rash to try to make a difference between principles of interpretation depending upon whether the treaties considered are bilateral or multilateral, law-making or contractual; the principles may apply differently according to the characteristics of the treaties concerned, but they necessarily remain the same. What international case-law does show is both far more modest and more interesting, i.e. that the courts examine groups of treaties covering similar subjects at a given time (see above, No. 81). Indeed, with regard to both vocabulary (especially technical terms) and some usual provisions (e.g. the most-favoured-nation clause), drafting practice reveals that drafters often look to existing treaties (especially in a bilateral context): hence it becomes possible to identify groups or types of treaties. The scope of clauses which recur from treaty to treaty or the meaning of a particular expression may thus be clarified in some complex cases, although here too considerable caution is required.(*)

2. Application

A. TERRITORIAL APPLICATION

149 The territorial scope of the rules laid down by a treaty has to be identified: in what territory or extraterritorial location are the situations and facts governed by such rules supposed to arise? Each treaty must define its territorial scope, otherwise it may be difficult to ascertain the parties' intention, especially for areas whose status has not yet been clearly defined as in the case of certain maritime or polar areas or of outer space. When a treaty refers to the territory of a State, in order to determine the scope of application of its rules, it must be regarded as covering the whole of the State's territory (article 29 of the 1969 and 1986 Conventions). Such a presumption cannot extend to international organizations since they do not have a 'territory'.

150 In the past, it was often the policy of colonial powers to exclude colonial territories from the application of their treaties by means of a final clause usually referred to as the 'colonial clause'. This practice has raised conflicting opinions from the legislative point of view. It is less relevant now that most colonies have become independent; but many States still practise a high degree of decentralization and usually exclude islands or remote areas from the application of certain treaty rules, especially for economic matters. No better example could be given than the provisions of the treaties of the European Communities involving the rules applicable to territories enjoying special relations with member States. Apart from the federal solutions which will be dealt with below, there are a number of highly specific situations which may derogate from the rule that a treaty, unless otherwise stipulated, applies to the whole of a State's territory.(*)

B. TEMPORAL APPLICATION

151 The conditions under which a treaty enters into force have already been discussed (see above, No. 10) and the next chapter (see below, Nos. 230 ff.) will consider the different situations in which the application of a treaty is suspended or terminated. The question is how to identify the temporal application of the treaty, or in other words how to connect the facts and situations governed by the treaty rules to a given period of time. As a general rule, there is no doubt that the parties are free to determine this for themselves and in principle are subject to no restriction, with regard either to the past or to the future. Yet treaty provisions are not always clear enough and the need has therefore been felt to lay down residual rules. It can be maintained that there is a general principle of law that, unless otherwise stated, legal rules apply only to the future and have no retroactive effect. But the problem is precisely how to determine the characteristics of retroactivity, how to identify and contrast a 'fact' and a 'situation', etc. The issues of intertemporal law and conflicts of law in time are extremely complex matters in all legal systems; they involve concepts and language hardly separable from a specific municipal order.(*)

152 The 1969 Convention, followed by the 1986 Convention, devoted several provisions to this problem. Under article 28, the provisions of a treaty 'do not bind a party in relation to any act or fact which took place or any situation which ceased to exist before the date of the entry into force of the treaty with respect to that party'. Under article 70 (1) (b) the termination of a treaty 'does not affect any right, obligation or legal situation of the parties created through the execution of the treaty prior to its termination'. Under article 71 (2) (b), the emergence of a new peremptory rule of international law 'does not affect any right, obligation or legal situation of the parties created through the execution of the treaty prior to its termination; provided that those rights, obligations or situations may thereafter be maintained only to the extent that their maintenance is not in itself in conflict with the new peremptory norm of general international law'.

Currently it is hardly possible to do more than restate these provisions: their content could only be clarified by a long judicial practice, but so far only very few relevant cases have been decided (see below, No. 271). In fact, the problem is to determine how a legal rule situates in time the concepts it involves, taking into consideration either the instantaneous or repetitious character of facts and the continuity of situations, as the case may be.

II Effects with regard to non-parties

153   Article 26 of the 1969 and 1986 Conventions provides that '[e]very treaty in force is binding upon the parties to it and must be performed by them...'. Treaties are therefore not binding upon third States and international organizations, and do not have to be performed by them (article 34) *(pacta tertiis nec nocent nec prosunt)*. These principles are obvious to the point of being tautological, or rather they are another expression of the definition of a treaty. But they do not express the whole reality. A review of practice in international society shows that in many ways third States and organizations are affected by treaties to which they are not parties. It should be noted from the outset that 'to be affected by treaties' is quite a vague expression which may cover very different situations. Some of these call for no objection of principle in justifying such effects; others on the contrary challenge what is still the basic principle in interstate relations, namely State sovereignty. To accept that the legal situation of a State or international organization may be modified by a treaty which it has never agreed to seems incompatible with the principle of sovereignty. It is therefore necessary to consider carefully, case by case, all the effects which may be felt by third States, to ascertain their true nature and to identify the legal mechanism from which they result. This is where the political dimension appears behind the doctrinal controversy and indeed throws some light on the debate: if all the effects of a treaty are consented to by the third State or organization, the principles are maintained; if there is no such consent, the principles are jeopardized; and if the third party is openly opposed to the treaty, the principles are flouted. The actual form of consent will be a crucial element in any analysis.

The rights and obligations which treaties may directly establish for individuals and which such individuals directly benefit from or have to perform (see above, No. 47) are quite distinct from the situations considered here, since the direct effects of a convention for individuals always derive from State authority, even where these rights and obligations are subject to international control mechanisms. They will therefore not be examined in this section.

The simpler cases will be reviewed first, i.e. those where the treaty purports, at least partly, to create rights and obligations for third States or international organizations, subject to their consent: this is the classical offer to stipulate rights and obligations for a third State under a treaty (Sub-Section 1). Next, a set of specific mechanisms will be discussed whereby treaties produce effects for third parties under special circumstances which might possibly amount to a derogation from the general principle (Sub-Section 2).(*)

1. Effects stemming from the consent of third parties

154 This is the only case (apart from the formation of a custom) to be contemplated by the 1969 and later the 1986 Convention. After laying down the principle that a treaty does not create either obligations or rights for a third State or organization without its consent (article 34), the Conventions deal separately with obligations (article 35) and rights (article 36) before considering the revocation or modification of obligations or rights of third States (article 37).

155 For both obligations and rights, the parties must have the intention of creating them by a provision, and the third State or organization must give its consent. A first difference is that whereas article 35 only provides for the creation of obligations for a single State or international organization, article 36 stipulates that the beneficiary of rights may be either a State, a group of States or all States, or an international organization, a group of them or all of them. It is not apparent why obligations might not be established with regard to a group of States or organizations, nor why rights or obligations might not be established with regard to a group comprising both States and organizations. A second very important difference is that obligations must be expressly accepted in writing, whereas it is enough for a third State or organization to assent to rights extended under a treaty, the assent of the State being 'presumed so long as the contrary is not indicated, unless the treaty otherwise provides', while the assent of the organization is 'governed by the rules of the organization'. Two reasons were given by the International Law Commission to justify this difference between States and international organizations. First, it is impossible in general to presume the assent of an entity whose capacity, unlike that of States, is limited. Secondly the 'rights' of international organizations are more closely linked to particular functions than those of States and it is only normal that an extension of the organization's functions should comply with its own rules. In fact, presumed consent is a technical device which goes beyond just introducing greater flexibility in the forms of consent.

156　These are reasonable rules; they do not, however, clarify the legal mechanism upon which they are based. The Special Rapporteur and the International Law Commission referred to a collateral agreement for the creation of obligations, but did not give any further clarification. As to the creation of rights, two theories were put forward during the discussion, one based on the collateral agreement, the other on *stipulation pour autrui*. By such a stipulation, third party beneficiaries would enjoy these rights immediately, regardless of their acceptance. The Commission was divided on this subject, with a slight majority in favour of the collateral agreement theory.

157　The mechanism of *stipulation pour autrui* involves a greater departure from the principle of the relative effect of conventions than the collateral agreement mechanism, which strictly adheres to the principle that it is impossible for a treaty to have any effect whatsoever on third parties. The choice between the two theories raises the issue of the effect in international law of unilateral acts — a promise, an offer or an undertaking — pending their consolidation by acceptance. It could be said that in international law, as opposed to private law, few situations recur frequently enough in similar circumstances, and that it is therefore more difficult to identify the standards of conduct entitling third parties to take unilateral acts into account. However, especially since the Judgment of the International Court of Justice in the *Nuclear Tests* case (*ICJ Reports 1974*, p. 267, paras. 42 ff.), it cannot be ruled out that a unilateral act comprising an intention to be bound under the terms of a declaration presents the character of a 'legal undertaking' without any *'quid pro quo'* or 'subsequent acceptance' being required. Hence there is no objection in principle to admitting that a treaty confers a right upon a third State, it being understood that, in relation to that State, the treaty is no more than a *collective unilateral act*. In fact, the Court went further than was required to justify a *stipulation pour autrui,* which in no way excludes acceptance by the beneficiary; its distinctive feature is merely to produce such effects immediately even though the beneficiary may reject them when they are brought to its knowledge. This is where *in practice* it may be more appropriate in some situations to choose one theory rather than the other.(*)

158　In fact, at least for the creation of rights, the Commission did not opt for any theory and the wording of article 36 of the 1969 Convention concerning States, which was later confirmed by the 1986 Convention with regard to organizations, can accommodate either explanation. But the commentary on the draft articles and the provision adopted for the creation of rights shows that the texts predominantly refer to the collateral agreement theory. Indeed, the beneficiary's assent exists even for the creation of rights, although such assent is *presumed,* involving therefore a presumed tacit agreement. As soon as the beneficiary takes a position on the effects of the stipulation, the presumed agreement becomes an explicit one if the effects are accepted, or disappears if they are rejected (retroactively it would seem, although the Vienna Conventions do not clarify this point). In any event, the collateral agreement is the crucial concept in the mechanism instituted by the Vienna Conventions.

159 It is therefore useful to take a closer look at how the agreement operates. It is entered into on the one hand by a State or organization accepting the obligation or right, and on the other hand by all the parties to the treaty. But how then should the intention of the parties to the treaty, which together constitute one of the parties to the collateral agreement, be regarded? In a way, this is a single intention which has previously been considered as giving rise to a collective unilateral act (see above, No. 157); but it is also a sum of individual wills and the analysis of this sum of wills is not without effect on the legal consequences of the collateral agreement.

160 The 1969 Convention dealt with this question partially and summarily in article 37 ('Revocation or modification of obligations or rights of third States') whose provisions were extended to treaties of international organizations under the 1986 Convention. But article 37 only covers one aspect of the issue. In the case of an obligation, revocation or modification requires, apart from the consent of the parties to the treaty, the consent of the third State or international organization; the collateral agreement is consolidated as a separate treaty. The same applies in the case of a right 'if it is established that the right was intended not to be revocable or subject to modification without the consent of the third State or the third organization' (to quote the 1986 Convention); if this condition is not fulfilled, the parties to the initial treaty may modify or revoke the right in question. The Conventions do not deal with the effects of a modification to the main treaty by withdrawal of one of the parties or for any other reason.

In fact, collateral treaties raise the problems relating to *groups of treaties,* i.e. treaties which do not necessarily all bind the same parties but which are connected by links of interdependence varying from case to case in nature or scope. There has been an increasing number of these groups of treaties in contemporary international relations, especially in the economic field; but the 1969 and 1986 Conventions made no attempt to include them and were based on past examples, mainly intent on protecting State sovereignty, yet without depriving States of the benefit of treaties seemingly directed at all States. Examples will be provided further on of categories of treaties to which the residual provisions of the Vienna Conventions do not apply (see below, Nos. 169, 177 and 178) and in one instance at least the 1986 Convention had to take this into account (article 74 (3)).(*)

161 The purpose of the 1969 and 1986 Conventions was not, however, to regulate in detail all the aspects of the law of treaties and many questions were left open, especially with regard to the effect of treaties on third States. This is the case *inter alia* of the application of different rules concerning rights and obligations: since most treaties include both rights and obligations for third States, will it be possible in practice to maintain different systems of acceptance for rights and for obligations, especially where the rights are conditional on the obligations (1969 Convention, article 36 (2); 1986 Convention, article 36 (3))? When rights and obligations are thus linked, which should apply: the more flexible rule concerning the acceptance of rights or the stricter rule concerning the acceptance of obligations?

2. Effects depending upon specific mechanisms

162 After dealing with these classical rules on the lack of effects of treaties on third parties, one usually turns to a number of cases which in varying degrees are presented as exceptions. In fact most of these do not amount to exceptions at all since the effects merely relate to facts, not to rights and obligations. Such is the case (A) when the treaty is merely referred to by a third State or organization as a yardstick for its own obligations (most-favoured-nation clause), (B) when the treaty constitutes an unlawful act with regard to a third State or organization in whose favour rules of international responsibility then apply, or again (C) when the treaty, apart from its conventional character, forms a precedent contributing to the development of a customary rule. Other cases, however, are more specific, notably (D) treaties relating to the appearance of a new subject of international law, or (E) treaties involving a composite entity. Finally some cases seem to constitute genuine exceptions to the *pacta tertiis* principle, i.e. (F) 'status treaties', 'objective régimes' or 'rights *in rem*'; but even these cases, rather than being considered as exceptions, are often given other explanations, especially by resorting to the concept of 'informal agreements' in the widest sense, which practice seems to accept.

A. REFERENCE TO ANOTHER TREATY (MOST-FAVOURED-NATION CLAUSE)

163 One of the best-known institutions in treaty practice is the most-favoured-nation clause whereby a State or organization undertakes to grant another State or organization all benefits it might subsequently grant any other State or organization. In fact, more generally speaking, the parties have determined their obligations not merely by describing them but by means of a parameter which varies according to such undertakings as may be assumed by them in other respects. The treaty therefore determines part of its effects by reference to another treaty. Many examples can be given. Thus a treaty between States A and B will normally apply to the entire territory of both (1969 and 1986 Vienna Conventions, article 29). Both territories may, however, be determined by treaties with neighbouring States. These treaties may be subject to modifications, and the territorial scope of the treaty between A and B will then following an accepted rule automatically change (article 15 of the 1978 Convention on Succession of States in Respect of Treaties). Treaties modifying in relation to third States the territory of State A or B are as between A and B mere facts implicitly taken into account by reference to an element — territory — defined in those treaties. A modification of the territory of A under a treaty with one of A's neighbours does not affect the treaty between A and B from outside, but from within, by way of the reference agreed between A and B themselves. In the case of the most-favoured-nation mechanism the reference is explicit, but even then it remains a simple fact. The effect of a treaty between A and C does not become part and parcel of treaty relations between A and B; there is no consolidation of the effects brought about by the most-favoured-nation clause, and as soon as the treaty between A and C ceases to produce any effects between A and C, its effect also ceases between A and B.(*)

B. THE TREATY AS AN UNLAWFUL ACT WITH REGARD TO THIRD PARTIES

164 Unlawful acts may consist not only in material facts, but in legal transactions such as treaties. The most straightforward example is a treaty between A and C violating A's obligations under another treaty with B (similar situations often arise in private law). From the point of view purely of the law of treaties, both agreements are valid; but as they conflict with each other, only one of them can be performed. Performance of this treaty will constitute a breach of the undertaking assumed by the other treaty and will entail an obligation to make reparation. This effect of the performed treaty on the non-performed treaty again results from a simple fact and does not amount to an exception to the principle that treaties have no effect on third parties. The example could be further elaborated, yet without altering the appreciation of the point at issue: if it is the *conclusion* of the later treaty that constitutes an unlawful act, one could always consider that the adequate reparation should be to eliminate it; this might work out if the later treaty were concluded in bad faith and in circumstances authorizing the other party to be regarded as an accomplice in the breach of A's prior undertaking, but that will rarely occur. This raises the problem of conflicting treaties (see below, No. 200).(*)

C. THE TREATY AS A PRECEDENT FOR CUSTOM

165 There are many and complex relations between treaty and custom, as has already been mentioned (see above, Nos. 32 and 67). Further on we shall consider the situation deriving from a treaty subsequent to a custom concerning the same subject-matter, in particular in the case of codification. But the present case is the opposite one, namely that of treaties dealing with a matter which is not the subject of a customary rule: can the provisions of such treaties give rise to a custom? Article 38 of the 1969 Convention merely states with great caution that '[n]othing in articles 34 to 37 precludes a rule set forth in a treaty from becoming binding upon a third State [the 1986 Convention adds 'or a third organization'] as a customary rule of international law, recognized as such'. Of course, treaties constitute practice, and any practice may constitute a precedent. But the nature of custom remains controversial in theory and the preliminary work of the 1969 Convention shows that this point was systematically avoided. In any event, it is very difficult from a practical viewpoint to prove that a custom has emerged on the basis of prior treaties alone. This can be shown by distinguishing between restricted bilateral or multilateral treaties and non-restricted multilateral treaties.

166   In the case of restricted treaties, in order to establish that a customary rule has been formed, great importance is attached to the number and repetition of such treaties in the practice of all States, in order to show that the rule laid down corresponds to a perceived need which is recognized as such. Although in the interpretation of such treaties, courts will take into account identical provisions in a series of particular treaties (see above, Nos. 81 and 148), they do not in general go so far as to infer from this uniformity an awareness of an obligation extending even to States not bound by such undertakings. France in the *Lotus* case (*PCIJ, Series A, No. 10*, pp. 25–27) and the United States in the case of the *Rights of Nationals of the United States of America in Morocco (ICJ Reports 1952*, p. 179) relied in vain *inter alia* on a series of concordant treaties concerning collisions at sea and capitulations, respectively.

For unrestricted multilateral treaties, the problem is different and no longer a matter of repetition. The difficulties arising out of non-ratification by some (often many!) States tend to be overcome by assuming that such treaties give rise to corresponding customary rules. As an example of rapid formation of customary law on the basis of major multilateral conventions, reference can be made to the development of outer-space law. However, the formation of a customary rule extending beyond the parties to the treaty is not in the first place determined by the treaty as such but by the fact that non-parties have applied its rules or recognized their customary character, or at least put up with their application by others in circumstances where they would normally have been expected to object. Concepts such as 'quasi-universal treaties' which have occasionally surfaced in judicial decisions (e.g. *Barcelona Traction, Second Phase, ICJ Reports 1970*, p. 32, para. 34) are not legally relevant.(*)

D. TREATIES CONCERNING A NEW LEGAL SUBJECT

167   New legal subjects always pose many theoretical and practical problems in any legal order, and this is also true in international law, especially the law of treaties. Two groups of treaties are concerned in such changes: (a) those relating to the creation of a new State or international organization; and (b) those which are binding upon the predecessor in the event of a succession of legal subjects. Can it be said that both groups of treaties have effects for third parties and, if so, do such effects amount to an exception to the *pacta tertiis* principle?

(a) Treaties relating to the creation of a new State or international organization

(1) New States

168 Many treaties, especially major peace treaties, have provided for the creation or rebirth of a State. When a State has been created in this way, it is not a party to the treaty. Yet can it be regarded as a third party? This type of question has been the subject of much theoretical and even judicial discussion, in particular when courts have attempted to determine the exact date of birth of the new State. Three points should be made. First, whatever the other effects of the treaty may be, it is not the treaty itself which breathes life into the State but the fact that the entity concerned fulfils all the actual requirements of statehood (a responsible government exercising stable control over a territory and its population). Second, a rejection of this viewpoint would amount to asserting that the State concerned is the object of the treaty, which is enough to establish specific links between the State and the parties to the treaty but not to make it a *party* to the treaty. Its situation in relation to the parties will depend on the terms of the treaty; and if the treaty entails rights and obligations for the new State, this will be by virtue of the undertakings it may have assumed when it came into being. Third, international practice shows that, before a State comes into being, a provisional situation usually prevails with an embryonic government exercising a varying degree of control over a territorial area and its population; this organized entity concludes agreements with States, and these acknowledge that they are bound by such agreements under international law; the very existence of such agreements means that the new State resulting from the provisional body will already be a party to international undertakings which concern it. This mechanism has frequently been used in the process of peaceful decolonization (see above, No. 126*). Yet the 1978 Convention on Succession of States in Respect of Treaties (articles 8 and 9) has made it a principle that even a treaty between a predecessor and a successor State (or for that matter a unilateral declaration by a successor State) does not necessarily regulate *all by itself* the effects of a treaty entered into by the predecessor State; this is yet another restatement of the relative character of the effects of treaties.(*)

(2) New international organizations

169 The same observations with certain adjustments may be made with respect to new international organizations. The essential difference is that an international organization is not in practice a product of nature, but the result of a treaty which sets out in detail all the conditions of its existence. Although it may appear rather strange to regard the organization as a third party in relation to its own constituent charter, it cannot be considered a *party* to that charter. The organization owes its legal existence to its constituent charter, and is governed by it; the charter can be invoked against it and it can itself invoke the charter. One cannot in this case simply rely on the general framework of articles 34 to 37 of the 1968 and 1986 Conventions.

The obligations of the organization could not possibly be regarded as deriving from its explicit acceptance, for the States would then be unable to modify its constituent instrument without its consent! Article 37 therefore does not apply and it must be accepted that the treaty has direct effects on the organization, simply because the organization is the object of the treaty; but it is not a party to its constituent charter. One is therefore faced with a situation where the simple alternative, either 'party' or 'non-party', does not cover all the effects of a treaty. Yet it would seem inappropriate to treat this as an exception to the *pacta tertiis* principle, which has never had the curious effect of preventing a treaty from creating a new legal subject.(*)

(b) Treaties relating to a succession of legal subjects (succession of States)

170 When a legal subject is succeeded by another, what becomes of its treaties? Assuming that they are transmitted to the successor, should this not be regarded as an exception to the *pacta tertiis* principle? The problem arises mainly in the event of State succession and is dealt with by the Convention of 23 August 1978 which has already been mentioned on several occasions (see above, Nos. 124*, 163 and 168). A 'succession' between a State and an international organization could also be discussed here, but it is enough to mention it in passing at this stage, since this situation will be examined below in relation to composite entities (No. 175).(*)

171 The transformation of States has always given rise to many problems. So far they have been resolved rather empirically and it is difficult to show that they proceed from a homogeneous legal theory. Solutions vary according to the different cases of State succession, the subjects concerned and the political circumstances. The 1969 Convention on the Law of Treaties and the 1978 Convention on Succession of States in Respect of Treaties (another Convention on Succession of States in Respect of State Property, Archives and Debts was adopted on 8 April 1983) will not change this situation for a long time to come. Certainly, by its general spirit, the 1978 Convention was fundamentally intended to ensure the complete freedom of States which had been former European colonial territories; for these 'newly independent States', as they are curiously called, there is no succession to the treaties concluded by the predecessor State, but only the possibility of simply and rapidly becoming a party to multilateral treaties to which the predecessor was a party except when, 'under the terms of the treaty or by reason of the limited number of the negotiating States and the object and purpose of the treaty, the participation of any other State in the treaty must be considered as requiring the consent of all the parties' (1978 Convention, article 17 (3)). In draft article 33 (3), the International Law Commission had provided that 'if a part of the territory of a State separates from it and becomes a State in circumstances which are essentially of the same character as those existing in the case of the formation of a newly independent State, the successor State shall be regarded for the purposes of the present articles in all respects as a newly independent State' (*YILC 1974,* vol. II (part 1),

p. 260), but the Conference rejected this extension of the privileges of decolonized States.

172 Essentially, the 1978 Convention provides either for the non-transmission of treaty obligations (clean slate) or for their transmission (continuity of undertakings) to the successor State. The clean slate solution applies to newly independent States, whereas continuity applies to the unification or separation of States (irrespective of whether or not the State which has undergone the separation remains in existence). These solutions derive not from the nature of treaty undertakings but from political considerations or equity, namely the concern to release decolonized countries from all commitments assumed by the colonial power, and the wish to prevent States from escaping prior commitments by merger or from repudiating by separation obligations which the State as a whole accepted when the treaty was concluded. Strict adherence to the principles of State personality and of the law of treaties would require the clean slate solution to be extended to all situations and treaties. In fact this has only been applied as a general solution to newly independent States, remaining exceptional in the case of unification and separation; and an attempt has been made to safeguard as far as possible the continuity of application of general law-making treaties. The régime of succession in matters of treaties must therefore be taken for what it is, a compromise based on political considerations. And yet the basic principle of sovereignty underlying the law of treaties essentially remains that a State cannot be bound without its consent by the will of others. When, in the case of unification or separation, it is apparently bound without any formal consent, this is either because the State cannot free itself from an undertaking by intentionally entering a union whose legal personality would bring about the termination of its previous treaties or because, having contributed to the formation of a State's commitment, a fraction of that State cannot free itself from those undertakings by acquiring a distinct personality by means of separation.

173 The basic characteristic of these rules which reflect common international practice is a realistic appraisal of State personality and this is the prevalent feature of the solutions adopted: when the personality of the new State expresses a genuine and autonomous social reality, commitments are not transmitted, but when it has in fact had a part in the formation of its predecessor's commitments there is a substantial continuity and commitments are transmitted to the successor State as far as compatible with their character. The solutions prevailing for State succession with regard to treaties are the result of an assessment of factual elements which leave a part to be played by both the fictitious and the real side of legal persons. In the case of unification or separation, the successor State is not really a third party in relation to certain commitments of the predecessor State whereas, morally and sociologically, newly independent States are. Once again it appears that certain effects a treaty may have on States which are not parties are due to reasons unconnected with the *pacta tertiis* principle which prevent them from being regarded as third States.

174 Succession to treaties relating to international organizations immediately involves a number of specific difficulties which are better considered in the more general context of international organizations (see below, Nos. 175 ff.). In fact, while there are many cases of succession from State to organization or even vice versa, it is far more difficult to contemplate succession from one organization to another. Indeed succession requires a natural continuity of some components from predecessor to successor. As between States, such components are territory and population. These do not exist for international organizations, which are completely abstract entities depending for their existence on the will of member States. Some treaties did transfer property from a dissolved organization to a new one (from the League of Nations to the United Nations, from OEEC to OECD, from one body established by a commodity agreement to another, etc.), but rather than proper cases of succession, these are isolated and empirical arrangements, none of which, moreover, has ever contemplated the 'passing on' of a treaty concluded *by* the organization.(*)

E. TREATIES RELATING TO COMPOSITE ENTITIES (INTERNATIONAL ORGANIZATIONS)

(a) General régime
175   The expression 'composite entities' may be used to describe political structures endowed with their own personality in international law but made up of component units which also to some extent enjoy an international legal personality. In decreasing order of centralization they are: federal States, confederations, international organizations exercising State functions, and ordinary international organizations. For reasons to be given below, interest is focused on international organizations exercising State functions. For all composite entities, the question is to identify the effects of a treaty concluded by the composite entity on its component units or of a treaty concluded by one of the component units on the composite entity and, if such effects exist, to determine whether or not they amount to an exception to the *pacta tertiis* principle.

176   It is easy to show the type of entity for which the issue is most relevant and controversial. In a federal State only the composite entity is itself a State under international law; the treaties validly concluded by the federal State are binding upon the provinces, cantons or republics whose association constitutes the State, unless the federal Constitution dispenses them from performing treaties concluded in specific fields, thereby in practice preventing a State from making commitments in such fields; the federal State then has to include in its treaties a 'federal clause' under which it merely undertakes to recommend a given line of conduct to its 'provinces'. But it makes no sense in international law to look upon cantons or provinces as third parties in relation to the treaties concluded by the federal State. Conversely, where a federal State very exceptionally allows a *Land* or a canton to conclude certain treaties, this is done with its agreement or under its control, in conditions such that the federal State cannot be regarded as a third party in relation to treaties performed on a portion of its territory. This is not the case with confederations, where both the confederation and its member States are entitled to make certain types of treaties. While this case is of merely historical interest, since this type of union has almost disappeared at the end of the twentieth century, the same theoretical problems as in former confederations are raised nowadays in a different political context by 'organizations' or 'communities' which tend to have an economic rather than a political or military purpose. In this study, these will be referred to as 'organizations with State powers' but they are often called 'supranational' or 'integrated' organizations; the most important example is the European Economic Community. Similar problems arise, but to a far lesser extent, and mostly not on the legal level, for organizations whose powers are not made up of renounced State powers. The essential difficulty with composite entities is first of all to identify clearly the respective powers of the overall structure and of its components. Moreover there is often a *de facto* interdependence between the powers exercised at different levels: hence, to be successful, a course of action requires decisions to be taken at these levels either upon consultation or even by way of subordination. This can be illustrated by two examples. When an organization such as the European Economic Community concludes a fishing agreement with a third State, it is up to the member States to control the application of the treaty by their maritime police. The member States cannot claim ignorance of the agreements of the organization; they are not properly speaking third parties in relation to such agreements. Another example concerns treaties determining privileges, immunities and obligations of States members of an organization in their relations with the State on whose territory the organization has its headquarters. Thus a Convention on the Privileges and Immunities of the United Nations was adopted by a General Assembly resolution on 13 February 1946 and was opened to the accession of all member States. The United Nations is not itself a party to such agreements, but the Secretary-General has correctly maintained that it is not a third party in relation to this Convention concluded under Article 104 of the United Nations Charter (see above, No. 169). The United Nations also concluded a headquarters agreement on 26 June 1947 with the United States of America which was immediately binding upon member States without their explicit written consent. Both examples show that some flexibility is called for with regard to the very strict provisions of articles 34 to 37 of the 1969 Vienna Convention.(*)

177   In what direction is such flexibility to be sought? Two types of sources shed some light on this point. First, the work and discussions of the International Law Commission and the 1986 Vienna Conference; and second, the treaty practice of the European Communities. While both these sources may have taken into account certain features of the other, they have nevertheless remained totally independent from each other. The question of the effect on member States of treaties concluded by an international organization was raised right at the beginning of the Commission's work in 1972; from 1977 onwards, it was the subject of lively discussions in the Commission and in the General Assembly's Sixth Committee, owing both to technical difficulties and to the opposition of socialist countries who perceived it as a stratagem by the European Communities. It then became the International Law Commission's draft article 36 *bis,* which, after some amendments making it much stricter, was adopted in 1980. Six years later, however, the Vienna Conference was more hesitant. The representatives of international organizations agreed that there was indeed a difficulty, but wished to avoid a rigid and general solution. The European Communities which had settled their problems on a case by case basis had no wish to be assimilated to international organizations, and feared that the proposed solution might have an adverse effect on their future prospects. Most government delegations had problems in evaluating the practical consequences of the proposed solution. Draft article 36 *bis* was therefore rejected and, following the proposal of international organizations taking part in the Conference, a third paragraph was added to article 74 to the effect that nothing in the Convention should 'prejudge any question that may arise in regard to the establishment of obligations and rights for States members of an international organization under a treaty to which that organization is a party'. As for the European Communities, they had considerably extended their treaty-making capacity since 1971 and become parties to many unrestricted multilateral treaties. In order to do so, they had to solve many problems arising out of the changing power distribution between the Community and its member States, the factual interdependence in the exercise of the powers of the Community and of member States, and the objections of other parties fearing that Community structures would prove a source of insecurity for them and a means for Community members to increase their influence in the management of conventions. Among the empirical solutions which were therefore devised, those adopted in Annex IX to the United Nations Convention on the Law of the Sea of 10 December 1982 were influenced by the final draft articles prepared that year by the International Law Commission and by the political problems characterizing the 1982 Convention.(*)

178   The following conclusions may be drawn from this brief review of a problem which has been the subject of much discussion during the last few years and has given rise to a number of solutions in international practice.

When an international organization concludes a treaty, three kinds of conventional relations are theoretically involved. The first concerns relations between the international organization and the other party, and these naturally play the major role. The second kind concerns relations between the international organization and its member States regarding the treaty; such relations may not exist when the member States reserve their right to ignore these undertakings; conversely member States may be bound to comply with certain obligations toward the organization, depending on the constituent instrument of each organization which is the source of the rights and obligations of member States. The third kind of relations is between member States and the other parties to the treaty concluded by the organization; such relations do not exist automatically, but they may exist and the point here is to assess the conditions and régime under which they arise.

Such relations are subject to the general rules of the law of treaties rooted in non-formalistic consensualism: the parties must be fully informed of their undertakings and must have given their consent; within this simple but basic framework any solution is conceivable.

Given this flexible and liberal approach, it is in each case up to those concerned to be as clear and complete as possible about their arrangements; no residual rule can be laid down in general. The respective interests of the other contracting parties, of the organization and of the organization's member States vary not only by the subject-matter of the treaties, by the number and influence of the States concerned, but above all by the organization's own features, i.e. according to how consistently and firmly it asserts its identity, or in other words its personality 'in detachment from its members', to use a well-known phrase coined by the International Court of Justice. This is easy to illustrate by a few examples.

(b) Examples

179 A first example is provided by a comparison between the Council for Mutual Economic Assistance and the European Economic Community, which in the wider sense are both furthering the development of economic solidarity between their member States, the CMEA by simple co-operation not affecting their formal sovereignty, and the EEC by an integration process based on the transfer of wide-ranging and constantly increasing powers. When a treaty is concluded between the CMEA and a third State, the treaty merely lays down principles and a general framework; it is negotiated with the participation of the member States which then approve the text, enabling the treaty to come into force, but do not formally become parties to it. A treaty implementing the principles of the CMEA treaty is then concluded between each State and the third State; this bilateral treaty comes into force and will remain in force irrespective of the treaty concluded between the CMEA and the third State, from which it is quite independent.

The EEC concludes treaties under widely varying conditions; under article 228 (2) of the Treaty of Rome, all these treaties 'shall be binding on... Member States'. The consent of member States has therefore been given to that principle once and for all in advance. The other parties are officially informed of this provision. This could be taken to mean that direct legal relations might arise between the member States and the other parties. While a *dictum* of the Court of Justice of the European Communities seems to accept this, some Community circles are reluctant to adopt the same view and hope that by its growing international responsibility and by exercising an international capacity to bring claims, the Community will be in a better position to assert its powers. Although the Community does conclude certain multilateral treaties by itself, in particular fisheries agreements, it concludes others to which its member States are also parties (mixed treaties). These raise many problems and occur in a great variety of situations. Normally, because of the power distribution between the Community and its member States, the object and purpose of such treaties require *all* member States to give their consent alongside the Community. Despite their multilateral character, these treaties tend to have a bilateral structure, with the Community and its member States on one side, and a State (association treaties) or even a group of States (the Lomé Convention of 8 December 1984 between ACP countries and the EEC and its member States) on the other. In the case of such treaties establishing between the organization and its member States on the one hand and a State or group of States on the other, a permanent and rather close relationship (treaties establishing a free-trade régime or 'economic co-operation' or an 'association'), the precise distribution of powers between the organization and its member States does not generally cause concern to the third State since such treaties are only conceivable in an atmosphere of mutual trust and co-operation. But things change when the EEC (or Euratom) takes part in a universal multilateral treaty, as was shown by EEC participation in the Convention on the Law of the Sea of 10 December 1982. The wish to have the Community and its member States become parties to the Convention, the risk of one or several member States refusing to be bound by the Convention, the distrust shown by socialist countries and some Third World States for Community institutions, and the sheer scope and diversity of the issues concerned, were enough to explain why it was accepted in Annex IX to the Convention that the Community could become a party to the Convention before all its members had done so. However, the Annex links the signature, formal confirmation or accession of the organization to those of the majority of its member States (articles 2 and 3) and as long as one of its member States remains a party, the organization cannot denounce the Convention, while conversely it is compelled to do so if none of its member States remains a party. The practice of other multilateral conventions concluded by the Community and its member States shows that normally all EEC members are parties. Without going into greater detail on the problems raised by 'mixed' treaties, it must be stressed that they do not alter the general conclusions reached above; whether a third State can directly require a Community member to observe obligations undertaken not only by the member State itself but also by the Community will depend on the undertakings of all those concerned.(*)

180   Other examples concern situations where questions of *succession* are raised along with questions deriving from the *composite structure* of one of the parties. The first case concerns organizations exercising certain powers on behalf of their member States in a specific field. What becomes of the treaties of member States concluded in that field *before* the participation of these States in the organization? The obligations flowing from a treaty between such a State and one not a member of the organization remain in force; they are not affected by entry into the organization, for a State cannot evade its obligations under a treaty by concluding another treaty with third States, *viz.* States which are parties to the constituent charter of the organization (for this type of conflicting treaties, see above, No. 164, and below, No. 227). On the other hand, the obligations of a State which had come into being prior to its entry into the organization cannot be ignored by the organization; the organization must either take over the obligations or open negotiations with the parties to the treaty in order to conclude another treaty on its own behalf. The *pacta tertiis* principle fully applies to prevent the State from repudiating its treaty obligations by means of another treaty making it a member of an organization; it does not authorize the organization to ignore a treaty which is binding upon one of its members, for it is not a third party in relation to its member States. International practice, both judicial and conventional, clearly reflects this view.(*)

181 The reverse case is less straightforward: what happens to the international agreements (and indeed to the contracts) of an international organization when it is dissolved? Dissolution of international organizations by treaty has occurred in practice (e.g. the League of Nations, the Permanent Court of International Justice, bodies responsible for the administration of a treaty governing a given commodity, and a few other cases), but all these cases were settled empirically as special situations. However, while the effects of such dissolutions on treaties between States or on contracts with private persons have occasionally been dealt with by the courts, it does not seem that so far the treaties of the dissolved organization have ever been. The fate of these treaties after the disappearance of the organization (as well as the effect of other substantial changes in the participation of States, in its financial resources or its constituent treaty) was discussed by the International Law Commission, which considered that such situations could not be the subject of draft articles; it merely provided for a reservation, which was confirmed by the 1986 Conference (article 74 (2) of the 1986 Convention), so as not to 'prejudge any question that may arise in regard to a treaty… from the termination of the existence of the organization or from the termination of participation by a State in the membership of the organization'. It could perhaps be assumed in the case of a 'mixed treaty' that the member States which are parties to such a treaty 'succeed' to the organization when it ceases to exist or is altered so as no longer to be in a position to perform the treaty; but there is no general rule to the effect that member States 'inherit' the treaties of the international organization once it has ceased to exist. A distinction must of course be made between succession to a treaty and succession to assets and liabilities; it would be quite normal for whatever property of a former international organization may remain to revert to its former member States.(*)

F. 'STATUS TREATIES', 'OBJECTIVE REGIMES', 'RIGHTS *IN REM*'

182 Many treaties entered into by a limited number of States create situations intended to produce lasting effects. While they may affect the interests of other States, occasionally of all States, such situations in fact prove to be permanent. Circumstances may arise where a State which is not a party to the treaty claims to derive a right from it, or on the contrary challenges the situation, or at least declares it irrelevant as against itself. This again involves the *pacta tertiis* principle and, for the legal validity of such situations to be established, exceptions to the principle have been invoked. Are these arguments sound? Are there really genuine exceptions to the relative effect of treaty undertakings? Or are the legal features of such situations dependent on considerations entirely foreign to the law of treaties?

183   Several explanations or theoretical conceptions will be discussed in this regard: 'international *de facto* governments', 'status treaties' or 'objective situations' or régimes, and 'rights *in rem*'. But some general observations are called for in order to attempt to identify the actual validity of such legal constructions. Words and concepts are far from irrelevant and they all carry their own implications and connotations; yet beyond words and concepts there are social realities leading to the assumption of a certain order based either on some degree of authority or on consolidation by lapse of time. Both aspects are linked to the mechanism of tacit consent. If tacit consent is viewed as a simple and reassuring explanation of how the effect of certain treaties may reach beyond the parties, this can be done without referring to anything else, even consolidation by lapse of time, which after all is merely indicative of the general assent resulting from the failure to object by those who can and should object. But other more ambitious interpretations seek to detect in the contemporary world treaty effects extending beyond the parties, as a partial and imperfect manifestation of authority to meet the pressing needs of modern society. Hence there are two types of legal explanation, one relying on the security of the past, the other turning to the uncertainty of the future. Mostly, always perhaps, they are interchangeable.

(a) International de facto governments

184   Analysing international relations in sociological terms leads to observations not always in keeping with the sovereign equality of States. Indeed, the Great Powers, either through the flexible system of the European Concert or through international organizations, often impose their will upon smaller or even middle-ranking States. Especially at the end of major conflicts or world crises, legal régimes acknowledged and accepted by all are set up by agreements between such Powers. A systematic explanation of this situation was occasionally attempted by the theory of international *de facto* governments originating in conceptions borrowed from constitutional and administrative law. The theory is based on the assumption that the acts of such international *de facto* governments were binding upon other States since they were acting in the general interest in circumstances where no other solution was possible. This is the reasoning put forward nowadays to justify the effects *erga omnes* of certain nineteenth-century instruments such as the Treaties of Vienna (1815) and Paris (1856). An even bolder position taken by some jurists was to consider certain United Nations bodies as organs of the 'international community', enjoying in that capacity powers not conferred upon them by the Charter. The theory of international *de facto* governments was criticized as unconvincing and unnecessary. Even with the detachment attained in some cases at least by the passage of time, it is by no means certain that the action of such *de facto* governments was as disinterested as was supposed; if it may occasionally have been the case, this is because the States which had not taken part in such treaties later agreed to recognize their effects. But then the explanation becomes superfluous, for the validity of agreements emanating from such *de facto* governments hinges on the consent of other States, and there is no real exception to the *pacta tertiis* principle.

185 It should, however, be noted that, leaving this terminology aside, the theory that the victors in a major world conflict enjoy some kind of special authority entitled to universal recognition is still accepted in contemporary international relations and is presently even further justified by another argument based on the punishment of aggression. After World War II in particular, certain measures concerning the defeated States were taken by virtue of agreements between the major victorious Powers without any participation by the defeated States. In some cases, such agreements took the place of peace treaties which failed to be concluded. To avoid such 'settlements' being challenged under the classical principles of the law of treaties, the International Law Commission put forward a saving clause which was inserted in both Vienna Conventions (1969 Convention, article 75; 1986 Convention, article 76). At the 1968–1969 Vienna Conference, this provision was strongly opposed by the States which felt directly concerned. Apart from the problems it raises and the developments it heralds in the field of international responsibility, it clearly buttresses the theory of international *de facto* governments which indeed underlies the whole structure of the United Nations.(*)

(b) Status treaties or objective régimes

186 In order to extend the effects of certain situations to States not parties to the treaties establishing them, such situations or régimes have been described as *objective*, or based on a status. Charles De Visscher coined the expression 'objective situation' to characterize, apparently for the first time, the Belgian neutrality in 1914 such as it derived from the Treaties of 15 November 1831 and 18 April 1839. The same idea recurs in the Advisory Opinion of the International Court of Justice concerning *Reparation for Injuries Suffered in the Service of the United Nations*: 'Fifty States representing the vast majority of the members of the international community, had the power, in conformity with international law, to bring into being an entity possessing *objective international personality,* and not merely personality recognized by them alone...' (*ICJ Reports 1949*, p. 185; italics added).

The term 'status' is similarly used for régimes intended to have permanent and general effects on territories, communications and neutrality. Occasionally it serves to designate in doctrinal studies situations which otherwise are referred to as objective. There is an obvious analogy between such situations and those arising in municipal law for family or real estate matters. To a large extent, situations are described as 'objective' when they concern subjects of international law or territories, just as in private law it is generally agreed that the status of persons or the ownership of real estate is valid *erga omnes*.(*)

187 Such explanations are, however, subject to rather serious reservations. First of all they are quite vague in that those terms are used merely to identify, rather than to explain upon clear legal grounds, a number of situations where certain effects on a treaty are felt beyond the parties. Moreover the terms are used interchangeably, especially in legal literature; they draw both on the idea of authority and on the special nature of the rights. They would seem to represent mere provisional labels until international practice and scholarly reflection reveal the true nature of the matter.

188 The analogy with municipal law is certainly attractive. But it should be borne in mind that the reason why in municipal law everyone is bound to acknowledge the status of persons and real estate is that they are ascertained and registered by an authority common to all legal subjects. There is no such common authority in international law; each State itself ascertains the status of legal subjects and territorial titles, and their binding character is dependent on recognition by the State. No 'objective situation' or 'status' is 'opposable' *per se;* only recognition by other States makes it so. That is why there is some reluctance to give weight to the idea of authority which is hardly in keeping with the basic principles of international law. Hence, all one actually does is either use a new terminology, or emphasize passive attitudes viewed as assent, recognition or acquiescence, or again ascribe the emergence of an objective situation to the passage of time measured not in absolute terms but by the density of events it has or should have elicited.(*)

(c) Rights in rem

189 The suggestion that some situations present a real character and that the treaties creating them therefore have an effect on States which are not parties is already latent in the concept of 'status' and 'objective situation'; but it emerges independently, first in connection with a number of specific problems involving merely two contiguous States, for instance enclaves in the territory of a foreign State. In private real estate law, enclaves are frequent and their status is regulated by law in all countries. It has been suggested by analogy that territorial enclaves between States may be governed in international law by a similar status based on specific 'real' rights. However, the suggestion that some situations could be treated as if they involved 'real' rights, i.e. rights *in rem,* rapidly goes beyond the minor problems bearing a close resemblance with private law cases; it tends to cover relations presenting considerable political and economic importance such as: delimitation of all boundaries, neutrality or demilitarization, international waterways and other aspects of the territorial basis of international communications. At this level, the analogy loses all its relevance and other explanations must be sought to justify the fact that régimes instituted by such treaties can be invoked against non-parties. The most important argument is that territorial situations are supposed in law to enjoy considerable stability. In a positive sense, they give a concrete definition to the configuration of States; in a negative sense, their preservation and protection are linked to the maintenance of peace. As will be seen later (see below, No. 276), article 62 (2) excludes the application of the effect of a fundamental change of circumstances to boundary treaties; the benefit and the observance of territorial situations must extend to all States engaged in the normal conduct of international relations. The connection with peaceful relations is often asserted in the guise of a *regional balance,* i.e. a compromise to be maintained between neighbouring States. The political intention behind the concept thus becomes clearer, but is this enough to endow the notion of a 'real' *right* with a technical content?

190 This appears rather doubtful. The concept of a right *in rem* is certainly familiar to all jurists. In common law systems, it still has the importance and creative power which it has lost in civil law systems, where codification has drawn up *ne varietur* a limited list of rights *in rem;* this is why it is often advocated by Anglo-Saxon writers on international law. However, there are no rights 'in things', for rights merely govern relations between subjects of law, and it is difficult to introduce such a concept in a legal order as 'decentralized' as the international legal order. A closer study of the relevant legal literature incidentally reveals that the concepts dealt with, i.e. objective situations, status, and international *de facto* governments are in fact put forward jointly, together with the idea of rights *in rem,* so as to justify specific solutions, and this certainly does not make for a clear legal construction.

191 The attempts at codification pursued in this field by the International Law Commission throw some valuable light on the matter. In the draft articles on the law of treaties submitted in 1964, Sir Humphrey Waldock, Special Rapporteur, mentioned treaties 'providing for objective régimes' (*YILC 1964,* vol. II, p. 26, article 63) but restricted his proposal to treaties where one of the parties had 'territorial competence with reference to the subject-matter of the treaty' and where all of the parties had the intention 'to create in the general interest general obligations and rights relating to a particular region, State, territory, locality, river, waterway, or to a particular area of sea, sea-bed or air-space'. Clearly these were all situations concerning territory although any reference to the concept of right *in rem* was avoided. The proposal was nevertheless discarded by the Commission on the general grounds that these effects were not due to the treaty as such but to the custom which might derive from the treaty. It reverted to the issue some ten years later in its work concerning State succession in relation to treaties. The Commission, later to be followed by the Vienna Conference on Succession of States in Respect of Treaties, had no difficulty in adopting what were to become articles 11 and 12 of the 1978 Convention on Succession of States in Respect of Treaties:

Article 11
Boundary régimes
A succession of States does not as such affect:
(a)   a boundary established by a treaty; or
(b)   obligations and rights established by a treaty and relating to the régime of a boundary.

Article 12
Other territorial régimes
1.   A succession of States does not as such affect:
(a)   obligations relating to the use of any territory, or to restrictions upon its use, established by a treaty for the benefit of any territory of a foreign State and considered as attaching to the territories in question;
(b)   rights established by a treaty for the benefit of any territory and relating to the use, or to restrictions upon the use, of any territory of a foreign State and considered as attaching to the territories in question.
2.   A succession of States does not as such affect:
(a)   obligations relating to the use of any territory, or to restrictions upon its use, established by a treaty for the benefit of a group of States or of all States and considered as attaching to that territory;
(b)   rights established by a treaty for the benefit of a group of States or of all States and relating to the use of any territory, or to restrictions upon its use, and considered as attaching to that territory.
3.   The provisions of the present article do not apply to treaty obligations of the predecessor State providing for the establishment of foreign military bases on the territory to which the succession of States relates.

192   Without in any way claiming to exhaust all the observations called for by these provisions (which in any case cannot be regarded as binding upon all States as customary rules, and still less as conventional rules), it could be alleged that they recognize the possibility for States to attach rights and obligations to a territory, which is tantamount to introducing the concept of rights *in rem*. But the effects of this concept are restricted to the field of State succession. All that the long text of article 12 provides is that the successor State takes over *qua* successor the territorial rights and obligations of the predecessor State as they stand. Significantly enough, the provisions on this point do not concern the law of treaties and refer only to State succession. In other words, States which are not parties to the treaties concerned remain in the same position in relation to it, with the exception of the successor State. For the latter, its situation as a successor prevails over its non-party status, unless it can show that the treaty which it objects to was concluded in breach of its rights or of a general rule of international law (articles 6, 13 and 14 of the 1978 Convention). However interesting these provisions may be with respect to the creation of rights attached to a territory, they do not therefore indicate by what legal mechanism treaty provisions concerning a territorial régime may be invoked against third States.(*)

193   If it is accepted that the rights attached to a territory are binding upon any third State unless it objects, the scope of the right *in rem* concept as introduced by these articles is widened. But even admitting that in general international law, except in case of objection, there is a special régime governing territorial status, this would not fundamentally affect the *pacta tertiis* principle: such an effect, instead of being due to a modified function of the will or in other words to treaty consensualism, would simply derive from the specific features of the treaty's *object*. This is probably the gist of the various theoretical views followed on this point by the International Law Commission, which regard certain legal effects not as a consequence of the treaty itself but of the *situation* established by the treaty. This subtle distinction is understood by some to show more clearly that the effect of a treaty on third parties is not due to the treaty itself but to some external mechanism.

194   More generally, the preceding paragraphs have attempted to emphasize that the rules of the law of treaties should never be read in isolation but in conjunction with one another. While the *pacta tertiis* principle remains one of the cornerstones of this law, its application in a given case depends on the essential elements of the treaty. Thus, as has been observed, if one of the parties is an international organization, some requirements become less stringent. But the main source of diversity in treaties indisputably stems from their purpose. Although many treaties purport to create and implement rules intended to be universal, a treaty has never been imposed upon a State which refused to be a party and to accept its effects. Conversely, many treaties define concrete situations and, when a territorial settlement is at stake, very naturally it should be possible to invoke such a situation against other States no less than the very existence of the States concerned whose actual configuration is thus determined — without prejudice to a territorial situation that a State regards from the outset as curtailing its rights. In any case, the limits to a more liberal application of the *pacta tertiis* principle in the world today are clearly apparent.

III Effects in relation to other legal rules

195   A treaty does not produce its effects in a legal vacuum. Surrounding each treaty, tightly or loosely as the case may be, there is an intricate web made up of all the treaties in force, of customary rules, and acts of international organizations. After considering the international treaty without reference to its systematic environment, we must now connect it to other acts and sources of law. Relations with other treaties will be dealt with in Sub-Section 1 and relations between a treaty and other acts and sources of law in Sub-Section 2. Some of these relations have already been mentioned (see above, Nos. 44, 144, 156, 158, 160, 163, 177), but there has been no general overview. Before presenting such an overview, it should be noted that the aspects which have been most often studied and elaborated concern the relations between treaties on the one hand and the possible conflicts between distinct acts and sources on the other. This should come as no surprise: there is no central legislature in international law; hence the many conflicting determinations, a very significant one of which has already been mentioned (see above, No. 164). But there is also another aspect which is just as important if less spectacular, namely that a number of treaties may be linked among themselves, as well as with other acts and sources of international law, with differing degrees of closeness and varying effects; this relationship has already been touched upon, in particular with reference to groups of treaties (see above, Nos. 68, 144, 160, 177) and to the development of a customary rule based on a treaty (see above, No. 165). A general view of these two aspects will be given in the following sub-sections.(*)

1. Relations between a treaty and other treaties

196   From a purely formal point of view, all treaties appear in relation to one another as independent and self-sufficient entities, like so many monads based on the rule *pacta sunt servanda*. A series of treaties does not, in mathematical terms, constitute an ordered 'set' but an 'accumulation'; this is the consequence of the nature of international society itself; nor has the creation of international organizations, however universal, changed this fundamental feature (see below, No. 227). In other respects, however, there are many points of contact between treaties: a great number are wholly or partly entered into by the same parties and many also cover the same subject-matter. This creates complex relationships between certain treaties which vary according to the intentions of the parties. Indeed, the main reason behind many treaties is another treaty in respect of which they have an ancillary or supplementary character; such is the case of agreements clarifying, complementing or performing a basic treaty, or 'amending' or modifying it: in principle these agreements are subordinated to the basic agreement, unless the parties intend them to be autonomous.

197   However, it should be pointed out that there can be an equally strong interdependence between treaties in no way subordinated to, but simply conditioned by, one another. From a purely legal point of view there are two solutions which, while formally different, must be regarded as equivalent. First, when a single treaty is concluded, and secondly when several formally distinct but interdependent treaties govern a specific situation (for examples, see above, Nos. 52 and 181). Moreover, intermediate solutions are conceivable depending on practical needs. The simplest situation is that of the single treaty; but, for various reasons, occasionally political but more often economic, complex solutions are preferred where a number of treaties are so closely linked that each one can be regarded as the 'consideration' of the others, so that they can only exist or disappear together.

198 Various subtle links may thus exist between treaties. Apart from the very close relationships just mentioned, there are others which are more superficial and may defy classification. The 1969 and 1986 Conventions did not ignore this aspect of the law of treaties, and both occasionally refer to it, for instance in article 31 (see above, No. 52), although merely for the purposes of treaty interpretation. However, the Vienna Conventions did not deal with these relations between treaties systematically and exhaustively; they confined themselves to the issues which arise most frequently in practice, and which can be subjected to some general guidelines.

199 In an elementary study, it is appropriate to follow the same method as the 1969 and 1986 Conventions which dealt with the subject in three different places (articles 30, 39 to 42, and 56 to 60), starting with the situations where one of the treaties concerned is least affected and ending with those which reduce its effectiveness most significantly. The Conventions did not fail to take into account the fact that the breach of a treaty by the conclusion of another treaty, while being largely a matter of State responsibility, should also be seen from the point of view of its effects on the breached treaty. But, as has already been pointed out (see above, No. 164), the treaty which is instrumental in the unlawful act must be regarded as a simple fact entailing the same consequences as any other unlawful act: as such it will therefore be dealt with in the next chapter (see below, Nos. 296 ff.). The Vienna Conventions start out with the simplest case (A) where, irrespective of any breach of one by the other, two treaties cover the same subject-matter without the later treaty being intended to modify or suspend the earlier one; they then go on to consider more specific cases, (B) where the treaties concerned deal with the same subject-matter, but the later treaty amends or modifies the earlier one which survives therefore only in some of its provisions or with regard to some of the parties, and finally (C) where the intention is even more radically to suspend or terminate the earlier treaty altogether by a new agreement.(*)

A. ORDER OF PRECEDENCE BETWEEN TREATIES RELATING TO THE SAME SUBJECT-MATTER

200 This question is covered by article 30 of the Conventions. A clear illustration of the situation has been given by the International Law Commission as follows: a consular convention is concluded by a number of States and provides for very broad consular privileges and immunities. Later on, the same parties conclude a consular convention with other States providing for far more restricted privileges and immunities. What are the relations between the two conventions? As shown by this example, there are two quite distinct aspects to be considered: the situation of States which are parties to two successive treaties on the same subject-matter, and the situation of States which are parties only to one of them.

201 Considering the situation of parties to two successive treaties, the simplest case is where all the parties to the first treaty are also parties to the second. The solution here is to be sought quite simply in the intention of the parties: if the treaties contain no clause or only obscure clauses on that point, the problem is merely one of interpretation. Normally, the provisions of the later treaty should prevail (article 30 (3)). But the cautious wording of the Conventions ('the earlier treaty applies only to the extent that its provisions are compatible with those of the later treaty') shows that this is at best a mere indication since 'compatibility' can only be gauged by reference to the parties' intention. The examples provided in paragraph 2 of the same article ('[w]hen a treaty specifies that it is subject to, or that it is not to be considered as incompatible with, an earlier or later treaty, the provisions of that other treaty prevail') can be supplemented by other considerations put forward during the 1968–1969 Vienna Conference. Thus when doubts were voiced about what was meant by 'treaties relating to the same subject-matter', the Expert Consultant pointed to a traditional principle on which, however, the Conventions remained silent: namely that the 'special' nature of one of the treaties concerned could possibly be taken into account as opposed to the 'general' nature of the other to give priority to the 'special' treaty. The rule of article 30 would therefore only apply to treaties with subject-matters of a comparable degree of 'generality' (*Official Records UNCLT, II, Summary Records...*, Committee of the Whole, 91st meeting, p. 253).(*)

202 Yet the most intricate problems arise where the two treaties are binding upon different groups of parties, in which case another criterion becomes relevant in addition to the intention of the parties, namely the one resulting from the *pacta tertiis* principle. The great difficulties encountered in this situation were dealt with quite differently by the various Special Rapporteurs of the International Law Commission. In accordance with the Commission's thinking, the Conventions attempted a solution in article 30 (4): that rule will first be presented before the situations where it applies are identified. The provision is based on the assumption that a distinction is possible between two sets of legal relations, i.e. those between the parties to both treaties, and those between a party to one treaty and a party to both treaties. If such a distinction is accepted, relations within the first group must be determined, as was stated earlier, simply by interpreting the intention of the parties; relations within the second group are governed by the treaty entered into by both parties.

203 But the crucial question is under what circumstances separating a treaty into two sets of legal relations is possible. The wording of article 30 (4) shows that the two treaties must be compatible with the separation and this is only possible if the multilateral treaty or treaties concerned (one at least is necessarily multilateral) can be divided into a series of independent bilateral agreements without losing their *raison d'être*. This appears to be possible — at least in most cases — for a multilateral consular convention or a convention unifying the national rules of private law. But it will not always be so, and in that case the second treaty will be seen as a breach of the first, or in other words performance of the second treaty will prevent performance of the first. What is at stake here is therefore no longer a question of precedence between treaties, to be solved by interpretation, but the various issues concerning the breach of treaties, which are to be considered in the next chapter. This is why article 30 had to make a reservation in its final paragraph for the possible application of a number of other rules, in particular all those bearing on international responsibility. The basic difficulty (to be dealt with in a general way further on) is that some multilateral treaties go beyond the framework of simple reciprocity and cannot be broken down into a collection of bilateral undertakings.(*)

B. AMENDMENTS TO TREATIES

204 Amendment introduces a new element in that the second treaty is *intended* to modify the first. It would be inaccurate to say in general that the first treaty is *replaced* by the second, although this can be achieved by the express intention of the parties. In most cases of multilateral treaties, normally both the initial and the modified treaty remain in force. But owing to their obvious connection, the two treaties form a conventional system and are in fact usually referred to (as indeed in the Vienna Conventions) as a *single* treaty with two versions, the original and the amended one.(*)

205 The considerable practical importance of amendments appears in the case of treaties concluded by more than two parties, especially treaties widely open to accession by new parties. Indeed such treaties, all more or less law-making in character, often need to be adapted. At one time, the parties could dispense with an appropriate amendment procedure, and merely amended the treaty by the same means used for its initial adoption; but this soon turned out to be insufficient. The revision procedure had to be made easier and as international organizations came to play an ever increasing part in the conclusion of treaties, it became normal also to make room for them in this procedure. More particularly, the unanimity rule for revision became too cumbersome to ensure the rapid adaptation of a treaty to changing needs. That is why in practice specific provisions have been introduced in the final clauses of most international conventions relating to their revision. These nearly always stipulate that revision is possible by a qualified majority decision; in some cases even a simple majority is enough, in others the amendment must also be accepted by States which are specially interested in the treaty (see above, No. 26). The clearest effect of this practice is that, once the amendment enters into force, there are two sets of

States or international organizations which are parties to the same treaty system: those bound by the initial convention alone and those bound by both the initial and the amended conventions. This is a consequence of the maintenance of State sovereignty coupled with the flexibility required in modern agreements. In this regard, the system has rightly been compared to the one brought about by the régime of reservations, especially under the liberal definition of the Vienna Conventions: both establish a treaty system incorporating obligations of different substance which are binding upon different sets of States. To avoid such an outcome, it should be provided — although this is seldom done in practice — that after each amendment the initial convention disappears and only the amended convention is left; the only choice for the parties would then be either to be freed of all their obligations under the convention or to accept the amended convention. This is the system used in certain postal conventions and by the United Nations Charter.(*)

206 The Conventions could have remained silent on the question of amendments to multilateral treaties, merely laying down the rules mentioned in Sub-Section A. But while they expressly stated that these rules are applicable to relations between the parties having accepted the amendment and the others (article 40 (4)), they also (a) laid down rules of procedure and substance for the specific amendment process, (b) organized within certain limits a régime of 'modifications' and (c) considered, without settling it decisively, the issue of the form of amendments.

(a) Rules of procedure and substance concerning amendments

207 The rules of procedure and substance concerning amendments are of a residual nature (article 40 (1)). The most important of all is the one allowing amendments to be made by an agreement between the parties (article 39), which authorizes the adoption of an amended text by a two-thirds majority (by reference to article 9 (2)). As for its entry into force, and since article 40 is silent, the combined effect of articles 39 and 24 would be, failing an express stipulation, to require the consent of all States and international organizations having negotiated the amendment. Although in fact States and organizations often contemplate and accept the entry into force of amendments not agreed by all parties, in principle the amendment must nevertheless have been devised, with a view at least *potentially* to governing relations between *all* the parties. If, on the contrary, the new text were from the outset directed only at some of the contracting parties, this would amount to a 'modification', and this change in terminology involves the application of stricter rules as laid down in article 41.

208 Concerning amendments proper, which constitute quite an important transaction in the life of a treaty, the main concern of the Vienna Conventions was to ensure full equality between the parties. That is why all parties are entitled to submit draft amendments and to take part in the decision whether to follow up the submission, as well as in the negotiation and conclusion of, or accession to, the amendment agreement. In order to ensure that this participation is effective, any draft amendment must be notified to all States and international organizations which are parties to the initial treaty. On the other hand, the Conventions have clarified somewhat the consequences of accession to an amended treaty by a State or organization which was not a party to the initial treaty; while confirming the right of a third State or international organization to become a party either to the initial treaty alone or to the amended treaty alone or to both, the Conventions have laid down a presumption which had long been accepted by the United International Bureaux for the Protection of Intellectual Property according to which a State or international organization acceding after the entry into force of an amendment is regarded as acceding to the amended treaty in relation to the parties having accepted the amendment and to the non-amended treaty in relation to the others (article 40 (5)).

(b) Modifications

209 With reference to 'modifications' as opposed to 'amendments', article 41 requires notification to be made to the parties of both the intention to 'modify' the treaty and the modification agreement. Moreover such an agreement is only admissible if modification is expressly contemplated or at least not prohibited by the treaty, nor incompatible with it. In this respect, article 41 clarifies a concept which has already been touched upon above, involving the separation of the relations in a treaty system into two sets of parties (see above, No. 203). Article 41 requires that the modification in question 'does not affect the enjoyment by the other parties of their rights under the treaty or the performance of their obligations' and 'does not relate to a provision, derogation from which is incompatible with the effective execution of the object and purpose of the treaty as a whole'. A similar wording is used in article 58 relating to suspension (see below, No. 214).

(c) Legal form of amendments

210 This issue was dealt with by the International Law Commission in a draft article and was subsequently considered in several parts of its final report, but the 1968–1969 Conference rejected the draft article. What then should be the legal form of amendments? In the first place, the treaty itself may contain some relevant provision. Yet, even when a treaty sets out a minutely described amendment mechanism, are not States and international organizations still entitled unanimously to agree on another modification procedure? The answer would seem to be in the affirmative since the parties may at any rate conclude another treaty which, bearing on the same subject-matter, will prevail over the earlier one. This has, however, been challenged where the revision procedure of the earlier treaty involves powers of the organization created by the treaty and the modifying treaty is concluded without resorting to this particular mechanism. The Vienna Conventions have provided a clear rule only for the termination of the treaty which may always be decided on by consent of all the parties (article 54).([*])

211 If the initial treaty is silent on that point, to what extent are the parties free to choose the form of the amendment? In its final report in 1966, the International Law Commission stated that any form could in general be resorted to. A treaty may be modified by another written treaty emanating from lower-ranking organs or by an agreement in a less solemn form. According to the Commission, a written treaty may even be modified by a treaty based on oral or tacit consent. In principle, this seems quite sound; another solution would hardly be conceivable since there are no requirements in international law as to the form of treaties. In any case, it is well established that the 1969 and 1986 Conventions provide in more than one place that treaties are supplemented and made more precise by related agreements which may be purely verbal (see above, No. 68).(*)

212 Draft article 38 submitted by the Commission provided that '[a] treaty may be modified by subsequent practice in the application of the treaty establishing the agreement of the parties to modify its provisions'. According to the Commission's final report (*YILC 1966*, vol. II, p. 238), the case contemplated amounted to a tacit agreement rather than to a custom. The 1968–1969 Vienna Conference rejected the draft article by 53 votes to 15, with 26 abstentions (*Official Records UNCLT, I, Summary Records...,* Committee of the Whole, 37th and 38th meetings, pp. 207–11), for several reasons: first to avoid recognizing officially a situation which must remain exceptional, secondly to back up the requirements of constitutional law against the encroachments of international law, and finally to resist unwritten international agreements in general (all the more fiercely as the requirements of practice prevail over any such resistance).(*)

C. TERMINATION AND SUSPENSION OF TREATIES

213 In these cases, the effect of the later treaty is greater than that of an amendment since it involves a temporary or permanent termination of its predecessor. The Vienna Conventions thus dealt in parallel with termination and suspension; they laid down far-reaching provisions concerning suspension, probably in order to increase the number of situations where the principle of the treaty is safeguarded, although this endeavour has hardly been so far sanctioned by practice. Subjecting termination and suspension to symmetrical rules, the relevant provisions of both Conventions (articles 54, 57, 58 and 59) confirm the solutions relating to treaties bearing on the same subject-matter, as has already been observed (see above, No. 200).(*)

214 A number of points should, however, be emphasized in this connection:

1. The possibility to terminate or suspend the treaty by consent of all parties is expressly provided for, and there are no formal requirements to that effect. Of course this rule only operates on the level of

international law; if a State or international organization — as indeed is the case for the United States of America — deems it proper under its constitutional law to observe given formalities, it must arrange for them to be fulfilled. Also, the later treaty may include, in addition to the former parties, States or organizations which had not been parties to the earlier treaty. Moreover States or organizations, having already expressed their consent to be bound by the initial treaty, but for whom it is not yet in force, must be consulted (*Official Records UNCLT, I, Summary Records...*, Committee of the Whole, 81st meeting, p. 476).

2. The application of a multilateral treaty can be suspended as between some parties only, under the same conditions as those governing its modification (article 58) (see above, No. 209).

3. A treaty may also be terminated or suspended implicitly by a later treaty. This is of course a mere problem of interpretation closely related to the case dealt with above under Sub-Section A. The question is whether the later treaty was intended to have this effect. Such an intention may be apparent either from that treaty itself, especially from the impossibility of applying both treaties at the same time, or from any other piece of evidence. Here again the later treaty may include other parties but it must include all the parties to the earlier treaty.(*)

2. Relations between treaties and other sources of law

215 Staying within general international law, the treaty will be considered in its relations with (A) custom, (B) general principles of law, and (C) peremptory rules of international law (*jus cogens*), the legal nature of which is still debated. Finally there are also some important aspects in the relations (D) between treaties and the law of an international organization.

A. TREATIES AND CUSTOM

216 The interaction between treaties and custom has already been touched upon several times. It has been shown (see above, No. 166) that in theory, if not always in practice, a treaty could contribute to the emergence of a customary rule. We shall now consider the opposite case where a custom is embodied in a treaty. First of all, however, a fundamental point should be emphasized: these relations are viewed in a different light according to the legal nature attributed to customary rules. If custom is regarded as a tacit agreement, as it is by some authors and especially in Soviet thinking, the problem is the same as with the relationship between an unwritten agreement and a written treaty; in that case, most governments hold that the written treaty prevails. The following paragraphs take the opposite view which is that treaty and custom are distinct sources of international law, having the same legal value: a later custom therefore prevails over an earlier treaty just as a treaty may modify or abrogate an earlier customary rule. These consequences must be viewed in the light of the other principles peculiar to each source of law (separability of the provisions of a treaty, relative effect of treaties, integrity of a customary régime, etc.). If therefore a treaty between two States terminates the application of an earlier customary rule as between these States, this rule will not cease to govern the relations between each of them and third States. For the opposite to be true — which would be very difficult to show in practice — such bilateral treaties would have to be numerous enough and serve as negative 'precedents' exerting a destructive effect on the custom.(*)

217   There is another question bearing on future codification whose practical importance has emerged in a recent case: can two separate rules with similar content, one being conventional and the other customary, be valid at the same time as between the same States (or international organizations)? An affirmative answer may be of some consequence if the rules in question have divergent effects in connection with other legal rules applicable between the States concerned, depending upon whether it is the custom or the convention which is at stake. This would be the case in particular if the régime of responsibility were found to differ according to whether a treaty or a custom is breached. When customary rules are codified in a treaty, they would survive along with new conventional rules of a similar content, and a State (or an international organization) could place itself on the conventional or on the customary level, depending on where its interests lie. Without going into every aspect, it must be observed from the outset that the question will hardly be of frequent practical importance since international responsibility, as was pointed out in the International Law Commission's early work on that topic, does not seem to vary in terms of the source of the obligation breached. Moreover the essential criterion in any solution can only be the intention of the States. To be sure, nothing prevents them from maintaining in force a customary rule while laying down a similar conventional rule. But it is difficult to see what could induce them to choose such an ambiguous and uncertain solution. On the contrary, there are obvious reasons for giving a clear and unequivocal preference to the more recent source, i.e. the codification treaty, for any codification clarifies, complements and modifies customary rules. Reservations are not ruled out for codification treaties unless expressly prohibited, and therefore, if the simultaneous validity of the customary rules were presumed, not only would the reservations be without effect even when accepted, but the very modifications of the customary rules brought about by the treaty would fall to the ground. In the case of *Military and Paramilitary Activities in and against Nicaragua* (*ICJ Reports 1986*, especially pp. 94–96, paras. 175–179), the International Court of Justice allowed Nicaragua to rely on customary law rather than on a later multilateral treaty of the same content so as to discard an objection to its jurisdiction predicated on a multilateral treaties reservation. To do this, the Court stated in very general terms (para. 179) that both sources of law continued 'to exist and to apply, separately'.

Regardless of whether the objection concerned was rightly rejected, it may be said that the statements of principle supporting that decision hardly seem convincing.(*)

B. TREATIES AND GENERAL PRINCIPLES OF LAW

218 For most authors, general principles of law are scarcely distinguishable from custom or have automatically gone through the customary stage; the problem is therefore the same as in the previous sub-section. Others believe that a distinction should be made between general principles deriving from municipal law and general principles of public international law, assimilation to custom being possible only for the latter category. Some again have pointed out that general principles of law have a character of permanence and generality which differentiates them from custom, but the problem of a potential conflict with treaty rules would then hardly arise. Still others hold that, precisely because of their fundamental character, a number of these principles in any case prevail over conventions, thus terminating treaties concluded before they were recognized as principles of international law and invalidating later treaties. This brings us to the broader issue of peremptory rules of international law.(*)

C. PEREMPTORY RULES OF PUBLIC INTERNATIONAL LAW (*JUS COGENS*)

219 Whether there are peremptory rules in public international law which cannot be derogated from is a very old issue; it was a standard question for the natural law school. In our own time, only a few authors and judicial decisions have referred to it, usually as a mere hypothesis, but it suddenly came to the fore again following the work of the International Law Commission and the 1968–1969 Vienna Conference. The 1969 Convention (followed by the 1986 Convention) devotes articles 53 and 64 to the subject. The 1968–1969 Conference was well aware of the hazards for the *pacta sunt servanda* principle inherent in the proclamation of peremptory rules to be determined by the will of States. The majority of States therefore only accepted these articles under the safeguard laid down in article 66 (a) providing that 'any one of the parties to a dispute concerning the application or the interpretation of article 53 or 64 may, by a written application, submit it to the International Court of Justice for a decision...'. In 1986, this provision was retained but supplemented by mechanisms enabling international organizations to seek from the Court an advisory opinion which is to be 'accepted as decisive by all the parties to the dispute concerned'. This safeguard was viewed from the outset as utterly illusory by certain States whose constant policy was to refrain from any international undertaking relating to *jus cogens;* indeed the recent accessions by socialist States to the 1969 Convention comprise a reservation excluding any recourse to the Court. Although article 53 defines a peremptory norm of general international law for the purposes of the Convention only, it is clear that a peremptory rule applying to treaties of international organizations also extends to their unilateral acts and prevails over customary rules. It must be taken into account in the field of responsibility (see below, Nos. 286 ff.) where it creates difficulties which are just as serious as in the law of treaties.(*)

220   Defined as a 'norm from which no derogation is permitted and which can be modified only by a subsequent norm of general international law having the same character' (article 53), the peremptory rule gives rise to a basic difficulty in that it draws on a concept applied to contracts in municipal law, i.e. in a legal system under a legislature authoritatively imposing general rules upon all legal subjects. In international relations, who could take the place of such a legislature and exert an authority above that of States? Asking the question is enough to point to the very source of controversy.(*)

221   How could such a peremptory rule come into existence in practice on the international level? Normally, care is taken not to be too specific on this crucial point which the International Law Commission purposely refrained from clarifying. The 1969 Convention — and later the 1986 Convention — seemed to hint that it is born out of custom since it provided that the rule is 'accepted and recognized by the international community of States as a whole'. This wording is perfectly consonant with a certain conception of the legal nature of custom. The peremptory rule therefore appears to be a custom with a particular kind of *opinio juris* expressing the conviction that the rule in question is of an absolute nature. The rule could thus apply even to States having not expressly recognized it as such; in other words the rule could be regarded as universally accepted even short of an express recognition to that effect by all States without exception. Going a step further, could such a rule be said to apply even to States which have consistently rejected it as a peremptory rule? Although views diverged on this point at the 1968–1969 Conference, it has been so strongly emphasized on many occasions that the customary process does not allow an obligation to be imposed upon a State which had not recognized the rule in question, that most States would certainly answer in the negative. As, however, it is in the nature of *jus cogens* to be recognized by all States, it would be difficult to claim that a rule is absolutely peremptory if several States do not agree. In accordance with this interpretation, the examples of peremptory rules most frequently given are the prohibition of slavery and of trading in human beings, as well as genocide and aggression.(*)

222   On this view, it is readily apparent that the theory of peremptory rules is relevant to the law of treaties in three different respects:

1. Technically such rules cannot be established nor possibly modified by treaty, for technically speaking, no treaty stands above the others, since there are no constitutional rules in public international law:

should a treaty which conflicts with a treaty establishing an absolute rule be regarded as modifying or breaching that treaty? This does not mean that a peremptory rule could not derive from a convention, and indeed a treaty may contribute to the formation of a customary rule as has previously been shown, but it is this customary process involving a particular type of *opinio juris* which causes the rule to become peremptory, and not the treaty mechanism preceding or accompanying it.

2. Not only do peremptory rules prevail over treaties which conflict with them, but they strip them of any legal validity: the 1969 and 1986 Conventions laid down strict rules on invalidity which will be considered with the other grounds of invalidity in the following chapter (see below, No. 270).

3. Can non-observance of an obligation based on a peremptory rule entitle the injured State to disregard it in turn by way of reciprocity in relation to the other State? Asking this fundamental question implies a shift from validity to non-application of treaties which will be considered further on (see below, No. 304). It is enough for the time being to stress that this point brings into question the very basis of peremptory rules. Indeed, as their validity is not dependent on State will, these rules are binding in any circumstances. In principle, therefore, the question has to be answered in the negative, and this is indeed the solution adopted in the narrow field of certain fundamental rules of humanitarian law (article 60 (5)). It is impossible at the same time to claim that certain obligations are absolute and yet to disregard them in response to their violation.(*)

223 If the above interpretation is accepted, one is unfortunately bound to acknowledge that peremptory rules are few in number and often somewhat nebulous. It would be difficult to reduce their content, not only because it is already so limited, but because the idea of a definite regression of human conscience is hard to accept. On the contrary, it would be desirable for international practice in all fields to comply more and more with higher standards which so far are only the subject of moral laws, and thereby to call forth peremptory rules by State recognition: there could and should normally emerge new *jus cogens*. Without insisting on this point, it is fairly clear that such a conception is rooted in the natural law tradition which has recently been given a new lease of life by the idea of natural law with a developing content. In that sense, too, it could be argued that peremptory norms have gone beyond the customary stage and reached the firmer status of general principles of public international law. This indeed is what is suggested by the International Court of Justice in its Advisory Opinion on the *Reservations to the Convention on Genocide*: 'the principles underlying the Convention are principles which are recognized by civilized nations as binding on States, even without any conventional obligation' (*ICJ Reports 1951*, p. 23).(*)

224 But this presentation would not be acceptable to all governments. Peremptory norms were claimed, in particular by the Soviet Union, to be based solely on the binding force of treaties, the only genuine source of international law according to this view. This assumption, if accepted, has a number of consequences. Peremptory rules then are binding only upon the parties to the treaty, or the States recognizing them at least implicitly, not upon States which refuse to recognize them. It is also difficult to argue that such rules embody a degree of obligation absent in treaty rules, for any treaty rule is binding. Their distinctive feature is alleged to lie in the sanction alone: whereas a treaty running counter to an ordinary conventional rule is not a nullity as such but an unlawful act giving rise to international responsibility, a treaty breaching a conventional rule made peremptory by its own provisions is radically null and void. By being elevated to the status of peremptory provisions, a series of treaty rules are thus endowed with a radical sanction and their exceptional importance is underlined.(*)

225 Another consequence of this view is that peremptory rules are not necessarily universal; they could be regional, or could more generally concern a community of States with close ties especially on the ideological level. Such peremptory rules would enable members of the community to regard as radically null and void any agreements running counter to them. While such invalidity, based as it is on conventional grounds, obviously cannot affect States outside the community, in view of the most definite rules of the law of treaties, it is binding among the members of the community itself. Thus the treaties establishing the fundamental links between the USSR and States affiliated to the Soviet system, such as the treaty of 6 May 1970 between the Soviet Union and Czechoslovakia, would invalidate any contrary treaty undertakings for the States which are part of the system.(*)

226 There is no doubt that the Vienna Conference of 1968–1969 gave rise to a great many illusions as to the revolutionary scope of *jus cogens*, which was seen by some as a legally flavoured argument to dispose of unsatisfactory treaties. Twenty years later, the achievement seems more modest. It consists of a reminder — which has been neither heard nor accepted by all — of the moral basis of law, and of an assertion of absolute humanitarian law limited in fact to a few really fundamental rights in the face of armed force. As soon as any attempt is made to widen the scope of such rights or to condemn, for instance, the use of nuclear weapons, present-day political divisions preclude any expansion of the scope of peremptory rules. Today, moreover, it is not in relation to invalidity and termination of treaties that the assertion of peremptory rules is of greatest significance, but with respect to the prohibition of reprisals in kind following their violation, and from this point of view their extension is very limited indeed (see below, No. 304).(*)

D. TREATIES AND OBLIGATIONS DERIVING FROM MEMBERSHIP OF AN
INTERNATIONAL ORGANIZATION

227 Obligations of a State deriving from membership of an international organization may either stem from the constituent instrument of the organization or from a unilateral act by one of its organs in conformity with the constituent instrument. In the case of a treaty concluded by a member State in violation of such obligations, a distinction must be made between two situations. If it is concluded with a non-member State, the relevant rules are those which have already been examined, flowing from the *pacta tertiis* principle (see above, Nos. 196 ff.), and they apply to both obligations, as well to the one deriving from the constituent instrument as to the one deriving from the treaty with the third State. An attempt was made, however, to enact a special rule for organizations such as the League of Nations or the United Nations. If, on the other hand, the treaty which conflicts with the constituent instrument is concluded between two members of the organization, the relevant rules of the organization will apply (article 5 of the 1969 and 1986 Conventions) and then a specific case deserves closer scrutiny, namely that of treaties whose object is to carry out the 'rules of the organization' (article 2 (1) (j) of the 1986 Convention).

228 Article 103 of the United Nations Charter provides:

> In the event of a conflict between the obligations of the Members of the United Nations under the present Charter and their obligations under any other international agreement, their obligations under the present Charter shall prevail.

Article 20 of the Covenant of the League of Nations went even further:

> The Members of the League severally agree that this Covenant is accepted as abrogating all obligations or understandings *inter se* which are inconsistent with the terms thereof, and solemnly undertake that they will not hereafter enter into any engagements inconsistent with the terms thereof.

With regard to a treaty concluded between members of the organization, such provisions involve the idea of a hierarchy of treaties, the constituent instrument of the organization acquiring as it were a constitutional character. With regard to a treaty between a member and a non-member State, Article 20 of the League Covenant is quite consistent with the *res inter alios acta* rule, whereas Article 103 of the Charter could be construed as purporting to extend to third States; this question, upon which legal opinion is divided, has lost much of its relevance since the United Nations has become quasi-universal. Article 103 was essentially meant to provide a legal justification for the suspension of treaties decided on as a 'sanction' against member States.

229 Any organization has its own legal order deriving from its constituent treaty and comprising all the acts of its organs as well as those of the member

States in their relations with the organization. These are mainly unilateral acts; but they may also include different forms of agreements, some of which are concluded by member States in pursuance of a unilateral act of the organization. Thus, in order to implement a Security Council resolution, two States may conclude an agreement. Hierarchically, this agreement is subordinated to the resolution it seeks to perform. It is therefore dependent on the resolution and is only valid in so far as the resolution is maintained. Consequently there are treaties between member States or between a member State and the organization which become part of the law of the organization and which may be dependent on a unilateral act of the organization. But this situation can only arise in organizations whose legal order is fully developed and articulated; examples could be taken from European Community law.(*)

Notes

136* The requirement of good faith is essential in all actions governed by international law and in the performance of any obligation. Both the 1969 and the 1986 Conventions have applied this principle to the conduct of parties or future parties in the *conclusion* of treaties (see above, No. 110). Treaties must be interpreted in good faith (art. 31, see No. 144). But the Conventions give no specific examples of the requirements of good faith in the *performance* of treaties. According to the ILC Report (*YILC 1966,* vol. II, p. 211) and the case-law mentioned, good faith implies the requirement to remain faithful to the intention of the parties without defeating it by a literal interpretation or destroying the object and purpose of the treaty. For a critical analysis, see E. Zoller, *La bonne foi en droit international public* (Paris, Pedone, 1977).

137* The term 'application' is rather ambiguous. (1) It is used as opposed to 'interpretation' to indicate that a treaty is so clear that it may be 'applied' as it is, without any need for interpretation: French administrative courts 'apply' treaties, and if necessary request the Foreign Ministry's 'interpretation'. (2) In other cases, it is used as opposed to 'interpretation' in so far as interpretation only provides the abstract meaning of a text, whereas application combines the outcome of prior interpretation with the facts: the Court of Justice of the European Communities is empowered by article 177 of the EEC Treaty to 'interpret' the rules submitted to it, but not to 'apply' them. (3) 'Application' is used as opposed to 'performance' in that performance involves not a ruling in a given case but merely the taking of supplementary legal and material action to ensure the full effect of a given rule. (4) In a very broad sense, however, which seems to be that of the 1969 and 1986 Conventions, application also includes performance.

138* Authentic interpretation, proceeding as it does from the authors of an instrument, is hardly distinguishable from modification, and this raises the question of its lawfulness and possible retroactive effect; see I. Voïcu, *De l'interprétation authentique des traités internationaux* (Paris, Pedone, 1968).

141* The analysis presented here is valid from a legal point of view, but more is involved than pure considerations of legal methodology. First of all, quite frequently there is no common intention of the parties, and the texts adopted are those ambiguous enough to accommodate opposite claims; moreover the parties often lay down only very general principles and the interpreter has to construe a whole series of intermediate categories between principles and facts. This creative role of interpretation appears in varying degrees in connection with any kind of legal rule (Ch. De Visscher, *Problèmes d'interprétation judiciaire en droit international public,* p. 28). There are thus several scientifically possible interpretations from among which one is chosen for non-legal reasons (H. Kelsen, *The Pure Theory of Law* (translation of 2nd edn.) (Los Angeles, Univ. of California Press, 1967), p. 348; S. Sur, *L'interprétation en droit international public* (Paris, Librairie générale de droit et de jurisprudence, 1974)). On interpretation in general, see R. Bernhardt, *Die Auslegung völkerrechtlicher Verträge* (Cologne, Heymann, 1963), and 'Interpretation and implied (tacit) modification of treaties', *ZaöRV,* vol. 27 (1967), p. 491.

142* It has often been said, especially at the time when universal organizations were expanding, that constituent instruments of international organizations called for a largely 'constructive' interpretation (D. Simon, *L'interprétation judiciaire des traités d'organisations internationales*). A close study of ICJ decisions shows, however, that the Court's interpretation always relies on *practice.* The real issue with respect to the interpretation of constituent instruments is to determine whether this practice includes only that of the organization or also that of member States; the question was clearly put by Sir Percy Spender in his Separate Opinion in the case concerning *Certain Expenses of the United Nations* (*ICJ Reports 1962,* p. 151). Even if, by virtue of its constitutive charter, the organization may take majority decisions, have the minority States maintained the right not to accept the organization's interpretation? Could they also reject an interpretation given by an international court or arbitral tribunal as being either *ultra vires* or against the law? This involves the issue of sovereignty. In any event, the work of the ILC and of the 1986 Vienna Conference has shown that an 'established practice' (the French text even says *'pratique bien établie'*) is a practice which member States have not objected to (P. Reuter, 'Quelques réflexions sur la notion de "pratique internationale" ', *Studi in onore di Giuseppe Sperduti,* p. 200.

143* On the Vienna Convention, see: Sir I. Sinclair, *The Vienna Convention on the Law of Treaties,* pp. 114-159; M.K. Yasseen, 'L'interprétation des traités d'après la Convention de Vienne sur le droit des traités', *RCADI,* vol. 151 (1976-III), p. 1; S. Rosenne, 'Interpretation of treaties in the Restatement and the International Law Commission's draft articles: a comparison', *Columbia Journal of Transnational Law,* vol. 5 (1966), p. 205. It should be noted that the rules of the 1969 Convention on interpretation constitute a useful framework and were referred to by several arbitral awards regarding them as traditional (*Beagle Channel Arbitration, ILR,* vol. 52, p. 93; *Young Loan Arbitration, ILR,* vol. 59, p. 494). Similarly, art. 33 (4) of the 1969 Convention provides that when a treaty has been authenticated in several equally authoritative languages, the meaning to be adopted is the one 'which best reconciles the texts, having regard to the object and purpose of the treaty'. See: J. Hardy, 'The interpretation of plurilingual treaties by international courts and tribunals', *BYBIL,* vol. 37 (1961), p. 72; M. Tabory, *Multilingualism in International Law and Institutions* (Alphen a.d. Rijn, Sijthoff, 1980). However, neither the ILC nor the Vienna Conferences retained the interpretative guidelines which had been mentioned in their work but only had a minor indicative value, such as the principle of 'effective interpretation' (*ut res magis valeat quam pereat*) (*YILC 1966,* vol. II, p. 219: according to the Commission this indication is no more than an application of good faith) or the Latin maxims on the relations between 'general' and 'special' provisions (see No. 201).

144* This provision reveals considerable drafting skill, most visibly by bringing four very substantial paragraphs together under one heading by use of the singular 'general rule of interpretation'. Rather open tendencies emerged during the ILC discussions (*YILC 1966*, vol. I (part 1), pp. 184 and 197). The deletion of art. 38 from the ILC draft is somewhat inconsistent with art. 31 (3) (b) (see No. 212). See: J.-P. Cot 'La conduite subséquente des parties à un traité', *RGDIP*, vol. 70 (1966) p. 61; W. Karl, *Vertrag und spätere Praxis im Völkerrecht* (Berlin, Springer, 1983).

146* Recourse to preparatory work in order to choose between discordant interpretations given by States which participated in the drafting of the convention and by those which have acceded later remains controversial (*Territorial Jurisdiction of the International Commission of the River Oder, PCIJ, Series A, No. 23; Commission arbitrale sur les biens, droits et intérêts en Allemagne*, vol. III, No. 70, p. 452; *Young Loan Arbitration*, 16 May 1980, *ILR*, vol. 59, p. 544, para. 34. Without actually taking sides, the ILC seems to have taken quite a liberal view (*YILC 1966*, vol. II, p. 223; S. Rosenne, 'Travaux préparatoires', *ICLQ*, vol. 12 (1963), p. 1378).

148* On interpretation by reference to similar treaties, see: *Rights of Nationals of the United States of America in Morocco, ICJ Reports 1952*, p. 191; *Constitution of the Maritime Safety Committee of IMCO, ICJ Reports 1960*, p. 169; *Interpretation of the Agreement of 25 March 1951 between the WHO and Egypt, ICJ Reports 1980*, p. 95, para. 47.

150* For federal entities, see Nos. 175 ff. For the situation in Berlin with regard to the treaties concluded by the Federal Republic of Germany, as regulated by the Kommandantura on 21 May 1952, see: W. Wengler, 'Berlin-Ouest et les Communautés européennes', *AF*, vol. 24 (1978), p. 217; J. Groux, 'Territorialité du droit communautaire', *Revue trimestrielle de droit européen*, vol. 23 (1987), p. 5.

151* P. Tavernier, *Recherches sur l'application dans le temps des actes et des règles en droit international public* (Paris, Librairie générale de droit et de jurisprudence, 1970); D. Bindschedler-Robert, 'De la rétroactivité en droit international public', *En hommage à Paul Guggenheim*, p. 184; M. Sørensen, 'Le problème dit du droit intertemporel dans l'ordre international', *Annuaire de l'Institut de Droit international*, vol. 55 (1973), p. 1, and vol. 56 (1975), pp. 339 and 536; S. Rosenne, 'The temporal application of the Vienna Convention on the Law of Treaties', *Cornell International Law Journal*, vol. 4 (1970), p. 1; G.E. do Nascimento e Silva, 'Le facteur temps et les traités', *RCADI*, vol. 154 (1977-I), p. 215. The retroactive effect of developments of general international law, which had already been laid down in the Advisory Opinion on *Namibia* (*ICJ Reports 1971*, p. 31, para. 53), was further specified by the ICJ in the case concerning the *Aegean Sea Continental Shelf* (*ICJ Reports 1978*, pp. 28 and 32, paras. 69 and 77). Art. 4 of the 1969 Convention had aroused considerable controversy: should it be interpreted as excluding the application of the Convention to multilateral treaties as long as all the parties to such treaties had not become parties to the Convention (*si omnes* clause of the 1907 Hague Conventions) or should the separability of treaty relations be accepted under art. 3 (c) of the 1969 Convention corroborated by art. 73 of the 1986 Convention? Commentators are faced with a dilemma, for while the former position would make the 1969 Convention inapplicable to major multilateral treaties (E.W. Vierdag, 'The law governing treaty relations between parties to the Vienna Convention on the Law of Treaties and States not party to the Convention', *AJ*, vol. 76 (1982), p. 779), the latter seriously affects the integrity of treaties (see Nos. 82 and 166).

153[*] G. Kojanec, *Trattati e terzi stati* (Padua, CEDAM, 1961); Ph. Braud, 'Recherches sur l'Etat tiers en droit international public', *RGDIP*, vol. 72 (1968), p. 17; Ph. Cahier, 'Le problème des effets des traités à l'égard des Etats tiers', *RCADI*, vol. 143 (1974-III), p. 589. As from 1964, the ILC quite rightly left aside the effects of treaties with respect to individuals, *YILC 1966*, vol. II, p. 227. In general, ILC Special Rapporteurs on the law of treaties took a far more open view of the situation than that which finally prevailed; see Sir Gerald Fitzmaurice, Fifth Report, *YILC 1960*, vol. II, p. 69; Sir Humphrey Waldock, Third Report, *YILC 1964*, vol. II, p. 26.

157[*] On *stipulation pour autrui*, see the statements by E. Jiménez de Aréchaga at the ILC and 'Treaty stipulations in favor of third States', *AJ*, vol. 50 (1956), p. 338. On unilateral acts, see: P. Guggenheim, *Traité de droit international public*, 2nd edn., vol. I, p. 279; J.-P. Sicault, 'Du caractère obligatoire des engagements unilatéraux en droit international public', *RGDIP*, vol. 83 (1979), p. 633; J.-P. Jacqué, 'A propos de la promesse unilatérale', *Mélanges offerts à Paul Reuter*, p. 327, and P. Reuter, 'Du consentement des tiers aux normes d'un traité', *Realism in Law-Making*, p. 155; see also above, No. 54. The cases most often referred to remain ambiguous: the case concerning the *Jurisdiction of the European Commission of the Danube* (*PCIJ, Series B, No. 14*) where the Court merely speaks of an 'unwritten *modus vivendi';* the *Free Zones* case (*PCIJ, Series A, No. 22*, p. 17) which subjects the creation of a right for the third State to its acceptance; similarly the Report of the Commission of Jurists relating to the Aaland Islands Question (League of Nations, *Official Journal 1920, Special Supplement No. 3*, October 1920, p. 18). Only exceptionally do the two conceptions entail practical differences, e.g. the controversy in the United States on the compensation owed by Finland, *AJ*, vol. 50 (1956), p. 355. But despite the commonly expressed doctrinal views, States parties to treaties concerning rights of passage in international canals have denied the very principle of a right for third States: R.R. Baxter and J.F. Triska, *The Law of International Waterways* (Cambridge, Mass., Harvard University Press, 1964).

160[*] Article 37 has not actually been criticized for *imposing* a solution — since it only applies if there is no contrary agreement between the parties — but because it is impossible to lay down a *general* residual rule: according to the Expert Consultant at the 1986 Vienna Conference, this was the main reason why the ILC had adopted the very controversial draft article 36 *bis* derogating from the residual rule in one particularly important case (*Report of the Commission to the General Assembly on the work of its 34th session*, Chapter II, Commentary to article 36 *bis*, *YILC 1982*, vol. II (part 2), pp. 43–7, and *United Nations Conference on the Law of Treaties between States and International Organizations, or between International Organizations*, Committee of the Whole, 25th meeting, A/CONF 129/C. 1/SR. 25). The Conference followed this view by deleting article 36 *bis* but qualifying article 37 by article 74 (3). On groups of treaties, see P. Reuter, 'Traités et transactions. Réflexions sur l'identification de certains engagements conventionnels', *Essays in Honour of Roberto Ago*, vol. I, p. 399.

163[*] *Anglo-Iranian Oil Co.* and *Rights of Nationals of the United States of America in Morocco, ICJ Reports 1952*, pp. 93 and 176; P. Pescatore, 'La clause de la nation la plus favorisée dans les conventions multilatérales', *Annuaire de l'Institut de Droit international,* vol. 53-I (1969), p. 1; all the Reports to the ILC by Special Rapporteur E. Ustor since 1973, as well as the final ILC draft adopted in 1978 (*YILC 1978,* vol. II (part 2), pp. 8–73) and submitted to the General Assembly which for political reasons postponed further action.

164* To mention only the Special Rapporteurs who considered the issue from the point of view of treaty law: Sir Hersch Lauterpacht provided for invalidity of the subsequent treaty if it involved a serious breach of the earlier treaty (*YILC 1953,* vol. II, p. 156, and *1954,* vol. II, p. 133 (art. 16)); Sir Gerald Fitzmaurice (*YILC 1958,* vol. II, pp. 41–45 (arts. 18–19)) rejected invalidity, unless the first treaty contained a formal prohibition and the second implied an express breach; Sir Humphrey Waldock, followed by the ILC, relied in particular on PCIJ decisions in *Jurisdiction of the European Commission of the Danube (Series B, No. 14)* and *Oscar Chinn (Series A/B, No. 63)* to reject invalidity (*YILC 1966,* vol. II, pp. 214 ff.). This issue is also being considered by the ILC from the point of view of State responsibility (see below, No. 285).

166* See above, No. 62. On the political objectives covered by the concept of 'quasi-universal' treaties, see: P. Reuter, *La Convention de Vienne sur le droit des traités,* p. 21; C. Deleau, 'Les positions françaises à la Conférence de Vienne sur le droit des traités', *AF,* vol. 15 (1969), p. 7.

168* The problem of new States has been presented with great clarity by P. Guggenheim, *Traité de droit international public* (1st edn.), vol. I, p. 216); all the practice is mentioned in J. Crawford, *The Creation of States in International Law* (Oxford, Clarendon Press, 1979), especially pp. 301 ff. and 387 ff. For an important historical case study, see D. Anzilotti, 'La formazione del Regno d'Italia nei riguardi del diritto internazionale', *Rivista di diritto internazionale,* vol. 6 (1912), p. 29. But situations may arise where the State is so artificial and so closely dependent on the treaty that it is in fact functionally more like an international organization than a State; such was the case of Danzig in the inter-war period.

169* The effects of a constituent instrument on an organization are governed neither by the 1969 Convention (which only concerns States) nor by the 1986 Convention (since constituent instruments are governed by the 1969 Convention). If the modification of a constituent instrument requires intervention by organs of the organization, even in a purely advisory or preparatory capacity, the conventional character of the instrument tends to be affected; it has been argued that in such cases the instrument can no longer be modified by an ordinary treaty between the States parties to it (see below, No. 210*).

170* Classical works on the subject are: D.P.O'Connell, *The Law of State Succession* (Cambridge, Cambridge University Press, 1967); K. Marek, *Identity and Continuity of States in Public International Law,* 2nd edn., (Geneva, Droz, 1968); the lectures by D.P. O'Connell, *RCADI,* vol. 130 (1970-II), p. 95, and M. Bedjaoui, *ibid.,* p. 455; A.G. Pereira, *La succession d'Etats en matière de traité* (Paris, Pedone, 1969); M.G. Marcoff, *Accession à l'indépendance et succession d'Etats aux traités internationaux* (Fribourg, Ed. universitaires, 1969). On the 1978 Convention, see M.K. Yasseen, 'La Convention de Vienne sur la succession d'Etats en matière de traités', *AF,* vol. 24 (1978), p. 59, and especially the Reports to the ILC by Special Rapporteur Sir Francis Vallat, *YILC 1974,* vol. II (part 1), pp. 1–89, and the ILC

Report, ibid. (part 2), pp. 162–269. For recent applications, see: Y. Lejeune, 'La succession du nouveau canton du Jura aux traités internationaux du canton de Berne', *RGDIP*, vol. 82 (1979), p. 1051; R. Sonnenfeld, 'Succession and continuation: a study on treaty practice in post-war Germany', *Netherlands Yearbook of International Law*, vol. 7 (1976), p. 91; D. Bardonnet, *La succession d'Etats à Madagascar* (Paris, Librairie générale de droit et de jurisprudence, 1970); Nguyen Huu-Tru, *Quelques problèmes de succession d'Etats concernant le Viet-Nam* (Bruxelles, Bruylant, 1970); A. Crivellaro, 'Continuità dei trattati e Stati non riconosciuti', *Rivista di diritto internazionale*, vol. 57 (1974), p. 29. What has sometimes been called 'succession of governments' was left aside here; this conception was put forward by certain governments claiming not to be bound by the international obligations accepted by the previous government, thus defeating the principle of State continuity; it is difficult to justify or even to provide a legal analysis of a position which amounts to an actual denial of the State; such a generalized conception would be coherent in an international society consisting of monarchs instead of States, where no monarch could ever bind his or her successor, and this system has actually operated to some extent at certain times. But this has nothing to do with the law of treaties, and is simply a retroactive refusal to *recognize* the legitimacy of a previous government and therefore the validity of the agreements it has concluded. See: Ch. Rousseau, *Droit international public*, vol. III (Paris, Sirey, 1977), p. 331; S. Bastid, 'Mutations politiques et traités: le cas de la Chine', *Mélanges offerts à Charles Rousseau*, p. 1.

174*   There have been many studies of the best-known cases (League of Nations–United Nations, OECE–OECD, ELDO–ESRO–ESA) but any general theory on the subject is bound to be a negative one. See: R. Ranjeva, *La succession d'organisations internationales en Afrique* (Paris, Pedone, 1978); ILC Report, *YILC 1980*, vol. II (part 2), paras. 6–11, pp. 92–93 (commentary to art. 73). The insolvency of the International Tin Council and the proceedings instituted in British courts against the States which were members of the Council concerns a case of succession between an organization and a State in relation to debts, not to treaties.

176*   Add to the references listed at No. 122*: C.T. Oliver, 'The enforcement of treaties by a federal State', *RCADI*, vol. 141 (1974-I), p. 331, and H.J. Geiser, *Les effets des accords conclus par les organisations internationales* (Berne, Lang, 1977). Concerning arts. 34 to 37 of the 1986 Convention, see the ILC's work presented annually in the ILC Yearbook: First Report, *YILC 1972*, vol. II, p. 189, para. 58; Second Report, *YILC 1973*, vol. II, p. 89, para. 89; Sixth Report, *YILC 1977*, vol. II (part 1), p. 129, and discussion (1438th–1442nd meetings), vol. I, pp. 124 ff.; 1978 discussion (1509th–1512th meetings) *YILC 1978*, vol. I, pp. 189 ff., and ILC Report, vol. II (part 2), pp. 132–137; Tenth Report, *YILC 1981*, vol. II (part 1), pp. 64–69; Eleventh Report, *YILC 1982*, vol. II (part 1), pp. 8–9, discussion (1702th–1707th, 1718th, 1719th and 1740th meetings), vol. I, pp. 23 ff., and ILC Report, vol. II (part 2), pp. 42–48. The work of the 1986 Conference has so far only been published provisionally in the form of documents; draft article 36 *bis* was discussed by the Committee of the Whole at the 19th, 20th, 25th and 27th meetings (A/CONF 129/C.1/SR 19, 20, 25 and 27).

177*   The final ILC text of article 36 *bis* rejected by the 1986 Conference was as follows (*YILC 1982*, vol. II (part 2), p. 43):

Article 36 bis. Obligations and rights arising for States members of an international organization from a treaty to which it is a party

Obligations and rights arise for States members of an international organization from the provisions of a treaty to which that organization is a party when the parties to the treaty intend those provisions to be the means of establishing such obligations and according such rights and have defined their conditions and effects in the treaty or have otherwise agreed thereon, and if:

(a) the States members of the organization, by virtue of the constituent instrument of that organization or otherwise, have unanimously agreed to be bound by the said provisions of the treaty; and

(b) the assent of the States members of the organization to be bound by the relevant provisions of the treaty has been duly brought to the knowledge of the negotiating States and negotiating organizations.

For the debates on article 36 *bis* at the 1986 Conference and the Expert Consultant's Statement, see the amendment submitted by the UN, the ILO and the IMF (A/CONF 129/ C.1/L 65), and the discussion by the Committee of the Whole (A/CONF 129/C.1/ SR. 19, 20 and 28); the final reasons for the EEC's indifference emerge in Ph. Manin, 'L'article 228 (2) du traité CEE', *Mélanges offerts à Pierre-Henri Teitgen* (Paris, Pedone, 1984), p. 289. For the growth of European Communities' competence in the perspective of the Commission of the European Communities, see J. Groux and Ph. Manin, *Les Communautés européennes dans l'ordre international*. For the historical background to EEC participation in the 1982 Law of the Sea Convention, see S. Rosenne, 'La participation à la Convention des Nations Unies sur le droit de la mer', in D. Bardonnet and M. Virally, eds, *Le nouveau droit international de la mer*, p. 287.

179* The pattern presented corresponds to the Agreement on co-operation between the CMEA and Finland of 16 May 1973 (*International Affairs*, October 1973, p. 123). See T. Schweisfurth, 'The treaty-making capacity of the CMEA in light of a framework agreement between the EEC and the CMEA', *Common Market Law Review*, vol. 22 (1985), p. 615. For the decisions of the Court of the European Communities referred to in the text, see the *Kupferberg* case, *ECR 1982*, p. 3641, para. 13. See also: D.C. Keefe and M.G. Schermers, *Mixed Agreements* (Deventer, Kluwer, 1983); K.D. Stein, *Der gemischte Vertrag im Recht der Aussenbeziehungen der EWG* (Berlin, Duncker und Humblot, 1986); P. Reuter, 'La Conférence de Vienne sur les traités des organisations internationales et la sécurité des engagements conventionnels', *Liber Amicorum Pierre Pescatore*, p. 545.

180* In the European Communities, treaties and subsequent regulations aim at striking a balance between observing treaties previously concluded by member States and enabling the Community to carry out its duties and to exercise its own right to conclude certain treaties instead of member States (ECSC Convention on the Transitional Provisions, arts. 16 and 20; EEC Treaty, arts. 111 and 234). Until the Community is able to exercise certain powers, undertakings of member States have been provisionally extended, and new agreements to be concluded by them automatically include a clause enabling them to free themselves from their obligations as soon as the Community exercises its competence. The Court of Justice of the European Communities has stated that the General Agreement on Tariffs and Trade is binding on the EEC, arguing that the General Agreement bound all its member States, that it was the members' intention to bind the Community when they created it, that the EEC had approved the same purposes as the General Agreement and that it had in fact acted within its framework, as was recognized by the parties to the General Agreement (cases Nos. 21 to 24/72, *ECR 1972*, p. 1219; 38/75, *ECR 1975*, p. 1439; 266/81, *ECR 1983*, p. 731; 267 to 269/81, *ECR 1983*, p. 801). Further problems involving succession to treaties and other mechanisms such as *stipulation pour autrui* have been raised in cases concerning proceedings against Spanish fishermen and have been the subject of numerous detailed and much commented Court decisions (cases Nos. 812/79, *ECR 1980*, p. 2787; 181/80 and 266/80, *ECR 1981*, p. 2961). See the note by Ch. Philip in *AF*, vol. 27 (1981), p. 322.

181* J.-P. Jacqué ('A propos de l'accord de Rome du 23 avril 1977. Etude de la survie de la Commission européenne du Danube', *AF*, vol. 27 (1981), p. 747) gives a very interesting example of measures putting an end to the existence and activity of an international organization by related agreements incorporated in a single instrument as 'Annexes'.

185* Art. 75 derived from a proposal by Professor Tunkin within the ILC. A Japanese proposal to replace art. 75 by a text which, although clearer, covered all the measures taken by the Security Council was rejected by the 1968–1969 Vienna Conference at the 76th meeting of the Committee of the Whole (*Official Records UNCLT, I, Summary Records...*, p. 453). The 1947 Peace Treaties with some of the defeated States, as a pure and simple expression of the domination by the victors, similarly provided for entry into force upon ratification by the victorious Great Powers, regardless of whether each defeated State had ratified them. In another interpretation, the League and the United Nations appear as *de facto* governments owing to their universality (P. Le Gal, *La Société des Nations et les Etats non membres* (Thesis, Rennes, 1938); Shou-Sheng Hsueh, *L'Organisation des Nations Unies et les Etats non membres* (Thesis, Geneva, 1953). This conception is reflected in the ICJ's Advisory Opinion on *Namibia* (*ICJ Reports 1971*, p. 56, para. 126; *Pleadings*, vol. II, p. 122).

186* Ch. De Visscher (especially in *Théories et réalités en droit international public*, 4th edn. (Paris, Pedone, 1970) although reasserting his general theory of objective situations and expressing reservations about the hegemonic character of the theory of international *de facto* government, has attributed increasing importance to objective situations deriving from the 'consolidation' of a territorial status. For a doctrinal analysis of the 'status' concept, see E. Klein, *Statusverträge im Völkerrecht* (Berlin, Springer, 1980; English summary, pp. 350–359).

188* In fact, to explain the effects of objective situations, several legal theories compete for doctrinal support: custom, prescription, recognition, acquiescence, consolidation of a legal title and, last but not least, tacit agreement which serves to explain almost anything; see P. Reuter, *Droit international public*, pp. 97 and 207.

192* In *Continental Shelf (Tunisia v. Libya)* (*ICJ Reports 1982*, p. 18), doctrinal hesitation and judicial caution concerning rights *in rem* are clearly apparent (para. 84, p. 65). For the land frontier (para. 84, p. 65), the Court noted the agreement between the parties and referred to the 1964 Cairo resolution of the Organization of African Unity (without mentioning the reservations by some African States) and to the Vienna Convention on Succession of States in Respect of Treaties (without citing the relevant provisions, in particular art. 6). Concerning the maritime boundary, the Court took into account a state of fact which it called in turn a '*de facto* compromise', a 'provisional solution' or a '*modus vivendi*'; without interpreting it as fixing a 'recognized maritime boundary', it considered it merely as evidence that a solution based upon it would be equitable (paras. 94 to 96 and 118). Judge Ago's view was that the maritime boundary existed *ab initio* and that the general principles of State succession were applicable; he probably had in mind the concept of 'acquiescence', to which there is a doctrinal reference (for a strong criticism in fact and in law, see the Dissenting Opinion of Judge Gros). It was because the opposability of some situations hinged on custom that in 1964 the ILC dropped the reference to 'dispositive treaties', 'objective situations' and similar expressions (*YILC 1964*, vol. II, p. 27, commentary to article 63).

195* M. Zuleeg, 'Vertragskonkurrenz im Völkerrecht', *German Yearbook of International Law,* vol. 20 (1977), p. 246, and vol. 27 (1984), p. 367; G. Roucounas 'Engagements parallèles et contradictoires', *RCADI* (to be published).

199* The ILC and the 1969 Vienna Convention took an approach which was both precise and subtle; and from the very beginning this gave rise to reservations (especially during the 1967 session of the Institute of International Law, *Annuaire de l'Institut de Droit international,* vol. 52-I (1967), in particular S. Rosenne's 'Rapport provisoire' (p. 25) and 'Rapport définitif' (p. 382)). There was undoubtedly some confusion during the debates at the 1968–1969 Vienna Conference: the extreme case — incompatibility between the treaties concerned — was in all minds whereas the article only covered the determination of precedence between treaties on the same subject-matter. Thus, on another point, the declarations of the BIRPI representative in fact concerned a question which was governed by art. 40 relating to amendments (*Official Records UNCLT, I, Summary Records...,* Committee of the Whole, 31st meeting, p. 165).

201* Following the explanation given by the Expert Consultant at the 91st meeting of the Committee of the Whole, paras. 39–40, (*Official Records UNCLT, II, Summary Records...* (Sales No. E.70.V.6, p. 253), 'for purposes of determining which of two treaties was the later one, the relevant date should be that of the adoption of the treaty and not that of its entry into force ... Another question, however, arose: that of the date at which the rules contained at article... would have effect for each individual party. In that connexion, the date of entry into force of a treaty for a particular party was relevant for purposes of determining the moment at which that party would be bound by the obligations arising under [that] article'.

203* Sir Gerald Fitzmaurice had clearly set forth in his third Report (*YILC 1958*, vol. II, A/CN.4/115, commentary to article 19) the concept of a treaty of an 'interdependent' type in which the maintenance of an obligation necessarily depends on the maintenance of the corresponding obligation of all the other parties (e.g. treaties concerning disarmament, nuclear tests, fishing methods, Antarctica); the 1969 Convention twice refers to that type of situation in arts. 41 (1) (b) (see No. 209) and 60 (2) (c) (see below, No. 301).

204* The ILC discarded the term 'revision' of treaties because of the political connotations it acquired after World War I. The clarification given in the general ILC Report (*YILC 1966*, vol. II, p. 232) shows that the term 'agreement' in draft article 35 was intended to cover the possibility of amendments in the most flexible form, including verbal or tacit agreement. But both the precedents mentioned by the ILC in its Report and its own statements show that international practice is reluctant to answer clearly by the question as to whether after an amendment there are one or two treaties: 'Two categories of parties to the treaty come into being: (a) those States which are parties only to the unamended treaty, and (b) those which are parties both to the treaty and to the amending agreement. Yet all are, in a general sense, parties to the treaty and have mutual relations under the treaty.' (ibid., p. 234).

205* See the United Nations Secretariat's *Handbook of Final Clauses* (ST/LEG/6), p. 135; J. Leca, *Les techniques de révision des conventions internationales* (Paris, Librairie générale de droit et de jurisprudence, 1961); A.O. Adede, 'Amendment procedures for conventions with technical annexes: the IMCO experience', *Virginia Journal of International Law*, vol. 17 (1977), p. 201.

210* The question was raised in connection with the revision of the ECSC Treaty in the Dutch Parliament. M. van der Goes van Naters ('La révision des traités supranationaux', *Netherlands International Law Review*, vol. 6 (1959), p. 120) argued that member States of the ECSC could no longer, by a new treaty concluded between all the parties, modify a treaty containing precise rules on powers and procedures without observing such powers and procedures; in practice this meant that in a revision procedure States could no longer do without the participation of certain organs of an organization if such participation was provided for in the treaty to be revised.

211* In its final Report (*YILC 1966*, vol. II), the ILC time and again refers to the *acte contraire* theory which it rejects (pp. 232 and 249). But many different meanings may be given to a theory (or principle?) going back to Roman law; the ILC in fact is only opposed to a formalistic approach to international agreements. According to the Commission, what has been established by a consensual act, can be undone by another consensual act, however different in form from the first one: thus the ILC does endorse a non-formalistic conception of the *acte contraire* theory. According to P. Chailley (*La nature juridique des traités internationaux selon le droit contemporain*), the *acte contraire* approach is central to the theory of treaties. French practice accepts that some provisions of a treaty ratified upon legislative authorization may be modified by a treaty not subject to such an authorization, provided the modifications do not concern a matter which in itself would require such an authorization.

212* Draft article 38 was acknowledged to confirm a principle accepted by the Arbitral Award of 22 December 1963 in the *Case concerning the Interpretation of the Air Transport Services Agreement between the United States of America and France, signed at Paris on 27 March 1946* (*RIAA*, vol. 16, p. 11); its rejection was clearly in contrast with all the other provisions of the 1969 Convention.

213* On suspension in the work of the ILC, see 'Modification et terminaison des traités collectifs (Rapport présenté par M. Shabtaï Rosenne)', *Annuaire de l'Institut de Droit International*, vol. 52-I (1967), p. 50. Although the French text of the 1969 Convention sticks to the expression *suspension de l'application d'un traité* (which is not an exact equivalent of 'suspension of the operation of a treaty'), 'suspension of a treaty' will be used for the sake of simplicity. International practice has primarily had to deal with suspension in connection with hostilities; the point is excluded from the 1969 Convention by article 73 and the late transformations of the *jus ad bellum* have hardly encouraged studies on the subject, especially since there is little consistency in the great number of national judicial decisions concerning the effects of war on treaties; see: Lord McNair, *The Law of Treaties*, p. 693; Lord McNair and

A.D. Watts, *The Legal Effects of War*, 4th edn. (Cambridge, Cambridge University Press, 1966); S.D. Bailey, *How Wars End* (Oxford, Clarendon Press, 1982). Suspension is generally preferred to a more radical solution as between the belligerent and neutral parties to a universal treaty. The 'sanctions' applied against Italy by the League of Nations in 1936 and those applied against Rhodesia by the United Nations as from 1966 'suspended' at least certain treaty provisions; the same can be said of certain coercive measures decided upon during the Falklands crisis (see the note by J.L. Dewost, *AF*, vol. 28 (1982), p. 215, and below, No. 296*). Article 103 of the U.N. Charter has answered the wish to implement the provisions of Chapter VII (UNCIO, *Documents*, vol. 13, p. 707; *Repertory of Practice of United Nations Organs*, vol. 5 (New York, United Nations, 1955), p. 303).

214* This is nothing more than an explicit application of the more general principle that a treaty of any form may modify an earlier treaty (see above, No. 199). The rule was previously set forth in a Dissenting Opinion by Judge Anzilotti (*Electricity Company of Sofia and Bulgaria, PCIJ, Series A/B, No. 77*, p. 92). On United States constitutional problems, see *YILC 1966*, vol. II, p. 249.

216* The inclusion in art. 38 after 'customary rule of international law' of the words 'recognized as such' and the declarations of the representative of the USSR (*Official Records UNCLT, I, Summary Records...*, p. 201) reflect a purely voluntarist approach to custom; see: R.R. Baxter, 'Treaties and custom', *RCADI*, vol. 129 (1970-I), p. 25; M.E. Villiger, *Customary International Law and Treaties* (Dordrecht, Nijhoff, 1985).

Concerning the question of desuetude (or obsolescence) in British practice, see C. Parry, 'The Law of Treaties', in M. Sørensen, ed., *Manual of Public International Law* (London, Macmillan, 1968), p. 235. J. Touscoz (*Le principe d'effectivité dans l'ordre international* (Paris, Librairie générale de droit et de jurisprudence, 1964), pp. 181 ff.) rejects the view that desuetude may derive from a tacit agreement and sees it as a pure fact. See also G. Scelle, *Théorie juridique de la révision des traités* (Paris, Sirey, 1936), and 'Rapport sur la révision des traités', *Annuaire de l'Institut de Droit international*, vol. 42 (1948), p. 1, as well as R. Pinto, 'La prescription en droit international', *RCADI*, vol. 87 (1955-I), p. 387. For judicial decisions, see *Minquiers and Ecrehos, ICJ Reports 1953*, p. 47 (especially Judge Levi Carneiro's Individual Opinion) and in a negative sense *Yuille, Shortridge and Co.* (Award of 21 Oct. 1861), in A. de Lapradelle and N. Politis, eds, *Recueil des Arbitrages Internationaux*, vol. II (Paris, Pedone, 1923), pp. 78 and 105. In fact, a custom modifying the existing law — whether conventional or customary — purports to create law by a breach of law, and although such a process is sound in theory, there is some reluctance to accept it as normal in practice.

217* The Court's view is in fact based on a notion transcending both treaty and custom, as can be seen from para. 181 of the judgment: 'The essential consideration is that the Charter and the customary international law flow from a common fundamental principle outlawing the use of force in international relations'. Moreover an important Separate Opinion referred to *jus cogens*. Therefore the only purpose of the distinction between treaty and custom so forcefully asserted in this case was to lead back to the concept of 'fundamental principle'. Does this refer to a third 'source' or does it rather tend to favour custom as a more convenient means than treaties to justify the existence of absolute peremptory rules (see Nos. 166 and 218)?

218* The appropriateness of mentioning in art. 38 of the 1969 Convention general principles of law as well as custom gave rise to a heated debate. The Expert Consultant had felt this was not required, since in his view general principles of law necessarily went through a prior customary stage; they were nevertheless included in the text at the first session (*Official Records UNCLT, I, Summary Records...*, Committee of the Whole, 14th meeting and 36th meeting, p. 201), but finally rejected at the second session (*Official Records UNCLT, II, Summary Records...*, 14th and 15th plenary meetings, pp. 63–71) after Soviet criticism of the general principles of law common to the national systems of capitalist countries.

219–226* The available literature is considerable. See e.g. J.A. Barberis, 'La liberté de traiter des Etats et le *jus cogens* en droit international', *ZaöRV*, vol. 30 (1970), p. 19; K. Marek, 'Contribution à l'étude du *jus cogens* en droit international', *En hommage à Paul Guggenheim*, p. 426; M. Virally, 'Réflexions sur le *"jus cogens"*', *AF*, vol. 12 (1966), p. 5; G. Morelli, 'A proposito di norme internazionali cogenti', *Rivista di diritto internazionale*, vol. 51 (1968), p. 108; J. Sztucki, *Jus Cogens and the Vienna Convention on the Law of Treaties: A Critical Appraisal* (Vienna, Springer, 1974); A.G. Robledo, 'Le *jus cogens* international: sa genèse, sa nature, ses fonctions', *RCADI*, vol. 172 (1981-III), p. 9; G. Gaja, '*Jus cogens* beyond the Vienna Convention', *RCADI*, vol. 172 (1981-III), p. 271. In two different cases, the ICJ characterized certain rules by reference to moral law of the 'conscience of mankind' (*Reservations to the Convention on Genocide, ICJ Reports 1951*, p. 23) or to 'elementary considerations of humanity, even more exacting in peace than in war' (*Corfu Channel, ICJ Reports 1949*, p. 22); a judgment of the 3rd Nuremberg Military Tribunal of 31 July 1948 regarded an agreement between Germany and the Vichy Government as '*contra bonos mores*' (*Trials of War Criminals,* (Washington, US Government Printing Office, 1949–1953), vol. 9, p. 1395). Since the settlements following World War II, the concept of peremptory rules gradually focused on the problems of responsibility, the generalization of the concept of international 'crime', the development of humanitarian law and, above all, the prohibition of the use of nuclear weapons (see below, No. 307).

For the Soviet positions, see: G.I. Tunkin, *Droit international public*, p. 127, and 'Remarks on the juridical nature of customary norms of international law', *California Law Review*, vol. 49 (1961), p. 419; O. Khlestov, 'The new Soviet–Czechoslovak Treaty', *International Affairs*, July 1970, p. 9; L. Alexidze, 'Legal nature of *jus cogens* in contemporary international law', *RCADI*, vol. 172 (1981-III), p. 219.

229* When the ILC discussed the possible inclusion in its draft articles on treaties of international organizations of a provision symmetrical to article 27 of the 1969 Convention, this was strongly resisted by some members. Apparently this position stemmed from an argument which had been invoked with regard to the maintenance of the effects of a cease-fire in the Middle East decided by the Security Council. Indeed, to make the practical arrangements for the end of hostilities, the Secretary-General, according to well-established practice, had concluded an agreement with one of the States concerned. Later, when the Security Council attempted to modify its resolution, this State claimed that the situation had been consolidated by treaty. Only at the end of its work on the subject was the ILC to adopt a draft article retaining the principle of article 27 of the 1969 Convention. A few months later the United Nations Conference on the Law of the Sea chose a similar solution in art. 4 (6) of Annex IX to the Convention of 11 December 1982 which provides that '[i]n the event of a conflict between the obligations of an international organization under this

Convention and its obligations under the agreement establishing the organization or any acts relating to it, the obligations under this Convention shall prevail'. The 1986 Vienna Conference followed the ILC draft and adopted for international organizations a provision symmetrical to the one concerning States: 'An international organization party to a treaty may not invoke the rules of the organization as justification for its failure to perform the treaty.'

Chapter 4
Non-application of treaties

I General observations

230 Treaty rules like any other rules must produce effects, which means that they must be applied, in the widest sense of the word. The fact is, however, that they are not always applied. Their non-application occurs in very different circumstances and with widely varying features, while an uncertain terminology only makes matters worse. This chapter will try to present an overall picture of non-application and point out some basic aspects of the problem, by considering first the causes and the effects of non-application in order to identify the different types of situation, and then to concentrate on the most important cases which will be further discussed in the subsequent sections.

1. Causes of non-application

231 The first essential distinction to be made is between causes stemming from some legal ground and causes stemming from a simple fact. A number of cases where a treaty is not applied owing to another legal rule (treaty, custom, unilateral act) more or less definitively precluding its application have just been described in Chapter 3 and will not be considered again, except to point out the precise effects of those other rules, especially where peremptory norms are concerned. The cases to be considered here therefore are those where non-application is due to a simple fact.

232 The most important cases of non-application arising out of a simple fact are as follows: a ground of invalidity vitiating the agreement; certain facts external to the treaty and the parties; and unlawful acts committed in the performance of the treaty. These three situations will be discussed in greater detail in the following sections. But there are others which also call for a few remarks. While most multilateral treaties only enter into force when there are a given number of parties, is it true to say that such treaties terminate merely because the number of the parties falls below that critical level as a result of withdrawals from the treaty? Article 55 of the 1969 and 1986 Conventions rules this out in cases where a treaty remains silent on the subject. Yet a series of withdrawals might deprive the treaty of its object and bring about its termination (see below, No. 283; see also article 74 (3) of the 1986 Convention). Treaties frequently include a termination date or a resolutive condition, in which case the treaty ends when the date is reached or the condition fulfilled.

233   A classical question arises in this respect: What does the lack of a termination date in a treaty mean? Does it imply that the parties will never be able to denounce a bilateral treaty or to withdraw from a multilateral treaty? Or are they free to do so at any time at their own discretion? The latter solution would really seem to make light of the binding force of international undertakings, to the point of destroying the actual concept of treaties, especially for unwritten agreements which hardly ever mention a termination date. Yet maintaining the absolute perennity of treaty undertakings disregards the fact that for obvious political reasons it is impossible to set a limit to the duration of certain undertakings which are not, however, regarded as everlasting by the parties. The problem is therefore essentially one of intention, but it is not an easy task to fix upon generally reliable signs of such an intention. Both Conventions nevertheless regard 'the nature of the treaty' as such a sign without being more specific (article 56 (1) (b)).(*)

234   Is it possible to categorize all the reasons for which a treaty fails to be applied? Although there is no logical impossibility, such an endeavour is fraught with difficulties owing to an uncertain terminology and to possible doctrinal implications. The question was raised in the International Law Commission because, by expatiating especially on the grounds of invalidity, the draft articles might seem to undermine to some extent the stability of treaty relations; in order to limit this threat, article 42 of both Conventions provides that issues of validity are to be settled exclusively 'through the application of the present Convention' and that '[t]he termination of a treaty, its denunciation or the withdrawal of a party, may take place only as a result of the application of the provisions of the treaty or of the present Convention'. Such provisions, which in any event have no bearing on matters as important as State succession, international responsibility and the effects of war on treaties, might lead to more than merely academic controversy.(*)

2. Effects of non-application

235   Three major aspects have to be considered under this heading: (A) effects of non-application in relation to time; (B) effects of non-application with regard to the provisions of the treaty; and (C) the automatic or non-automatic character of non-application depending on its causes.

A. EFFECTS OF NON-APPLICATION IN RELATION TO TIME

236   First of all, non-application may be final as far as one or several States are concerned. This is the case when a party forfeits, or is deprived of, its status as a party to a multilateral treaty which continues to apply as between the other parties, and also when, in the same situation, the treaty ceases to be binding for all the parties to a multilateral treaty, or when a State or an international organization ceases to be a party to a bilateral treaty. In the usual terminology, this is called 'withdrawal' or 'termination'; these are relatively simple situations. From the point of view of the effects in time, two features emerge: the effect occurs as soon as the cause is taken into account and, in principle, it is final; it is not retroactive but with regard to the State concerned the treaty will in principle never be in force again unless an entirely new procedure is followed.

237 In another situation, there is merely a suspension. The treaty is not challenged as such, but simply ceases for a time to produce any effects with regard to one, several or all the parties. Whether this is called 'suspension of the operation of a treaty' as in both Vienna Conventions or 'suspension of the treaty' is immaterial: what really matters is that the treaty may again become fully operative. Therefore only the 'obligation to perform' the treaty is suspended while the legal relations between the parties established by the treaty remain otherwise unaffected. Moreover, the parties must 'refrain from acts tending to obstruct the resumption of the operation of the treaty' (article 72 (2)); indeed, if this were not so, the term 'suspension' would be inaccurate. Intentionally preventing suspension from ending therefore infringes an obligation of good faith.(*)

238 Suspension is basically meant to provide in a great number of cases an acceptable alternative to termination while avoiding its radical effects. This is why suspension — previously restricted essentially to the case of hostilities — was given such prominence by the International Law Commission and later by both the 1969 and 1986 Conventions. Both of them, except when a treaty is radically void, practically always provide for suspension along with termination, no doubt in the hope that it might appear sufficient. In some cases, suspension alone is mentioned, for instance in relation to the possibility of affecting the operation of a multilateral treaty by agreement between some of the parties only (see above, No. 208; article 58 of the Conventions) or in relation to the measures a party is entitled to take as an individual reaction to the breach of a multilateral treaty (article 60 (2) (b) and (c)). It should be noted that multilateral economic treaties mostly include temporary derogation clauses enabling a party, when faced with possible economic difficulties, to disregard temporarily certain treaty requirements. However, such clauses are nearly always applied by an international organization or an equivalent body. In this particular context, the operation of specific obligations is frequently suspended for this type of attenuated *force majeure* situation.(*)

239 No question is more delicate than the one raised by invalidity. It involves several concepts originating in municipal legal systems; closely linked as they are to such rigidly structured systems, they are not easy to apply in public international law. Moreover the rules on invalidity vary considerably from country to country and the distinctive vocabulary of each legal system concerned is a frequent source of misunderstanding and miscalculation in international law. In any event, applying rules on invalidity to conventions always remains a most delicate task. For all these obstacles, the 1969 Convention (followed by the 1986 Convention) is the first international instrument to set out rules on invalidity on such a scale, a fact which caused some misgivings about their potential repercussions on the stability of treaties.(*)

240 Time is a central element in all matters of invalidity. A legal transaction cannot be invalid unless there was a substantial defect from the outset. This defect may be invoked from the start and the transaction will never have any effect, but this is not the most frequent situation. In practice, owing to appearances and circumstances, it will generally have produced some effects by the time the defects are revealed, and the essential difficulty with any rules on invalidity is to eliminate the consequences of a transaction which, on account of its defective character, should have lacked any effectiveness from the outset. Hence the considerable variety of the rules governing invalidity in different legal systems; whereas insistence on the lawfulness of transactions will lead to frequent cases of invalidity and indeed to the most absolute system of nullification, conversely the security of social relations and the necessary protection of legitimate interests call for milder solutions. The last consideration may be even more relevant in public international law, given the scope of the collective interests at stake. Moreover, even where invalidity is supposed to be merely acknowledged, avoidance still involves an authoritative decision. Yet, except in the case of some international organizations, invalidity is declared by States themselves for want of any jurisdictional authority. This is why rules on invalidity are bound to cause concern and misgivings. In the end, therefore, the crucial factor is the effect of invalidity on the past; this governs all its practical aspects. In other words, who can invoke a given ground of invalidity? In which cases can the right to invoke it be renounced? What elements of the transaction are affected by it? To what extent is it supposed to restore the past?(*)

B. EFFECTS OF NON-APPLICATION WITH REGARD TO TREATY PROVISIONS

241 When considering the different grounds of non-application, the question arises whether the treaty should be regarded as indivisible or whether non-application only extends to a number of specific provisions. This leads us back to the problem of 'integrity' and 'separability' which has already been mentioned in connection with reservations (see above, No. 135). To accept separability is, however, a more serious matter here. In the case of reservations, a State party to a treaty may challenge another State's view as to the separability of the treaty: all it has to do is refuse to consider the reserving State as a party. But with non-application, the problem arises between States which have fully accepted as between themselves a coherent and integral transaction of which there is a risk of one element disappearing. The same problem arises when non-application follows amendments and modifications and very precise rules must therefore be laid down to govern the situation (see above, Nos. 205 ff.).(*)

242 With no firm guidance to be found in State practice or case-law, the integrity of treaties must be upheld as the basic principle. Separability can only be accepted exceptionally, either to allow in certain cases for the maintenance of essential treaty provisions in the face of situations the parties had failed to contemplate, or because an agreement may contain regulations covering matters so different that they can be dissociated without difficulty. The exceptional case of separability thus hinges on a reconstruction of the parties' probable intention in concluding the treaty. But in addition to this criterion, an entirely separate idea must be taken into account which, although applying to certain specific mechanisms of the law of treaties, originates from concerns which have nothing to do with the law of treaties as such, and which relate to international responsibility. Failure to comply with a treaty may indeed be prompted by an unlawful act: coercion, fraud, conclusion procured by corruption, disregard of a peremptory rule, non-performance of a treaty, etc. In such cases, the rules governing separability and integrity may be adapted to allow for the principles of responsibility, especially by favouring the injured party or even in some cases by inflicting a penalty on the author of an unlawful act, regardless of the interests of the injured party. (*)

243 By and large, the 1969 and 1986 Conventions followed these principles (article 44). First of all, as a general rule, the principle of integrity prevails. When the possibility not to apply a treaty any longer (either by denunciation, withdrawal or suspension) derives from the common intention of the parties as expressed in the treaty or otherwise, or as implied by the nature of the treaty (article 56), non-application extends understandably enough to the treaty as a whole. Since in that case the ground of non-application is of a conventional character, it can very naturally be assumed that if the parties had wished to allow for partial non-application, they could easily have said so, or implied it in one way or another (article 44 (1)).

244 The presumption that a treaty is to be regarded as an indivisible whole prevails with respect to all the grounds of non-application which are due not to the common intention of the parties but to a vitiated act, a breach of the treaty by one party, or any extraneous fact. In this case, however, the presumption as a rule is not absolute. If the ground only concerns certain treaty provisions and if the provisions are clearly individualized within the treaty, it only applies to those provisions. These features are necessarily twofold: separability must be both material and intentional. Material separability means that the rest of the treaty remains applicable despite the lapse of the provisions concerned (article 44 (3) (a)). Intentional separability refers to what the parties presumably intended to commit themselves to. It is no easy task to assess intentions which may vary from party to party. To use the terms of French private law, separability could be said to imply that the 'cause' of the commitment must not be affected. Alternatively, from a more objective point of view, an attempt could be made to identify in specific types of treaties 'essential' as opposed to purely accidental elements, however elusive such a distinction may prove. The International Law Commission and both Vienna Conferences restricted separability to the case where the clauses to be deprived of their effect were not 'an essential basis of the consent of the other party or parties to be bound by the treaty as a whole' (article 44 (3) (b)). But taking up a United States amendment, the 1968–1969 Conference, later to be followed by the 1986 Conference, added a new subparagraph, apparently with a view to striking the necessary balance between rights and obligations in a contract, which is a well-established idea in common law. This conception, which more or less clearly underlies the theory of unequal treaties, is to be found nowhere else in the Vienna Conventions: separability is admitted only so long as 'continued performance of the remainder of the treaty would not be unjust' (article 44 (3) (c)).

245   Finally, as pointed out earlier, separability as recognized in general terms by both Vienna Conventions clearly allows for the idea of sanction in some particular situations. Where fraud or corruption only affect certain clauses, which under the above-mentioned criteria could normally be separated from the rest of the treaty, the injured party may choose to invoke the fraud or corruption either with respect to these clauses alone, thereby availing itself of separability, or with respect to the treaty as a whole; radically terminating the treaty might indeed go against that party's interests. But separability is ruled out altogether in cases of unlawful coercion of a State or its representative, or violation of a peremptory rule of international law (article 44 (5)). Such a strict solution does not necessarily favour the injured party and can only be explained as a sanction inflicted in the interest of international society as a whole.

C. IS NON-APPLICATION AUTOMATIC OR NOT?

246   A treaty may fail to be applied by a party for a variety of reasons, as has just been seen — in particular termination, withdrawal of a party, invalidity, or suspension. Any one of these grounds may be challenged by one or several of the other parties. This gives rise to a classical type of international dispute between the party or parties seeking non-application and those in favour of applying the treaty. If a purely objective definition of legal disputes is accepted, this would be a typical legal dispute. After a period of time, the dispute may or may not be adjudicated upon or settled, as the case may be. But what happens to the treaty in the meantime? Under the general principles of public international law, any State or international organization as a rule has the right to define legal situations of its concern; accordingly, a treaty may be held by some States or organizations to apply while others think it does not. The parties are of course free to settle the problem by themselves according to such general commitments or special clauses as may be included in the treaty. If the dispute is settled at law by some arbitral or judicial means, the treaty will be affected not as from the date of the ruling but as from the time when the ground of non-application first appeared. Especially if the treaty is declared null and void, it is deemed not to produce any effects as from the moment the ground of invalidity arose.(*)

247 Such are the traditional principles still valid today in this field. Yet they met with strong objections during the 1968–1969 Vienna Conference. In its work on the subject, the International Law Commission put forward a limited proposal — which the Conference endorsed without opposition — instituting a special procedure in case a party invokes 'a defect in its consent' or 'a ground for impeaching the validity of a treaty, terminating it, withdrawing from it or suspending its operation' (article 65 (1)). This procedure involves: notification, a statement of the legal grounds and, except in cases of special urgency, a three-month period during which the treaty should continue to be applied. If, at the end of this period, the parties fail to reach an agreement, general international law becomes applicable again. If a State wishes to draw the consequences of its claim, it must state its position with regard to the treaty by an 'instrument' communicated to the other parties (article 67 (2)); in other words, the procedure is solemnized, and becomes more formal and objective. As for international organizations, after some hesitation about the length of the period under article 65 (2), the International Law Commission, followed by the 1986 Conference, assimilated their case to that of States.(*)

248 The Commission's 1966 draft articles provided for no particular procedure for the settlement of disputes arising out of the interpretation or application of the articles. Yet relying on certain terms used in draft articles 39, 46 to 50 and 62, some States pursued the matter further at the 1968–1969 Vienna Conference. Could it not be said indeed in the field of treaties that an established title has a provisional authority (*provision est due au titre*) and that therefore so long as the grounds of non-application have not been 'established', i.e. in a way which is binding on those concerned, the treaty remains applicable? This statement immediately leads to another point, namely the obligation to resort to an arbitral or judicial solution, whereby certain effects of the treaty could be maintained even beyond the three-month period if interim measures of protection were indicated by an international tribunal. Relying on some inconsistencies and ambiguities in the provisions relating to invalidity, these same governments perceived the draft articles as purporting to make a distinction between void treaties and a kind of voidability which at least partially justified their position.(*)

249 There is little doubt that the listing in the draft articles of all the grounds of non-application and their definition in very general or even extremely vague terms could generate some concern that the main result of those articles would simply be to foster uncertainty about the binding force of treaties. The question of peaceful settlement of disputes was in fact an element of a wider political struggle which was even to jeopardize the outcome of the Conference. The solution adopted in article 66 and in the Annex to the Convention presupposes the entry into force of the Convention; it contains highly original features: compulsory jurisdiction of the International Court of Justice for disputes involving peremptory rules; compulsory conciliation for disputes concerning other articles of Part V; and the dominant role of the Secretary-General of the United Nations in the conciliation procedure. The International Law Commission was equally divided when it came to discuss the procedure for settling disputes relating to treaties of international organizations. Relying on a post-1969 practice, the Commission added to its 1982 draft articles an Annex providing, in the spirit of the 1969 Convention, for a conciliation procedure and an Arbitral Tribunal to take the place of the International Court of Justice, under whose Statute international organizations have no *locus standi*. The solution adopted by the 1986 Conference is closer still to that of 1969 in so far as it replaces the application to the Court by a request for an advisory opinion which the parties undertake to regard as binding.(*)

250   The lively debates of 1968–1969 and 1986 which could have deadlocked the Conferences spell out two opposing conceptions of the development of international law. The first considers that, failing procedures for an objective settlement of disputes, the proclamation of new rules in the guise of vague 'principles' is ineffective and can only bolster those who prevail because of their power or their numerical advantage. The second considers that 'objectivity' is either inconceivable or at least beyond the reach of present-day institutions. It should also be noted that since 1969, or rather since 1980, the procedures instituted by the 1969 Convention have had no occasion to stand the test of international practice and that recent accessions to the Convention have done away with procedural constraints by means of reservations which destroy the balance painstakingly struck in 1969.(*)

II Grounds of invalidity

251   The possible grounds of invalidity will now be briefly discussed in the order followed by the Vienna Conventions, which on this point were at pains to be exhaustive if not always very precise. They are: consent invalid under municipal law, error, fraud, corruption of the representative of a State or international organization, coercion of a representative, coercion of a State or organization by the threat or use of force, and conflict with a peremptory rule of international law. For each case we shall consider (partly by cross-references) the nature of the vitiating factor, its features and its effects (who may invoke it and whether it may be renounced).(*)

252   A number of preliminary observations should, however, be made. The first concerns the elementary character of such considerations. There is an almost total lack of practice in this field, which is just as well. As for theoretical studies, they are few in number and rarely give a general view of a subject, which should cover juristic acts as a whole rather than just treaties. The second observation is more a matter of vocabulary but nevertheless has substantive implications: the fact is that there is still no international terminology on the subject. The terms used are those of municipal law, but it must be emphasized that none of them has quite the same meaning as in a given national legal system.(*)

253 This is true in particular of the fundamental term 'invalidity' which the Conventions use often but not consistently with the same meaning. Behind the actual term, the substance is what matters. Clearly all the cases to be considered involve an initial flaw of such importance that the whole transaction is liable to be quashed from the very beginning. This is what invalidity means when it is defined by its effects. And this is what the Vienna Conventions mean to do by describing in article 69 the consequences of invalidity. Yet the rudimentary character of this provision shows how difficult it is to give a definition and to develop a theory.

254 Thus while some grounds of invalidity may cause a bilateral treaty simply to lapse, things are more complex with multilateral treaties. To be sure, it may happen that the consent of only one of the parties is defective so that invalidity merely affects the relations between that party and the others (article 60 (4)); but this is not decisive: in addition there is the question of whether cancelling the conventional link as to one party allows the treaty to subsist as between the others, and also whether the other parties or some of them played an active part in bringing about the ground of invalidity. Again, eliminating the invalid treaty theoretically entails the elimination of all transactions and situations based on it; but this theoretical consequence does not take into account the conduct of the contracting party which may have acted either in good or bad faith. Invalidity is too severe a penalty in the former case and too lenient in the latter. In any event, invalidity is only simple in abstract terms, and reconstructing a situation after invalidation is always very complex, as can be seen in municipal law especially with respect to acts which have had a whole series of legal consequences.

255 These questions are hardly clarified by international practice. Cases of invalidation are in practice settled by *ad hoc* conventions depending on the interests of the States concerned, which is hardly conducive to the elaboration of general rules. The Vienna Conventions merely laid down a few very general principles: situations changed by the treaty are 'as far as possible' restored; acts performed in good faith by a contracting State on the basis of an invalid treaty are not unlawful; and no rights accrue to a contracting party from a nullity originating in its own unlawful act (article 69 (2) and (3)).

1. Consent invalid under municipal law

256   The much-debated and well-known problem of so-called 'imperfect ratifications' or 'unconstitutional treaties' has already been dealt with (see above, No. 37), as has the solution afforded by the Conventions. Although in principle treaties are invalid if concluded in violation of the municipal law of a State or the rules of an international organization, such invalidity, as shown by international practice, can only become effective in quite exceptional cases. The nature of the defect concerned is quite clear: the consent of a legal entity (in this case a State or international organization) is essentially the result of a legal procedure. If the procedure has not been observed, there is no consent.(*)

257   This question depends on a State's municipal law or on the rules of an organization, as the case may be. The entity concerned is the only one which may invoke invalidity, and this may possibly be a case for separability of treaty provisions (article 44). But there is a difference between States and organizations. A State may at any time renounce its right to invoke invalidity either explicitly or by its conduct (article 45). That is why the issue is not very relevant in practice. Indeed, as has already been observed, if the State declares that its consent was given irregularly from the start and before the treaty is performed, things will be as if the treaty had never been concluded; yet this is an unrealistic hypothesis. The question only arises after at least partial performance, usually following domestic political changes; but precisely in that case, even if invalidity were assumed to exist, it could no longer be invoked since it would have been precluded by acquiescence. International law here is less concerned with protecting the other States' good faith than with sanctioning the conduct of a State that gave rise to a legitimate belief of which it must bear the consequences. Thus, although it must be regarded as a case of vitiated consent, this form of invalidity is heavily tinged with international responsibility. As for international organizations, the 1986 Convention, following the draft article of the International Law Commission, adopted a more protective solution: renunciation by conduct is only taken into account if it emanates from the *competent organ*, i.e. the one explicitly entitled to renounce, as opposed to the ones entrusted with the performance of the treaty. Moreover this conduct has to spell out renunciation, not just acquiescence, and must therefore be quite conclusive.

2. Error

258   Error is the clearest case of vitiated consent in its most classical sense. It vitiates the very substance of consent if it concerns a decisive element which forms an 'essential basis' of consent, whether of a State or of an international organization (article 48). Errors merely relating to a text (in French '*erreurs de rédaction*') do not come under article 48 but are subject to correction procedures (1969 Convention, article 79; 1986 Convention, article 80). Less conclusively than in the previous situation, but still significantly, the conditions of invalidity here too involve elements of responsibility: the injured party cannot avail itself of the error if it is to some degree responsible for it, either because it contributed to the error by its own negligence or failed to take into account circumstances which made it possible (article 48 (2)). Yet error does remain above all a factor vitiating consent, exerting its effects as such. A substantial error may be committed either by one of the parties alone or by several of them.(*)

259 In international practice, errors seldom occur in this specific sense except in the particular field of treaties delimiting or transferring territories on the strength of inaccurate geographical descriptions or maps, as shown by some judicial cases. Yet instead of appearing in the treaty itself, errors often materialize only in subsequent acts carried out in application of the treaty. Rarely is the error a sufficient ground for formal invalidation; still less will the issue of invalidation become the subject of contentious proceedings.

260 As a typical vitiating element, error can only be invoked by the injured party. It can be remedied by the explicit consent of that party or simply by its conduct. Separability applies under its usual conditions (article 44). Although the effects of an error come into play from the start, the mitigations resulting from good faith (article 69 (2)) apply most sweepingly, in particular when territorial changes are required to correct an error in delimitation.

3. Fraud

261 In almost every municipal legal order, deceit in matters of contract is sanctioned under various conditions; without being quite equivalent, the English concept of fraud and the French notion of *dol* both apply to a deceitful conduct whereby a person is induced to conclude a contract. Like error, fraud thus implies an inaccurate view of things in one of the parties. But unlike error it clearly involves an unlawful element of deceit. Accordingly, claiming fraud rather than error could only be in the injured party's interest in two cases: either if the conditions regarding the error involved in a case of fraud are less exacting, or if the effects of fraud benefit the injured party more than the effects of error. As will soon be seen, the latter is certainly true, whereas the former is merely probable, given the lack of any international practice.(*)

262 Error as such without any unlawful element only amounts to a ground of invalidity if there is firm evidence that an essential element of consent is at stake. This is not easy to establish since the 'essential basis of consent' is not always clearly apparent. If on the contrary a party claims that there has been fraud, it is as it were the author of the fraud himself who will have shown by his very conduct that the resulting error was an essential condition of the agreement. In fact, this has perhaps less to do with the extent of the error than with the burden of proof. Despite the lack of practice, there is one historical case where the concept of fraud is indeed relevant. The Munich Agreement of 1938 may for a variety of reasons be regarded as invalid *ab initio* by Czechoslovakia; but with regard to France — a signatory of the agreement — invalidity *ab initio* cannot be based on error; it can, however, be based on fraud since it was later shown that from the outset one of the parties regarded the agreement as simply the easiest means of achieving total domination over Czechoslovakia, and was already preparing to breach it.

263 Fraud remains close to error inasmuch as it is up to the deceived party either to invoke it or to confirm the treaty by its express consent or by its conduct. The difference lies in the more stringent effects of fraud, which unlike error involves an internationally wrongful act. Indeed, where the general provisions on separability prove applicable, the deceived party is given a choice under the Conventions: it can opt according to its best interests either for separability, maintaining part of the treaty in force, or for complete invalidity, the latter course being clearly intended to penalize the author of the fraud. There is yet another option open to the deceived party, namely to ask for the elimination of all acts performed under the invalidated treaty, without having to do so in every case. Such elimination cannot be requested by the State or international organization to which the fraud is imputable (article 69 (3)). More generally a treaty involving fraud is indeed a wrongful act with all the legal consequences this entails.

4. Corruption of the representative of a State or international organization

264 This case of invalidity was considered by the International Law Commission at a rather late stage in its work on treaties between States, and its existence as a distinct ground of invalidity was challenged: according to some members of the Commission, all cases of corruption were fully covered by the notion of fraud, while others regarded corruption as merely a form of coercion on the person of a State representative. Yet both Vienna Conferences adopted a separate provision on corruption (article 50). This seems quite justified, for while corruption does involve an element of deceit, it is a peculiar and particularly serious kind of fraud. On the other hand, while corruption is a step closer to coercion, it is still some appreciable distance away. The rationale behind this case of invalidity is distinct: through corruption, the representative of a State or international organization in fact loses his very status as a representative, although the State or organization is not aware of this.

265 For corruption to be a vitiating factor, its effect must have been to lead to the acceptance of the treaty as it is: even if it has affected only a single clause, and an inessential one at that, but one which a loyal representative would not have accepted, the treaty is still vitiated. The most difficult question is to determine from whom the act of corruption should emanate to have such effects. Article 50 requires that 'a negotiating State or a negotiating organization' should be responsible for the corruption. The problem is mainly due to the fact that potential examples of corruption are borrowed above all from the field of economic relations, where private interests are particularly concerned by ongoing negotiations, and where in some cases (investments, arms shipments, equipment contracts) a treaty between States may even be accompanied by agreements between private or State enterprises. The difficulty should be resolved under the general principles of international responsibility, which prevail in the case of corruption even more than in that of fraud. The act of corruption must be attributable to the negotiating State or organization, although it need not be committed by one of its official representatives: it is sufficient for it to be committed by a person acting under its control and on its behalf or merely with the State or organization's complicity.

266 The effects of corruption are exactly the same as those of fraud; both grounds of invalidity indeed closely depend on the unlawful nature of the act. Again therefore the injured party's exclusive interests are dominant; as in the former case, it enjoys extensive rights owing to the unlawful character of the vitiating factor.

5. Coercion of the representative of a State or international organization

267 When coercion is openly directed at the representative of a State or international organization in his official capacity, both the representative as a person and the entity represented are concerned, and the invalidity of the treaty derives from this dual character. These acts or threats may, however, be aimed at a representative personally rather than as an organ of the State or organization. As such they are not public; they may affect the physical well-being, career, or reputation of the representative or of his close relatives. Article 51 applies specifically to the second alternative. A case in point was that of the threats used against President Hacha of Czechoslovakia in March 1939 to induce him to accept the end of his country's independence.

268 Like corruption, this form of coercion perverts the legal relationship between a State or international organization and its representative who tends to negotiate more as a private individual than as an organ. However, the International Law Commission and the 1968–1969 Conference regarded it as worse than corruption, and therefore its effects were subjected to stricter rules. Indeed, whatever form it might take, coercion was seen as the major crime. Not only is it a wrongful act like fraud or corruption, but it is the most serious form of wrongful act, of the kind giving rise to penal sanctions in national legal systems; for coercion does not simply affect relations between the parties concerned but also between all the other States or, to use another concept, however unclear its legal construction may still be, the international community as a whole.

269 In this perspective, it matters little who is actually responsible for coercion. Whereas fraud or corruption must be imputable to a 'negotiating State' or 'negotiating organization', no such condition is laid down by the Conventions for coercion. As for the effects of coercion, they are clearly stated in article 51 of the Conventions: expressions of consent thus procured are 'without any legal effect'. The treaty is deemed never to have existed; its defectiveness cannot even be remedied by the injured party's consent; technically speaking, if the injured party wishes to retain some of the consequences of such a transaction, it can only do so by an entirely new treaty which could in no way be regarded as confirming the former one.

6. Coercion of a State or international organization by the threat or use of force

270 The rule invalidating treaties concluded under this type of coercion (article 52) raises three equally important questions: the nature of unlawful coercion, the application of the rule in time, and its effects.

A. THE NATURE OF UNLAWFUL COERCION

271 Not all uses of coercion in the conclusion of a treaty are sufficient to bring about invalidity; if this were the case, all peace treaties would be null and void. Formerly this had proved a doctrinal stumbling block, but now it is accepted that only the unlawful use of force can invalidate a treaty. Invalidity can therefore hardly be regarded as a result of vitiated consent; it is rather a sanction of an international offence deemed sufficiently important by some to fall within the category of 'international crimes' entailing special penalties for the individuals and States that have committed them.

272 In which situations is the use of coercion unlawful? This is no easy question to answer. Should the emphasis lie on the means of coercion and therefore only armed coercion be condemned, whereas economic or psychological coercion would remain lawful? Or should it lie on the ends that coercion is supposed to achieve? If this were the case, any coercion, even armed coercion, would be admissible provided it were applied for the good of the coerced party whereas any coercion, however small, exerted to secure a harmful or unequal treaty would be unlawful. It is easy therefore to move from relatively straightforward cases to less clear ones and eventually to challenge a great number of treaties. Incidentally, this type of reasoning may imply a shift towards another case of invalidation, not covered by coercion, i.e. the case of unequal treaties involving an imbalance in the parties' mutual obligations and benefits. Such inequality would then either be regarded as a separate ground for invalidity — like undue influence in common law systems or *laesio enormis* in civil law systems — or as sufficient evidence of unlawful coercion. The theory of unequal treaties, although never clearly and firmly articulated in legal terms, has often been put forward especially in Soviet and Chinese legal literature, to do away with concessions or capitulations.(*)

273 The International Law Commission and later the Vienna Conferences faced all these problems. The Commission, to avoid giving a complete and precise definition of unlawful coercion, simply referred to violation 'of the principles of the Charter of the United Nations', meaning that these principles were applicable already before the Charter and regardless of the Charter. The Vienna Conference of 1968–1969 emphasized this tendency by referring in article 52 to the 'principles of international law embodied in the Charter of the United Nations'. Clearly therefore the 1969 Convention refers to the legal situation existing before the Charter. An abortive attempt was made by an important group of countries to push through a provision governing all forms of coercion. To give them at least moral satisfaction, the Conference adopted a Declaration on the Prohibition of Military, Political or Economic Coercion in the Conclusion of Treaties which was annexed to the Final Act of the Conference. This Declaration '[s]olemnly condemns the threat or use of pressure in any form, whether military, political, or economic ... in violation of the principles of the sovereign equality of States and freedom of consent' (*Official Records UNCLT, Documents of the Conference* (UN Pub., Sales No. E. 70.V.5), p. 285).

274 The difficulty in formulating the prohibition of coercion in practical terms was clearly apparent in the Declaration on Principles of International Law concerning Friendly Relations and Co-operation among States adopted by the General Assembly on 24 October 1970 (resolution 2625/XXV). The lengthy and confused part of this Declaration dealing with the principle of non-use of force apparently failed to confront directly the problems raised by the use of unarmed coercion, but the question was mentioned indirectly elsewhere, in particular in connection with the sovereign equality of States. It would seem reasonable to conclude from all these endeavours that what the Conventions have in mind from the point of view of treaty invalidity is armed coercion, and perhaps exceptionally unarmed physical coercion of an unmistakable nature (see in this respect the judgments of the International Court of Justice in the *Fisheries Jurisdiction* cases (*ICJ Reports 1973*, p. 14)). This is not to say that the possible use by some States or groups of States of their dominant economic position would not call for protective measures to prevent or restrict unfair market practices; but this is another matter which can only be dealt with in a firmly organized context such as UNCTAD or the European Communities.

B. APPLICATION OF THE RULE IN TIME

275 The actual wording used in the Conventions implies that the rule existed before the Charter entered into force. Since there is little doubt that most modern States, even new ones, were constituted or enlarged by the use of armed force in conditions which are no longer admissible today, it would seem particularly important to establish exactly when the rule came into force. This date would indeed determine in theory which treaties are too remote to be challenged and which should be eliminated; the importance of this point in the context of territorial treaties scarcely needs to be stressed. Article 4, which stipulates that both Conventions only apply to treaties concluded after their entry into force, has no bearing on the problem, since what is at stake here is a rule of general international law simply codified by article 52.

276 In its 1966 Report, the International Law Commission gave some indications on this point (*YILC 1966*, vol. II, pp. 246–247). The rule is said to have emerged from the League of Nations, the Pact of Paris for the renunciation of war, the treaties establishing international military tribunals, Article 2 (6) of the Charter, and United Nations practice; it has certainly been an established rule since the Charter and perhaps even before; moreover 'the Commission did not think that it was part of its function, in codifying the modern law of treaties, to specify on what precise date in the past an existing general rule in another branch of international law came to be established as such'. These indications of the Commission were borne out by the pronouncements of the International Court of Justice in the case concerning *Military and Paramilitary Activities in and against Nicaragua, Jurisdiction and Admissibility* (*ICJ Reports 1984*, p. 392) and *Merits* (*ICJ Reports 1986*, p. 14).

C. EFFECTS OF THE RULE

277 As in the previous case (coercion of a representative), the sanction is particularly heavy: all the provisions of the treaty are null and void and separability is excluded (article 45). The International Law Commission's 1966 commentary seems to imply that others beside the injured State might raise this ground of invalidity; in any case they have the right and even the obligation not to recognize a situation brought about by a treaty concluded in such circumstances (*YILC 1966*, vol. II, p. 247). Since the 1986 Convention, this applies also to international organizations. Should the victim of coercion wish to maintain in its favour all or part of the vitiated treaty, it cannot renounce the benefit of invalidity in any way. As with coercion of a representative, a new agreement of similar content must be concluded, a solution explicitly laid down by the Commission in its 1966 Report.

278 A possible difficulty might arise in this last case if it is argued, as some governments have done, that the prohibition of coercion constitutes a rule of *jus cogens* (see *YILC 1966*, vol. II, p. 247). Could it not be contended that, owing to its peremptory character, the rule in question precludes the revival in a new treaty of all or part of a treaty which infringed such a rule? As has just been noted, the Commission does not go so far, and this seems to be the right solution. Indeed a treaty freely agreed upon, containing provisions identical to those procured under duress, may be regarded as perfectly valid without for that matter running counter to the peremptory rule prohibiting certain forms of coercion.

7. Breach of a peremptory rule

279 The general problems raised by the concept of peremptory rules in the law of treaties were already dealt with earlier on (No. 219); something should now be said about the sanctions provided in articles 44, 45, 53, 64, 69 and 71. If the drafters of the Conventions had merely contemplated the simple case of a treaty concluded in breach of an existing peremptory rule, there would be no need to labour this point since none but the strictest rules would be applicable, i.e. separability is precluded, subsequent acceptance cannot validate the treaty, and its invalidity can be claimed by all the parties (there is actually no real 'victim' of the breach of a peremptory rule). Clearly, all this is beyond the scope of vitiated consent and would in fact rather seem to amount to sanctioning a criminal offence committed against the international community as a whole, especially if the new tendency to generalize the concept of 'international crimes' in the field of responsibility is taken into account.

280 But the Conventions also contemplate a very different type of situation apparently rooted in vague political aspirations, namely the effects of a *new* peremptory rule on existing treaties. Obviously, this is no longer a case of invalidity but a difficult question of intertemporal law. As has been pointed out earlier (see above, No. 151), a great deal of rigour and precision cannot be expected in this regard of formulations whose scope could only be determined on the basis of judicial practice. At any rate, the wording of article 71 (2) is not satisfactory (especially in the French version). Indeed it seeks at the same time firmly to proclaim that the termination of a given treaty has no retroactive effect and yet that rights, obligations or situations brought about by its correct application prior to its extinction are not allowed to survive inasmuch as their maintenance would be 'in itself in conflict with the new peremptory norm of general international law'. Instantaneous effects of the terminated treaty would accordingly survive, whereas permanent situations set up by it would lapse. Thus, for instance, if the right to self-determination were to be recognized by a peremptory rule, all the effects of territorial conquests confirmed in defiance of that right by treaties concluded prior to the entry into force of the 1969 Convention and before the emergence of this new rule would be set at nought. No doubt the laborious contradictions on the right to self-determination which are to be found in the 1970 Declaration on Friendly Relations and Co-operation among States show this to be a moot point. Ultimately the effects of *jus cogens* appear to be as uncertain as the concept itself.(*)

III Non-application of a treaty for extraneous reasons

281   Apart from the grounds of non-application previously presented in Chapter 3 and Section II of this chapter, a number of other grounds remain to be considered. All of them consist of mere facts and do not involve a juristic act. Of the two categories to be distinguished, the first includes grounds arising from the conduct of one or several parties to the treaty and entailing a question of responsibility; these will be discussed in Section IV below. The second category includes grounds arising independently of the will and conduct of the parties; with regard to the treaty and for the parties, they are extraneous grounds. They play an important part in municipal contract law, although with considerable differences from one legal system to another. International law, being less developed, only takes these grounds into consideration in two cases which will be reviewed in this section: impossibility of performance and fundamental change of circumstances.

1. Impossibility of performance

282   Impossibility to perform a treaty leads by definition to non-application, but this is only true if there is genuine impossibility. At first sight, this would appear to be the case strictly speaking only of material impossibility. That is probably why, in article 61, the Conventions merely refer to the case of 'the permanent disappearance or destruction of an object indispensable for the execution of the treaty'. In its 1966 Report, the International Law Commission gave as examples the submersion of an island, the drying-up of a river, and the destruction of a dam or hydro-electric installation when such objects are concerned by a treaty or involved in its performance. This is no doubt a sound basis to which it is always possible to revert, but which requires closer scrutiny and a wider perspective if a general picture is to be provided. The assessment should bear in turn on the object of the treaty, the theory of *force majeure* and the theory of responsibility.

283   The object of the treaty is a far broader concept than the 'object indispensable for the execution of the treaty' within the meaning of article 61. The object of the treaty is made up of all the obligations stipulated by the treaty, and it is in this wider sense that the Conventions, following the International Court of Justice, very often refer to the object and purpose of the treaty (see in particular No. 79 above). In this sense, the object of a treaty can be frustrated in a far greater variety of circumstances than by the mere loss of a physical object required to perform the treaty, e.g. extinction of one of the parties or coercion by a third State (for example interruption of an economic relationship essential to performance of the treaty). But these two situations, though quite relevant, raise difficult issues of State succession and the effect of hostilities on treaties; both issues were purposely left aside by the Conventions (article 73 of the 1969 Convention and article 74 (1) of the 1986 Convention), which in itself explains their relative discretion but emphasizes the need to go beyond the formulation of article 61. Thus under article 55 a multilateral treaty will normally remain in force even if the parties drop below the number required for its entry into force (see above, No. 218); yet the very number of withdrawals or even the weight of some withdrawals may frustrate its object and purpose, and thereby cause it to lapse.

284 In some cases therefore, one is led to rely on the doctrine of *force majeure*. This concept has three characteristics: *force majeure* must be irresistible, unforeseeable and external to the party relying on it; within that general framework it allows for a certain refinement of treaty theory. As it also provides one of the grounds of exemption for responsibility (a subject equally discarded by articles 73 of the 1969 Convention and 74 of the 1986 Convention), it was not even mentioned in the Conventions. As for the characteristics of *force majeure* which have just been listed, the judicial decisions concerning international responsibility would require a lengthy discussion; but, for reasons to be set forth further on, the theories of international responsibility and of treaties should as far as possible be kept apart. Only one observation will therefore be made here on the irresistibility of *force majeure*. The impossibility of performance must be absolute: this is the very essence of *force majeure* distinguishing it from neighbouring concepts, especially when it is considered in the context of treaties. However, it must be granted that international law allows some flexibility for this requirement in certain treaty systems governing international economic relations, which occasionally acknowledge (even using the term *force majeure*) that an impossibility may exist under criteria falling short of absolute material impossibility (some economic difficulties or unforeseen developments being assimilated to impossibility). But what is called *force majeure* in these cases serves in fact more as a safety valve.(*)

285 As will be shown later in Section IV, the points of contact and interactions between the theory of treaties and the theory of responsibility are both numerous and intricate. Still, they remain distinct sets of rules separated by a basic difference: the rules of the law of treaties chronologically and logically come first, or rather are *primary* rules, whereas the rules of responsibility come later, or in other words are *secondary*, applying only once a primary rule is breached. The rules concerning the impossibility of applying a treaty are primary rules, but there are secondary rules on responsibility which may *per se* lead to the non-application of a treaty. Examples have just been given above in connection with fraud and corruption (Nos. 261 and 264): the primary rules relating to the formation of consent might not by themselves justify invalidity in such cases, but since in addition there is a *breach* of international law, the treaty is declared invalid as a result of an unlawful act. Conversely, in some cases impossibility of performance is clearly established under primary rules, but its benefit cannot be claimed because it is due to the breach of an international obligation (article 61 (2)). The treaty will not, however, be performed since impossibility has been established. The final balance-sheet of the parties' rights and obligations following the termination of treaty relations will not be based on justified non-performance (article 70) but on unlawful non-performance.(*)

286 The effects of *force majeure* vary according to its permanence and scope. If it is temporary, it can only be invoked to suspend the treaty (article 61 (2)); if it is permanent, it can be invoked to withdraw from a treaty or to terminate it. Suspension or termination are effective from the moment impossibility arises, and not when *force majeure* is alleged. Indeed, *force majeure* is independent of any will of the parties; the only thing they can do is endure it, otherwise it would not be *force majeure*. In some cases, under the general principles codified in article 44, *force majeure* may also affect only part of the obligations in a treaty.(*)

2. Fundamental change of circumstances

287 A fundamental change of the circumstances prevailing when the treaty was concluded is a ground for termination or suspension (article 62). Long regarded as the effect of a condition subsequent implied in treaties (the *clausula rebus sic stantibus*), it is now seen as the effect of an autonomous ground of non-application. What distinguishes it from *force majeure* is the lack of irresistibility, although it possesses the other two features of *force majeure*, namely externality (a State cannot invoke a change which it has brought about by unlawful conduct) and unforeseeability (article 62 (1)).(*)

288 How should the change of circumstances be defined and established? This is one of the many issues of the law of treaties where, in spite of statements to the contrary, procedure does affect the substance. A liberal approach to non-application based on change of circumstances would go against the principle of the binding force of treaties; conversely, ruling out non-application in such cases would sever the law from social reality. If there were some authority above States, be it legislative, judicial or both, a number of satisfactory procedures might be devised, but there is no such authority in international law. The Covenant of the League of Nations included a specific provision (article 19) under which the Assembly was entitled to invite members 'to advise the reconsideration by Members of the League of treaties which have become inapplicable'; however, two attempts to implement this provision met with little success. No provision specially devoted to this matter is to be found in the Charter; instead, the general provisions on the settlement of disputes and the adjustment of situations endangering the maintenance of peace will apply, and hence the specific aspects of the issue are ignored. Nor has the question been frequently brought before international tribunals: when the allegation was not clearly regarded as unfounded, as in the *Fisheries Jurisdiction* cases (*ICJ Reports 1973*, p. 17), tribunals have seemed rather embarrassed by the subject, as in the *Free Zones* case (*PCIJ, Series A/B, No. 46*, p. 157).

289 Two aspects should be distinguished: the correct definition of change of circumstances and its effects. The first is easier to deal with. Obviously, to be taken into consideration, the change must be such as to upset radically the circumstances on the basis of which an agreement was concluded. This implies both a qualitative and a quantitative element. Qualitatively, the change must affect the very facts on which consent was based; this aspect of the law of treaties is somewhat analogous to the common law concept of 'consideration' and the civil law concept of '*causa*'. More clearly the Conventions specify that the circumstances must have constituted 'an essential basis of the consent of the parties to be bound by the treaty' (article 62 (1) (a)). From a quantitative point of view the change must be sufficiently far-ranging to alter completely the conditions of the agreement and affect its *raison d'être* or, as the Conventions put it, 'radically to transform the extent of obligations still to be performed under the treaty' (article 62 (1) (b)). Accordingly, two fundamental concepts are taken into account: 'consideration' ('*causa*' in civil law) and contractual balance.

290 There is hardly any theoretical reason why certain treaties should *a priori* escape a possible challenge due to a change of circumstances. Yet an exception seems traditionally to be made for treaties operating territorial settlements. The 1969 Convention, intent as usual on securing the position of the victors of World War II, also ruled out a treaty which 'establishes a boundary' (article 62 (2) (a)). If the whole of the law of treaties is to depend on interpreting the presumed intention of the parties, the exception will be easy enough to accept: there are in fact treaties the parties to which are quite reasonably held *ab initio* to have excluded any challenge based on change of circumstances, and treaties concerning territorial settlements are a good example of this. The territory defines the very essence of the State; it can therefore be presumed that the parties intended to disregard any subsequent change of circumstances. One might perhaps add that in a more sophisticated state of international law, the only changes which could lead to a modification of territorial sovereignty would derive from the right to self-determination; unfortunately it is difficult to accept that this principle of political ethics has already been incorporated into the precise set of rules and institutions which would be required in order to endow it with a legal character. The 1986 Convention, though following in article 62 the wording of the 1969 Convention, restricted the exception contained in paragraph 2 (a) to boundary treaties between 'two or more States and one or more international organizations', thereby apparently implying that two States at least are needed to establish a boundary by treaty. This formulation, which was accepted after lengthy debates within the International Law Commission, is still in line with the powers that international organizations are currently recognized to enjoy, although the situation may change in the future. Furthermore neither Convention had to determine whether any doctrine of fundamental change of circumstances should apply to unilateral acts of international institutions such as judicial decisions, or to customary rules.

291   In any case, to determine whether a treaty can be challenged on the grounds of a change of circumstances, a series of appraisals are needed which should be conducted objectively and therefore might depend upon the decision of a judicial authority. There is nothing to prevent States or international organizations from bringing such a case before an international tribunal. It is true, however, that some treaties are essentially prompted by political situations, and it is difficult to ask a judicial body to decide whether a fundamental change has indeed occurred in this field. For instance, assuming that in 1966 France's denunciation of certain agreements concluded under the 1949 North Atlantic Treaty was justified only by a change of political circumstances, it would still be difficult to submit the matter to judicial assessment. But except for treaties containing mainly political commitments such as the North Atlantic Treaty, it remains true that if States so wish there is no technical obstacle to prevent a judicial appraisal of the change of circumstances.(*)

292   The effect of the change of circumstances as defined above is the termination of the treaty, which is easy to understand: a radical change calls for a radical consequence. The Conventions only allow one milder effect: a party entitled to claim termination or to withdraw may, if it so desires, only claim suspension. In any case, despite the cautious wording of the Conventions and the procedure laid down in article 65, the decision will be taken unilaterally. This is not a satisfactory solution. It is also reasonable to believe that in many cases treaties could be maintained by introducing changes negotiated by the parties. Yet this perspective is so alarming for the stability of treaties that it was not contemplated by the International Law Commission or by the Conventions. This can be explained partly on historical grounds. World War II originated in a claim for revision of the treaties concluded at the end of World War I. Not only was the word 'revision' therefore banished from the law of treaties, but no attempt was made to transfer to international law all the concepts enabling municipal systems to achieve a better contractual balance by adapting their contracts (e.g. the doctrine of *imprévision*). The key to any improvement of international law in this field lies in the recourse to international justice and it is worth trying to see how a development could be achieved in this direction.

293   Instead of describing fundamental change of circumstances as extinguishing a treaty *de plano*, it would be more accurate to say that it entails for the parties concerned an obligation to negotiate. But what if negotiations fail? As has just been stated, in such a case, after a brief period the Conventions leave the question to the discretion of the parties. They therefore prevent neither a unilaterally proclaimed termination nor a refusal by the other party to recognize this unilateral decision. One could, however, go further, as indeed France did in the *Free Zones* case before the Permanent Court of International Justice. France accepted the provisional authority of an established title (*provision est due au titre*), and hence the validity of the treaty pending recognition of the change of circumstances 'by some effective transaction fixing the legal position between the States concerned', i.e. either 'an agreement recognizing the change of circumstances and its effect on the treaty or a decision by an international judicial authority if there is one'. This theory, interesting though it may be, can hardly pass muster unless bolstered by an international judicial authority. In the *Free Zones* case, the Court was not satisfied that a fundamental change of circumstances had occurred; but it is still useful to pursue this line of thought and try to assess the role an international judge might play if he were to exist.

294 This again raises more fundamentally the question of the effect of a fundamental change of circumstances. In some cases the change is so far-reaching that no adjustment of the treaty commitment is possible or even conceivable. This will usually be the case with political treaties. A fundamental change of circumstances cannot but terminate the treaty and a tribunal is perfectly entitled to draw such a conclusion. If, in the absence of a tribunal, the decision were made unilaterally, it would be purely declaratory, and termination would take effect as from the time when the fundamental change of circumstances occurred.

295 Yet such a drastic conclusion is not always unavoidable: a treaty may be disrupted in its general structure or its very purpose and still be adjustable to a new situation without wholly disappearing. Should this case be assimilated to the previous one, the parties concerned being trusted to adopt the necessary changes? Or should the treaty not rather be deemed to remain in force until they have negotiated the relevant adjustments? Negotiations can only fail as a result of one of the parties' intransigence. In that case, a court could in no way itself decide what changes the treaty should undergo, for such power is clearly not part of the judicial function; but it could either pronounce the treaty terminated if the State whose interest it was to maintain it in force had failed to comply with its obligation to negotiate; or it could on the contrary declare that the treaty remains in force if the State seeking modification has not fully discharged its duty to negotiate. Such solutions could rely on the judicial precedents of the *Lake Lanoux* or the *North Sea Continental Shelf* cases (see above, No. 109*) as well as on a number of transnational arbitrations (e.g. *Kuwait v. Aminoil, ILM*, 1982, p. 976); they do, however, imply a clear infringement of the duty to negotiate, a condition which will seldom be fulfilled in fact.

IV The law of treaties and international responsibility

296   The idea of providing exhaustively, in a single convention on the law of treaties, for all the consequences of a breach of treaty obligations was never envisaged by the authors of the codification, nor has it been advocated by subsequent commentators. As has been pointed out, the 1969 Convention (article 73) does 'not prejudge any question that may arise... from the international responsibility of a State...' and the same solution was adopted by the 1986 Convention (article 74 (1) and (2)) with regard to international organizations. Such a division between the law of treaties and the law of responsibility is in the nature of things and commends itself for practical reasons. International responsibility relates to the breach of obligations and its general principles are the same, whatever the source of the obligation (treaty, custom, or unilateral act). Moreover, in view of the material restrictions faced by codification conferences, it is preferable wherever possible not to cover too extensive a subject-matter in the same instrument. Nevertheless, the distinction between these two branches of general international law cannot be absolute: not only do they border on each other but in several instances they overlap, which is why certain aspects of international responsibility referred to in the 1969 and 1986 Conventions should also be dealt with here.(*)

297   Some of the possible consequences of a breach of the obligations relating to negotiation (see above, Nos. 67, 110 and 295) or conclusion (see above, Nos. 242, 258, 261, 265, 268, 271 and 279) of treaties have already been mentioned, more particularly in connection with invalidity. As has been shown, the rules concerning invalidity of treaties do not exclusively derive from the principles of consensualism but to a great extent take into account the various elements involved in the parties' responsibility as well as the sanction of basic rules governing the international community. We shall not come back to this point. Yet some general aspects of the law of responsibility, concerning especially the consequences of wrongful acts, are quite closely linked to the law of treaties: both branches pursue an identical goal which is to contain as far as possible the effects of the anarchical structure of international society. They could be said to converge, as indeed the history of codification tends to show. Some rules were laid down in article 60 of the 1969 Vienna Convention whose scope was subsequently expanded by the 1986 Convention. The principles and aims which gave rise to article 60 were restated and extended after 1982 in the second part of the International Law Commission's work on the international responsibility of States, dealing as it does with its 'content, form and degrees', i.e. with the consequences of the attribution to a State of a wrongful act.

298   A wrongful act is in itself a disturbance which has to be stopped, repaired and, in the worst cases, according to modern views on international responsibility, punished. But its negative consequences go further than the breach of an obligation: beyond the actual *obligation,* a wrongful act may affect the very *source* of the obligation, the rule from which it derives. Indeed, under the general principles of responsibility, it is up to the injured State to react to the wrongful act; if the defaulting State is not willing to put an end to the offence and repair the damage, the injured State will take measures which can consist in refusal to perform some of its own obligations. Such measures are likely to be challenged by the defaulting State which in turn may take other measures. There is therefore a risk that non-performance will spread from the initial obligation to such others as are connected to it and to others still further afield. Third States not concerned by the initial offence may become involved in the escalation. When performance of the obligations can simply be suspended, the normal course of legal relations may be re-established, but the obligations can also disappear permanently if their actual source is affected, and this will be the case in particular for obligations deriving from a treaty. A bilateral treaty may be regarded by the injured State as definitively extinct following the breach of its stipulations. With multilateral treaties, the injured State can simply withdraw. What limits could be set to the discretionary power of the States in this regard? Technically speaking, the problem is a complex one, and politically it involves State sovereignty; on the level of codification, it was first considered in relation to the law of treaties (article 60 of both Conventions), and was later taken up again directly with regard to the law of responsibility which, by its more general and thorough approach, emphasized some of the difficulties raised by article 60.

299   Article 60 is basically simple and its mechanisms easily described. Fundamentally, the draft proposals of the International Law Commission aimed at saving what deserved above all to be saved in the process following the breach of a treaty, namely the treaty itself. To that effect, the Commission made a general distinction and went on to deal with the most important case, that of multilateral treaties.

300   The distinction bears on 'material' and 'other' breaches. Material breaches may constitute 'a ground for terminating the treaty or suspending its operation in whole or in part'. Article 60 does not state what the possible consequences of a non-material breach would be. This silence makes it necessary to refer back to the general principles of responsibility under which certain measures taken by way of reciprocity are not precluded; such measures will appear justifiable for a State which considers itself injured, amounting as they do to a suspension of the performance of the infringed obligation or of some equivalent undertaking. If for instance a bilateral consular convention exempts consuls from paying certain taxes and one State applies this immunity according to its own interpretation, the other State may challenge this interpretation as contrary to the treaty, yet apply it immediately by way of reciprocity to the consuls of the first State while maintaining its own interpretation: therefore although compliance with an obligation is suspended, there is normally no breach of the treaty. In English legal terminology the word 'breach' (which is stronger than its French counterpart *'violation'*) reinforced by the epithet 'material' only covers, under article 60 (3), '(a) a repudiation of the treaty not sanctioned by the present Convention; or (b) the violation of a provision essential to the accomplishment of the object or purpose of the treaty'.(*)

301 With regard to bilateral treaties, article 60 (1) entitles the injured party 'to invoke the breach as a ground for terminating the treaty or suspending its operation in whole or in part'. With multilateral treaties things are more complex. Article 60 (2) provides three types of measures: a collective measure, which alone can lead to termination, and two individual measures applying in different situations. The collective measure is the more challenging and innovative one. It is based on the assumption that the parties to a multilateral treaty are all united by a common interest and form an inchoate legal community entrusted with the administration and management of the treaty; the party which has committed a material breach is precluded from taking any part in a decision on the consequences of its act, but the other parties are entitled by unanimous consent to take whatever measure they think appropriate, i.e. to 'suspend the operation of the treaty in whole or in part or to terminate it either: (i) in the relations between themselves and the defaulting State or international organization, or (ii) as between all the parties'. The party 'specially affected by the breach' is only entitled to suspend the operation of the treaty in whole or in part in the relations between itself and the defaulting party. As for integral treaties (see above, No. 82), any party other than the defaulting one is only entitled to suspend the operation of the treaty in whole or in part with respect to itself; but if its appraisal is felt to be well founded, the other parties, apart from the defaulting one, are likely to follow suit, and once the situation becomes permanent they will concur in terminating the treaty.(*)

302 Under the 1966 draft of the International Law Commission these rules were to apply only in the absence of stipulations to the contrary in the treaty. But before considering the provision as it was eventually drawn up by the Vienna Conference of 1968–1969, a few general observations should be made about the trends which have emerged in legal thinking and especially in the work of the Commission. The convergence of efforts and the similarity of legal techniques is striking. And how could it have been otherwise? The purpose of international responsibility is to sanction the law, not to abolish it. *Restitutio in integrum,* which remains its foremost aim when it is materially possible, satisfies the same fundamental concerns as the 1969 Convention. The chronological sequence of the Commission's work spells out the unity of its efforts in both fields. It was just after the 1968–1969 Conference that the Commission, with Professor Ago as Special Rapporteur, embarked on the first part of its draft articles on State responsibility for internationally wrongful acts. The first reading of the 35 draft articles constituting Part I was approved by the Commission in 1980 (*YILC 1980,* vol. II (part 2), pp. 26 ff.), just as the 1969 Vienna Convention entered into force, and Professor Riphagen was appointed Special Rapporteur for the second and third parts of the topic, concerning the 'content, form and degrees of State responsibility' and the 'implementation of international responsibility and settlement of disputes'. While the Commission, for lack of time, has so far done no more than consider the draft articles presented by the Special Rapporteur, these articles nevertheless closely reflect present trends in codification.

303 These new trends are leading towards a system of international responsibility which is both more substantial and less homogeneous than before. Yet is that not precisely what can be observed everywhere in municipal law? In varying degrees, depending on the period and country, the law of responsibility consists, on the one hand, of a number of quite heterogeneous parts, on the other, of certain general unifying principles which help to coordinate the most diverse elements and to provide bases upon which to resolve newly arising problems. Present-day international law certainly inclines towards the diversification of the various régimes of international responsibility: international crimes as opposed to ordinary international torts ('international delicts') (article 19 of Part I of the draft articles on the internationally wrongful act of a State), the emergence of a régime of liability for activities which are not unlawful, the international criminal responsibility of individuals, etc. Even apart from these developments which would each constitute a new type of responsibility, it may be observed on a more restricted scale that responsibility is increasingly diversified according to the obligations it is supposed to sanction. This trend is already perceptible in the 1969 Vienna Convention (and later in the 1986 Convention) whenever it touches upon questions of responsibility, for it takes into account the object and character of the obligation breached. Whether implicitly (invalidity for coercion against a party or its representative: articles 51 and 52), or in more general if unspecific terms (invalidity for breach of a peremptory rule: article 53), or again in more restrictive though still uncertain terms (special régime for provisions of a humanitarian character: article 60 (5)), an emerging distinction is noticeable between international rules according to their *importance* and their *value*. This evolution was soon confirmed in Part I of the draft articles on international responsibility (article 19) which introduces for the most serious wrongful acts the concept of 'international crime' without yet determining its legal consequences. In 1980, in the case of *United States Diplomatic and Consular Staff in Tehran* (*ICJ Reports 1980*, pp. 40 and 41), the International Court of Justice asserted 'the fundamental character of the principle of inviolability' with regard to the premises of a diplomatic mission and to the immunity of its members, as well as 'the imperative character of the legal obligations incumbent upon the Iranian Government', and it based its decision in part on this consideration. The trend is thus unmistakable, however uncertain its practical consequences and legal articulation may still be. In his draft articles on the second part of the topic of State responsibility presented to the International Law Commission, Professor Riphagen endeavoured to clarify these elements and to build them into a synthetic framework.(*)

304 It may be useful to recall the essential elements of Professor Riphagen's draft articles 8 to 12 in order to clarify the scope of article 60 and especially paragraph 5. The Special Rapporteur began with an essential distinction according to whether suspension of performance concerns obligations which 'correspond to, or are directly connected with, the obligation breached', or other obligations. In the former case, action is taken by the injured State 'by way of reciprocity' (article 8); in the latter, the effects of the suspension must not 'be manifestly disproportional to the seriousness of the internationally wrongful act committed' (article 9) and the injured State must have exhausted all possible means of reaching a peaceful settlement (article 10). But in either case such suspension will hardly apply to a great number of obligations. For one thing, certain types of obligations in multilateral treaties cannot be suspended, such as integral obligations, obligations safeguarding the collective interests of the parties, or obligations protecting individuals irrespective of their nationality (article 11 (1)). This amounts to laying down a presumption of what the parties intended; if adopted, these articles would go further, except for integral obligations, than article 60 of the 1969 and 1986 Conventions, where these points are left to be freely determined by the parties in the treaty itself. Nevertheless, in theory at least, there is nothing in these draft articles to prevent the presumption from being reversed by an explicit treaty provision. The Special Rapporteur, relying on the idea of peremptory rules, went on to state (article 12) that obligations deriving from such rules cannot be suspended either by way of reciprocity (article 8) or by way of counter-measures (article 9). The injured State thus has to grant the defaulting State the benefit of a peremptory rule even if it has been infringed to its detriment.(*)

305 These proposals, on which the Commission was divided, go further than the 1969 and 1986 Conventions, without prejudice to what will be said further on about article 60 (5). Yet they follow the lines and spirit of these Conventions. Clearly article 60 and other provisions of the Conventions were one of the main sources of inspiration for the Special Rapporteur. The development of the law of international responsibility as contemplated by the draft articles is highly desirable. These articles do, however, constitute a 'development' of present international law, owing to the very precision and firmness of the rules providing for the right to suspend certain obligations. No doubt, States are ready to recognize some necessary relationship between breaches of the law and the reactions thereto; they are ready to forgo part of their freedom in that field through particular stipulations; but they are reluctant to subscribe to general commitments and usually deny courts or organizations any say in their application. As for peremptory rules, their origin, régime and effects still remain to be determined. A relatively recent occurrence demonstrates how much caution must be exercised when appraising the prospects for developing the law of State responsibility. On 26 April 1986, the Soviet Union, soon followed by other socialist countries, acceded to the 1969 Vienna Convention with substantial reservations under a Declaration appended to its accession in which it 'reserve[d] the right to take any measures to safeguard its interests in the event of the non-observance by other States of the provisions of the Vienna Convention on the Law of Treaties'. Objections were raised by the United Kingdom on 3 April and by Japan on 5 June 1987. This highlights the links between the Vienna Convention and international responsibility as well as the great reluctance of major States to accept ahead of time in a general form even slight limitations on their ability to react to what they consider a breach of the law.(*)

306   The interpretation of article 60 (5) of the 1969 Convention (restated by the 1986 Convention) provides an eloquent illustration of the prevailing tensions in the development of international law and in the legal thinking which is striving to order it. This provision is controversial with regard both to its legal basis and to its scope. Concerning its *legal basis,* it has been viewed — and this is the most straightforward solution — as merely conventional: by declaring that paragraphs 1 to 3 do not apply to certain provisions of some categories of treaties, paragraph 5 lays down the presumption that the parties to such treaties intended a different régime to apply, and it illustrates this at once by giving the example of provisions prohibiting any form of reprisals against persons protected by treaties of a humanitarian character. But for many commentators paragraph 5 must be read in the light of the existence of peremptory rules; hence positions vary according to the possible conceptions of such rules. Some hold that article 60 (5) spells out an already existing peremptory rule, thereby reinforcing the idea that such rules create obligations which cannot be suspended either on the grounds of reciprocity or by way of reprisals; others for whom a rule cannot derive its peremptory character from a conventional mechanism, hold that article 60 (5) merely reiterates the possibility for the parties to a treaty to stipulate in each convention that some of its provisions cannot be suspended by way of reprisals, as provided by the relevant provisions of humanitarian conventions.(*)

307   Similar differences prevail as to the *scope* of article 60 (5). What are 'treaties of a humanitarian character' and 'provisions relating to the protection of the human person'? In view of the origin of this provision which was proposed by the Swiss Government and inspired by the International Committee of the Red Cross, it might be considered only to cover a rather narrow field. But again a great many equally controversial extensions can be thought of, depending on whether the legal basis of this provision is seen as conventional or as founded on a peremptory rule. Two somewhat related examples may be given. Even though humanitarian law concerns first and foremost armed conflicts, it also involves human rights, and article 60 (5) has been claimed also to cover the protection of human rights in the most general terms. It may be noted in this regard that no measure of suspension taken by way of reciprocity or of reprisals would be admissible in the European system, whether in the European Court of

Human Rights or in the Court of Justice of the European Communities. Another example concerns nuclear weapons, i.e. both atmospheric nuclear tests and the use of nuclear weapons as such. An unsuccessful attempt was made during the negotiation of the Protocols additional to the 1949 Geneva Conventions to secure a universal prohibition of the use of nuclear weapons on a conventional basis; but such a prohibition was also advocated on the basis of peremptory norms whose existence was asserted to some degree on the strength of article 60 (5). These attempts contributed in some countries to discredit the concept of *jus cogens;* they certainly emphasized the permanence of the problem raised by nuclear disarmament; but they have so far not succeeded in bringing about any such prohibition on a legally defined basis accepted by all.(*)

Notes

233* There was some hesitation on the problems dealt with in art. 56, both within the ILC and at the 1968–1969 Vienna Conference (H.W. Briggs, 'Unilateral denunciation of treaties', *AJ,* vol. 68 (1974), p. 51). The question was what kind of presumption should be established: should reference be made simply to the intention of the parties (art. 53 of the ILC draft: *YILC 1966,* vol. II, p. 250) or is it possible to rely on more objective criteria (Report by the Special Rapporteur, Sir Gerald Fitzmaurice, *YILC 1957,* vol. II, p. 22; 1963 draft art. 39: *YILC 1963,* vol. II, pp. 67 and 200)?

The text finally adopted takes into account both the parties' intention and the 'nature of the treaty'. For the actual determination of this 'nature', see in particular Sir Humphrey Waldock's demonstration that no conclusion should be drawn from the absence of any denunciation clause in general codification treaties (*YILC 1966,* vol. II, pp. 250–251), relying mainly on a comparison between the opposite solutions adopted in the 1958 Geneva Conventions on the Law of the Sea or the Vienna Conventions on Diplomatic and Consular Relations on the one hand, and in the 1949 Geneva Conventions and the Genocide Convention on the other. At the 1968–1969 Vienna Conference, statements by Cuba and Spain based on well-known specific concerns identified, among the treaties where withdrawal or denunciation is possible in any case, agreements concerning bases, unequal treaties, treaties of alliance and trade agreements; the Soviet Union excluded peace and boundary treaties. In the *Fisheries Jurisdiction* cases (*ICJ Reports 1973,* p. 14), the Court mentioned, without considering it in depth, the question of whether treaties on judicial settlement or declarations of acceptance of its compulsory jurisdiction might by their nature be denounced unilaterally in the absence of an express provision concerning their duration; the question also arose in connection with the headquarters agreements of international organizations in the procedure relating to the Advisory Opinion on the *Interpretation of the Agreement of 25 March 1951 between the WHO and Egypt (ICJ Reports 1980,* p. 73). See K. Widdows, 'The unilateral denunciation of treaties containing no denunciation clause', *BYBIL,* vol. 53 (1982), p. 83.

As for *constitutional* rules relating to denunciation, they vary from country to country, but the right to denounce is generally vested in the Executive when it possesses discretionary treaty-making power; for the United States, see Ch. Rousseau, *RGDIP,* vol. 24 (1980), p. 613, and for the 'derecognition' of Taiwan, see D.J. Sheffer, *Harvard International Law Review,* vol. 19 (1978), p. 931, and A. Manin, *AF,* vol. 26 (1980), p. 141.

The observance of a reasonable period of notice had already been proposed by Sir Gerald Fitzmaurice in the ILC, and the period prescribed in art. 56 (2) is based on the Havana Convention on the Law of Treaties (*Sixth International Conference of American States, Final Act,* Havana, 1928, p. 135).

Whether the mention of an unlimited period amounts to a perpetual undertaking or not depends on the circumstances; for the interpretation of art. 240 of the EEC Treaty, see P. Reuter, *Organisations européennes* (Paris, PUF, 1965), pp. 231 and 285, and case No. 7/71, *ECR 1971,* p. 1018, para. 19.

234* For instance, in relation to desuetude, which was rather hastily equated with a tacit agreement (art. 54 of the 1969 Convention, see above, No. 217) by the general report of the ILC (*YILC 1966,* vol. II, p. 237), or to succession of States (see No. 173). Another point was whether complete performance of a treaty having produced all its effects was a cause of 'termination'. On this question, see the report by S. Rosenne ('Terminaison des traités collectifs') in *Annuaire de l'Institut de Droit international,* vol. 52-I (1967), p. 25, as well as the observations by Fitzmaurice, Morelli, Briggs and Castrén.

237* At the Institute of International Law (ibid., p. 290), Morelli criticized the term 'suspension de l'application', preferring 'suspension des effets' and later 'suspension du traité'.

238* S. Rosenne in his aforementioned report emphasized the innovative character of this wider use of suspension; see also Lord McNair, *The Law of Treaties,* p. 573. On the question of suspension of certain economic obligations, see P. Reuter, *Droit international public,* p. 163, and *Organisations européennes,* p. 197, and A. Manin, 'A propos des clauses de sauvegarde', *Revue trimestrielle de droit européen,* vol. 6 (1970), p. 1.

239* and 240* On the question of validity, see the still fundamental studies by J. Verzijl, 'La validité et la nullité des actes juridiques internationaux', *Revue de droit international,* vol. 15 (1935), p. 284, and especially P. Guggenheim, 'La validité et la nullité des actes juridiques internationaux', *RCADI,* vol. 74 (1949-I), p. 191; see also Ph. Cahier, 'Les caractéristiques de la nullité en droit international public et tout particulièrement dans la Convention de Vienne de 1969 sur le droit des traités', *RGDIP,* vol. 76 (1972), p. 645; J. Verhoeven, *Les nullités du droit des gens* (Paris, Pedone, 1981).

241* and 242* Judicial decisions have been mentioned on separability, but only with regard to interpretation (see above, No. 194); moreover, they are scarcely conclusive (*PCIJ, Series A, No 1,* p. 24 and *Series A/B, No. 46,* p. 140). As for doctrinal opinions on such alleged cases of partial invalidity, they mainly stem from Judge Lauterpacht, who was not followed by the ICJ (*Norwegian Loans, ICJ Reports 1957,* p. 55, and *Interhandel, ICJ Reports 1959,* pp. 57, 77 and 116). See P. de Meuse, *La divisibilité des traités internationaux* (Thesis, Paris II, 1977) and P. Reuter, 'Solidarité et divisibilité des engagements conventionnels', *Studies in Honor of Shabtai Rosenne* (to be published).

246* Certain statements made at the Vienna Conference, especially on articles 39, 62 and 62 *bis* of the draft articles, indicate that an international organization entitled to act on behalf of the international community might also be entitled to challenge the validity of a treaty (see below, Nos. 254, 263 and 265). Links between the substantive aspects of invalidity and the corresponding procedures to establish invalidity were discussed during the 1968–1969 Vienna Conference. During the first session, at the 39th meeting, Australia (*Official Records UNCLT, I, Summary Records...*, Committee of the Whole, para. 13, p. 216) referred to the 'indissoluble link between the question of settlement machinery and the substantive grounds for invalidity'; Cuba and the United Kingdom (paras. 21, p. 217, and 26, p. 218) commented on the distinction between absolute and relative invalidity; New Zealand (para. 38, p. 219) held that art. 39 lays down a presumption of validity; the Soviet Union (para. 55, p. 220) stated that invalidity is absolute only in the case of articles 48 to 50, while in the other cases treaties are merely voidable. At the 40th meeting, after a clarification by Denmark (para. 9, p. 222), Sweden (paras. 18–21, p. 223) insisted on the need to *establish* invalidity; the Expert Consultant (para. 66, p. 227) emphasized the distinction between invalidity of consent and invalidity of the treaty as laid down in arts. 49 and 50. At the 68th meeting, reverting to the links between arts. 39 and 62, Japan (para. 5, p. 402) claimed that questions of *jus cogens* involved the interests of the entire community of nations and could not be the subject of a limited settlement; France (paras. 9 ff., p. 402) again referred to the distinction in the draft articles between absolute invalidity (arts. 48 to 50 and 61) and relative invalidity (arts. 43 to 47); the United States (para. 49, p. 406) explained the scope of the Annex on the settlement of disputes. At the 69th meeting, the Soviet Union (paras. 57–58, p. 413) criticized the compulsory settlement of disputes; and Israel (para. 65, pp. 413–414) opposed the Japanese view. Finally the general debate was held at the 71st to 74th, 80th and 83rd meetings and, during the second session, at the 92nd to 98th meetings of the Committee of the Whole, and at the 25th to 30th plenary meetings. See R.J. Dupuy, 'Codification et règlement des différends. Les débats de Vienne sur les procédures de règlement', *AF,* vol. 15 (1969), p. 70; S. Rosenne, 'The settlement of treaty disputes under the Vienna Convention of 1969', *ZaöRV,* vol. 31 (1971), p. 1.

247* This kind of moratory period is reminiscent of the method used by the Bryan Treaties. Explicit legal justification of unilateral acts as a controlling factor is continuously expanding in the most varied fields of international law, e.g. when States refuse to introduce certain regulations proposed by specialized agencies (ICAO, WHO), or in cases of denunciation as contemplated by treaties relating to the non-dissemination of nuclear weapons or to the demilitarization of the sea-bed. Of course, in integrated organizations such as the European Communities, explicit legal justification plays a still greater role on account of a complete and strict system of judicial review of the legality of regulations and decisions taken by the organs of the Communities. M. Gounelle, *La motivation des actes juridiques en droit international public* (Paris, Pedone, 1979).

Whether art. 65 (3) of the 1969 Convention involves the loss of the right to object to a measure taken after the expiry of the three-month period is debatable. In its final Report of 1982, the ILC had advocated a clear-cut negative solution for the new Convention by means of a slight change of wording, but the Conference reverted to the 1969 version.

248*–250* In fact the dispute, which threatened the 1969 Convention had distinct political overtones; P. Reuter, *La Convention de Vienne sur le droit des traités,* p. 24.

251* G. Wenner, *Willensmängel im Völkerrecht* (Zurich, Polygraphischer Verlag, 1940); P. Reuter, 'La nature des vices du consentement dans la Convention de Vienne sur le droit des traités', *Liber Amicorum Elie van Bogaert* (Antwerp, Kluwer, 1985), p. 203.

252* The uncertainty of the practice appears for instance with respect to the definition of *inexistence* as distinct from invalidity (P. Guggenheim, *RCADI*, vol. 74 (1949-I), p. 191, and G. Morange, 'Nullité et inexistence en Droit international public', *La technique et les principes du droit public. Etudes en l'honneur de Georges Scelle* (Paris, Sirey, 1950), vol. II, p. 895. Practice does, however, resort to the concept: see Court of Justice of the European Communities, cases 1/57 and 14/57, *ECR 1957–1958*, p. 105; case of the Munich agreement (Y. Zourek, 'Annulation ou inexistence', in P. Reuter, *La Convention de Vienne sur le droit des traités*, p. 80); Advisory Opinion in the *Namibia* case (*ICJ Reports 1971*, p. 22, para. 20); G. Morelli, 'Aspetti processuali della invalidità dei trattati', *Rivista di diritto internazionale*, vol. 57 (1974), p. 5.

256* To the references listed above at 40*, add, for an analysis of the rather inconclusive international case-law, *YILC 1966*, vol. II, p. 241; Ph. Cahier, 'La violation du droit interne relatif à la compétence pour conclure des traités comme cause de nullité des traités', *Rivista di diritto internazionale*, vol. 54 (1971), p. 226; Th. Meron, 'Article 46 of the Vienna Convention on the Law of Treaties (*ultra vires* treaties): some recent cases', *BYBIL*, vol. 49 (1978), p. 175.

258* International practice is especially abundant concerning errors due to insufficient geographical knowledge relating to treaties on territorial questions, and above all measures taken to apply such treaties. The most important cases are: *Legal Status of Eastern Greenland, PCIJ, Series A/B, No. 53; Temple of Preah Vihear, Preliminary Objections, ICJ Reports 1961*, p. 30 (error of law); and *Temple of Preah Vihear, Merits, ICJ Reports 1962*, p. 26. Although it is a vitiating factor for any legal instrument, error is of course subject to quite different rules in unilateral, especially jurisdictional, acts; see *Arbitral Award Made by the King of Spain on 23 December 1906, ICJ Reports 1960*, p. 216. See also Decision of 14 March 1978 in the *Case concerning the Delimitation of the Continental Shelf between the United Kingdom and France* (interpretation of decision of 30 June 1977), *RIÂA*, vol. 18, p. 271.

261* Concerning the Munich agreement and the disagreement between Germany and Czechoslovakia in this connection, see the references listed above at No. 238*, and the following: J. Markus, 'Le traité germano-tchécoslovaque du 15 mars 1939 à la lumière du droit international', *RGDIP*, vol. 46 (1939), p. 653; Ch. Rousseau, 'L'accord de Munich et le droit international', *Casopis pro mezinárodní právo*, 1966, p. 105; and P. Dmochowski, *Le statu quo en Europe centrale et sa normalisation* (Thesis, Paris II, 1979).

272* H.G. de Jong, 'Coercion in the conclusion of treaties', *Netherlands Yearbook of International Law*, vol. 15 (1984), p. 209; A. Holmback, 'Principles of international morality (unequal treaties)', *37th Conference of the Interparliamentary Union (1948);* M.H. Haekal, 'Les traités inégaux', *Revue égyptienne de droit international*, vol. 5 (1949), p. 1; A.N. Talalayev and V.G. Boyarshinov, 'Unequal treaties as a mode of prolonging the colonial dependence of the new States of Asia and Africa', *Soviet Year-Book of International Law*, vol. 4 (1961), p. 156; A. Lester, 'Bizerta and the unequal treaty theory', *ICLQ*, vol. 11 (1962), p. 847; E. Kordt, 'Ungleicher Vertrag und Annexion im sozialistischen Völkerrecht und in der Staatenpraxis sozialistischer Länder', *Festschrift Hermann Jahrreis* (Cologne, Heymann, 1964); I. Detter, 'The problem of unequal treaties', *ICLQ*, vol. 15 (1966), p. 1069. According to G. Napoletano, *Violenza e trattati nel diritto internazionale* (Milan, Giuffrè, 1977), inequality constitutes in fact a presumption of violence in a wider sense.

280* The French version of article 64 ('tout traité existant qui est en conflit avec cette norme devient nul et prend fin') involves a contradiction in terms.

284* A Mexican proposal to extend art. 61 to all cases of *force majeure* was rejected by the Vienna Conference for fear of seriously undermining the security of treaty relations between States. *Force majeure* regarded as a justification from the point of view of responsibility was considered by the ILC in particular in connection with draft art. 31 on responsibility presented by Professor Ago (ILC Report, *YILC 1979*, vol. II (part 2), p. 122). The ILC Secretariat conducted a survey of practice in ' *"Force majeure"* and "fortuitous event" as circumstances precluding wrongfulness', *YILC 1978*, vol. II, (part 1), p. 61. See also above, No. 224*, and P. Reuter, *Droit international public*, p. 255.

285* For all the questions of principle raised here, see the Reports of Professor Riphagen on State responsibility: Second Report, *YILC 1981*, vol. II (part 1), p. 79; Third Report, *YILC 1982*, vol. II (part 1), p. 22; Fourth Report, *YILC 1983*, vol. II (part 1), p. 3; Fifth Report, *YILC 1984*, vol. II (part 1), p. 1; Sixth Report, *YILC 1985*, vol. II (part 1), p. 3; *YILC 1986*, vol. II (part 1), p. 1.

286* The effect produced as from the moment *force majeure* comes into existence must not be confused with the procedural duties which the States concerned might have to observe, especially under the Vienna Conventions; see *YILC 1966*, vol. II, p. 256.

287* Among the modern precedents which do not result from judicial decisions, the French Chamber of Deputies' Resolution of 14 December 1932 concerning international debts arising out of World War I is often cited. Many internal judicial decisions have been rendered in federal States concerning interprovincial treaty relations (*YILC 1966*, vol. II, p. 257, footnote 253). At the PCIJ, the question was raised in several cases: *Nationality Decrees Issued in Tunis and Morocco, Series B, No. 4 (Series C, No. 2*, pp. 187 and 208); *Denunciation of the Treaty of 2 November 1865 between China and Belgium, Series A, No. 16 (Series C, No. 16-I*, p. 52); *Free Zones of Upper Savoy and the District of Gex, Series A/B, No. 46, (Series C, No. 17-I*, pp. 89, 250, 283, 443, *No. 19-I*, pp. 67–70, 192, 324–326, 383–389, and *No. 58*, pp. 109–113, 405–416, 463, 586). In the *Free Zones* case, the PCIJ only gave its view on a limited number of points, since it considered that the changes which had taken place did not affect situations whose maintenance formed the basis of the parties' undertaking. The ICJ was able to decide important questions of principle in the *Fisheries Jurisdiction* cases, recognizing the customary character of the rule laid down in art. 62 of the 1969 Vienna Convention (*ICJ Reports 1973*, p. 21, para. 43). The Court accepted the relevance of a fundamental change in the applicable law, but not the effect of the change on a compromissory clause (pp. 17 and 20). The termination of the General Act of Arbitration was invoked in the following cases, but without being considered by the ICJ: *Nuclear Tests* (*Pleadings*, vol. II, p. 348), *Trial of Pakistani Prisoners of War* (*Pleadings*, p. 143), and *Aegean Sea Continental Shelf* (*Pleadings*, pp. 203, 316 and 347). See also G. Haraszti, 'Treaties and the fundamental change of circumstances', *RCADI*, vol. 146 (1975-III), p. 1; A. Vamvoukos, *Termination of Treaties in International Law. The Doctrines of Rebus Sic Stantibus and Desuetude* (Oxford, Clarendon Press, 1985); Ph. Cahier, 'Le changement fondamental de circonstances et la Convention de Vienne de 1969 sur le droit des traités', *Essays in Honour of Roberto Ago*, vol. I, p. 163.

291[*]   French denunciation of certain military agreements relating to the North Atlantic Treaty of 4 April 1949 gave rise to controversy about the existence of a fundamental change of circumstances. See: E. Stein and D. Carreau, 'Law and peaceful change in a sub-system. "Withdrawal" of France from the North Atlantic Treaty Organization', *AJ*, vol. 62 (1968), p. 577; J. Charpentier, 'Le retrait français de l'O.T.A.N.', *AF*, vol. 12 (1966), p. 409; Ministère des Affaires étrangères, *La France et l'OTAN* (Paris, 1967).

296[*]   For the purposes of this *Introduction*, it is not necessary to go into a detailed account of the terms which are generally used and are still rather ill-defined (retorsion, reciprocity, reprisals, countermeasures); the term 'response' will be used to describe the measures taken by States following a wrongful act. The rather frequent recourse in recent years to such 'responses' even outside the framework of the United Nations has prompted a number of new studies: B.P. Sinha, *Unilateral Denunciation of Treaty Because of Prior Violations of Obligations by Other Party* (The Hague, Nijhoff, 1966); E. Zoller, *Peacetime Unilateral Remedies. An Analysis of Countermeasures* (Dobbs Ferry, Transnational Publishers, 1984); S. Rosenne, *Breach of Treaty* (Cambridge, Grotius Publications, 1985). The most significant international cases are: *Tacna and Arica, RIAA*, vol. 2, p. 129; *Diversion of Water from the Meuse, PCIJ, Series A/B, No. 70; Case concerning the Air Services Agreement of 27 March 1946 between the United States of America and France* (Decision of 9 December 1978), *RIAA*, vol. 18, p. 417; *United States Diplomatic and Consular Staff in Tehran, ICJ Reports 1980*, p. 28. For the references to the ILC work, see above No. 285[*].

300[*]   The term 'repudiation' (*'rejet'* in French), encompassing all the means whereby a State might try to free itself unlawfully of its treaty obligations, was maintained despite strong criticism (*Official Records UNCLT, II, Summary Records...*, Plenary, 21st meeting, p. 112, para. 23, and p. 115, paras. 69–77). While in its Advisory Opinion in the *Namibia* case (*ICJ Reports 1971*, p. 47) the Court stated that the rules laid down in article 60 'may in many respects be considered as a codification of existing customary law on the subject', it might prove difficult (see below, No. 306[*]) to agree on a principle of proportionality between offence and authorized response in the event of a 'non-material breach', although practice in general accepts such a principle (see the award in the *Case concerning the Air Services Agreement*). Indeed it has been argued that the measures taken against a defaulting State could constitute a means of exerting pressure upon it to resume performance of its obligations.

301[*]   *Official Records UNCLT, I, Summary Records...*, Committee of the Whole, 60th and 61th meetings; *Official Records UNCLT, II, Summary Records...*, Plenary, 21st and 30th meetings. In the provisions of art. 60, one of the points which bears most deeply on the mechanisms of responsibility concerns the concept of a 'party specially affected' by the breach of a multilateral treaty. There is a tendency in some teachings on international responsibility to minimize the relevance of the 'damage' as an element of responsibility. However, since international responsibility does not follow the lines of criminal responsibility, damage and reparation are precisely what make it possible to define the 'specially affected' entity and its rights. The same question arises for the legal interest of the applicant, as was shown in *South West Africa, Second Phase* (*ICJ Reports 1966*, p. 6). In 1985, the ILC considered a precise definition of the affected State based on the Special Rapporteur's draft art. 5, presented in his fifth report (*YILC 1984*, vol. II (part 1), p. 1).

303* This is not the place for an exhaustive study of the ICJ's Judgment in the *United States Diplomatic and Consular Staff in Tehran* case, but the Court's cautious approach should be noted. It has been argued that the Court relied in this case on the concept of peremptory rules (G. Gaja, '*Jus cogens* beyond the Vienna Convention', *RCADI*, vol. 172 (1981-III), p. 271, and Sir I. Sinclair, *The Vienna Convention on the Law of Treaties*, p. 212); and yet a treaty regularly concluded between States so as to drastically restrict diplomatic privileges and immunities could not be said to be void. If therefore peremptory rules were to exist in this field, it would not be within the meaning of art. 53. More correctly, diplomatic and consular immunities should be regarded by their very nature as established on the common understanding that they would escape reprisals. A similar explanation was given in the above-mentioned case (*ICJ Reports 1980*, p. 28): the ICJ stated that no 'response' could justify the suspension of treaty provisions relating to the peaceful settlement of disputes. But it could also be argued that in this case some of the treatments inflicted upon diplomatic and consular officials in Tehran violated certain fundamental human rights.

304* Also in draft art. 12, the Special Rapporteur seems to suggest that obligations concerning the immunities to be granted by the State of residence to diplomatic and consular missions and their personnel should be subject to the same régime as those deriving from peremptory rules; on this point, see above, No. 303*.

305* The general influence of the 1969 Convention is also apparent in the third and last part of the draft articles on '[t]he implementation of international responsibility and the settlement of disputes'. Thus under arts. 1 and 2, suspension measures are subject to a mechanism based on art. 65 of the 1969 Convention. The second part also includes art. 16 (a) under which '[t]he provisions of the present articles shall not prejudge any question that may arise in regard to: (a) the invalidity, termination and suspension of the operation of treaties'. This is symmetrical to article 73 of the 1969 Convention, but it would obviously be premature to discuss its scope.

306* In his reports to the ILC on the law of treaties, Sir Gerald Fitzmaurice had mentioned peremptory rules in the context of a breach of treaty obligations (*YILC 1957*, vol. II, pp. 31 and 54). The ILC did not deal with the issue as it was confident that very few rules presented this character. It was raised again by Finland and Lebanon during the first session of the 1968–1969 Conference (*Official Records UNCLT, I, Summary Records...*, Committee of the Whole, 60th meeting, p. 352, para. 60; 61st meeting, p. 360, para. 85), while Switzerland raised the question of humanitarian law. The Expert Consultant held that conventional law *per se* could not confer a peremptory character on a rule and therefore expressed serious reservations; only custom emerging out of a treaty could generate a rule giving rise to obligations precluding suspension in any circumstances. The ensuing debate proved inconclusive (81st meeting, p. 478, paras. 23 ff.) At the second session, however, following a drafting amendment submitted by Switzerland (*Official Records UNCLT, II, Summary Records...*, 21st plenary meeting, p. 112, para. 20), the text of art. 60 (5) was adopted without difficulty (p. 115, para. 68) although without further clarification.

307* G. Barile, 'The protection of human rights in article 60, paragraph 5, of the Vienna Convention on the Law of Treaties', *Essays in Honour of Roberto Ago*, vol. II, p. 3; E. Suy, 'Droit des traités et droits de l'homme', *Festschrift für Hermann Mosler* (Berlin, Springer, 1983), pp. 935 and 939. For humanitarian law, see J. de Preux, 'The Geneva Conventions and reciprocity', *International Review of the Red*

Cross, vol. 25 (1985), p. 25; S.E. Nahlik, 'Le problème des représailles à la lumière des travaux de la Conférence diplomatique sur le droit humanitaire', *RGDIP,* vol. 82 (1978), p. 130; International Committee of the Red Cross, *Commentary on the Additional Protocols of 1977 to the Geneva Conventions of 1949* (in particular paras. 1838 ff. and 3440 ff). The theory occasionally put forward that the use of nuclear weapons is already prohibited by a non-conventional peremptory rule is weakened not only because Western powers do not recognize this rule but because two other nuclear powers have undertaken by unilateral decisions to refrain only from *first use* of nuclear weapons.

Appendix I
Vienna Convention on the Law of Treaties (23 May 1969)

The States Parties to the present Convention,

Considering the fundamental role of treaties in the history of international relations,

Recognizing the ever-increasing importance of treaties as a source of international law and as a means of developing peaceful co-operation among nations, whatever their constitutional and social systems,

Noting that the principles of free consent and of good faith and the *pacta sunt servanda* rule are universally recognized,

Affirming that disputes concerning treaties, like other international disputes, should be settled by peaceful means and in conformity with the principles of justice and international law,

Recalling the determination of the peoples of the United Nations to establish conditions under which justice and respect for the obligations arising from treaties can be maintained,

Having in mind the principles of international law embodied in the Charter of the United Nations, such as the principles of the equal rights and self-determination of peoples, of the sovereign equality and independence of all States, of non-interference in the domestic affairs of States, of the prohibition of the threat or use of force and of universal respect for, and observance of, human rights and fundamental freedoms for all,

Believing that the codification and progressive development of the law of treaties achieved in the present Convention will promote the purposes of the United Nations set forth in the Charter, namely, the maintenance of international peace and security, the development of friendly relations and the achievement of co-operation among nations,

Affirming that the rules of customary international law will continue to govern questions not regulated by the provisions of the present Convention,

Have agreed as follows:

Part I Introduction

ARTICLE 1 SCOPE OF THE PRESENT CONVENTION

The present Convention applies to treaties between States.

ARTICLE 2 USE OF TERMS

1. For the purposes of the present Convention:

(a) 'treaty' means an international agreement concluded between States in written form and governed by international law, whether embodied in a single instrument or in two or more related instruments and whatever its particular designation;

(b) 'ratification', 'acceptance', 'approval' and 'accession' mean in each case the international act so named whereby a State establishes on the international plane its consent to be bound by a treaty;

(c) 'full powers' means a document emanating from the competent authority of a State designating a person or persons to represent the State for negotiating, adopting or authenticating the text of a treaty, for expressing the consent of the State to be bound by a treaty, or for accomplishing any other act with respect to a treaty;

(d) 'reservation' means a unilateral statement, however phrased or named, made by a State, when signing, ratifying, accepting, approving or acceding to a treaty, whereby it purports to exclude or to modify the legal effect of certain provisions of the treaty in their application to that State;

(e) 'negotiating State' means a State which took part in the drawing up and adoption of the text of the treaty;

(f) 'contracting State' means a State which has consented to be bound by the treaty, whether or not the treaty has entered into force;

(g) 'party' means a State which has consented to be bound by the treaty and for which the treaty is in force;

(h) 'third State' means a State not a party to the treaty;

(i) 'international organization' means an intergovernmental organization.

2. The provisions of paragraph 1 regarding the use of terms in the present Convention are without prejudice to the use of those terms or to the meanings which may be given to them in the internal law of any State.

ARTICLE 3 INTERNATIONAL AGREEMENTS NOT WITHIN THE SCOPE OF THE PRESENT CONVENTION

The fact that the present Convention does not apply to international agreements concluded between States and other subjects of international law or between such other subjects of international law, or to international agreements not in written form, shall not affect:

(a) the legal force of such agreements;

(b) the application to them of any of the rules set forth in the present Convention to which they would be subject under international law independently of the Convention;

(c) the application of the Convention to the relations of States as between themselves under international agreements to which other subjects of international law are also parties.

ARTICLE 4 NON-RETROACTIVITY OF THE PRESENT CONVENTION

Without prejudice to the application of any rules set forth in the present Convention to which treaties would be subject under international law independently of the Convention, the Convention applies only to treaties which are concluded by States after the entry into force of the present Convention with regard to such States.

ARTICLE 5 TREATIES CONSTITUTING INTERNATIONAL ORGANIZATIONS AND TREATIES ADOPTED WITHIN AN INTERNATIONAL ORGANIZATION

The present Convention applies to any treaty which is the constituent instrument of an international organization and to any treaty adopted within an international organization without prejudice to any relevant rules of the organization.

Part II Conclusion and entry into force of treaties

Section 1 Conclusion of treaties

ARTICLE 6 CAPACITY OF STATES TO CONCLUDE TREATIES

Every State possesses capacity to conclude treaties.

ARTICLE 7 FULL POWERS

1. A person is considered as representing a State for the purpose of adopting or authenticating the text of a treaty or for the purpose of expressing the consent of the State to be bound by a treaty if:

   (a) he produces appropriate full powers; or
   (b) it appears from the practice of the States concerned or from other circumstances that their intention was to consider that person as representing the State for such purposes and to dispense with full powers.

2. In virtue of their functions and without having to produce full powers, the following are considered as representing their State:

   (a) Heads of State, Heads of Government and Ministers for Foreign Affairs, for the purpose of performing all acts relating to the conclusion of a treaty;
   (b) heads of diplomatic missions, for the purpose of adopting the text of a treaty between the accrediting State and the State to which they are accredited;

(c) representatives accredited by States to an international conference or to an international organization or one of its organs, for the purpose of adopting the text of a treaty in that conference, organization or organ.

ARTICLE 8 SUBSEQUENT CONFIRMATION OF AN ACT PERFORMED WITHOUT AUTHORIZATION

An act relating to the conclusion of a treaty performed by a person who cannot be considered under article 7 as authorized to represent a State for that purpose is without legal effect unless afterwards confirmed by that State.

ARTICLE 9 ADOPTION OF THE TEXT

1. The adoption of the text of a treaty takes place by the consent of all the States participating in its drawing up except as provided in paragraph 2.
2. The adoption of the text of a treaty of an international conference takes place by the vote of two-thirds of the States present and voting, unless by the same majority they shall decide to apply a different rule.

ARTICLE 10 AUTHENTICATION OF THE TEXT

The text of a treaty is established as authentic and definitive:

(a) by such procedures as may be provided for in the text or agreed upon by the States participating in its drawing up; or
(b) failing such procedure, by the signature, signature *ad referendum* or initialling by the representatives of those States of the text of the treaty or of the Final Act of a conference incorporating the text.

ARTICLE 11 MEANS OF EXPRESSING CONSENT TO BE BOUND BY A TREATY

The consent of a State to be bound by a treaty may be expressed by signature, exchange of instruments constituting a treaty, ratification, acceptance, approval or accession, or by any other means if so agreed.

ARTICLE 12 CONSENT TO BE BOUND BY A TREATY EXPRESSED BY SIGNATURE

1. The consent of a State to be bound by a treaty is expressed by the signature of its representative when:

(a) the treaty provides that signature shall have that effect;
(b) it is otherwise established that the negotiating States were agreed that signature should have that effect; or
(c) the intention of the State to give that effect to the signature appears from the full powers of its representative or was expressed during the negotiation.

2. For the purposes of paragraph 1:

(a) the initialling of a text constitutes a signature of the treaty when it is established that the negotiating States so agreed;
(b) the signature *ad referendum* of a treaty by a representative, if confirmed by his State, constitutes a full signature of the treaty.

ARTICLE 13 CONSENT TO BE BOUND BY A TREATY EXPRESSED BY AN EXCHANGE OF INSTRUMENTS CONSTITUTING A TREATY

The consent of States to be bound by a treaty constituted by instruments exchanged between them is expressed by that exchange when:

(a) the instruments provide that their exchange shall have that effect; or
(b) it is otherwise established that those States were agreed that the exchange of instruments should have that effect.

ARTICLE 14 CONSENT TO BE BOUND BY A TREATY EXPRESSED BY RATIFICATION, ACCEPTANCE OR APPROVAL

1. The consent of a State to be bound by a treaty is expressed by ratification when:

(a) the treaty provides for such consent to be expressed by means of ratification;
(b) it is otherwise established that the negotiating States were agreed that ratification should be required;
(c) the representative of the State has signed the treaty subject to ratification; or
(d) the intention of the State to sign the treaty subject to ratification appears from the full powers of its representative or was expressed during the negotiation.

2. The consent of a State to be bound by a treaty is expressed by acceptance or approval under conditions similar to those which apply to ratification.

ARTICLE 15 CONSENT TO BE BOUND BY A TREATY EXPRESSED BY ACCESSION

The consent of a State to be bound by a treaty is expressed by accession when:

(a) the treaty provides that such consent may be expressed by that State by means of accession;

(b) it is otherwise established that the negotiating States were agreed that such consent may be expressed by that State by means of accession; or

(c) all the parties have subsequently agreed that such consent may be expressed by that State by means of accession.

ARTICLE 16 EXCHANGE OR DEPOSIT OF INSTRUMENTS OF RATIFICATION, ACCEPTANCE, APPROVAL OR ACCESSION

Unless the treaty otherwise provides, instruments of ratification, acceptance, approval or accession establish the consent of a State to be bound by a treaty upon:

(a) their exchange between the contracting States;

(b) their deposit with the depositary; or

(c) their notification to the contracting States or to the depositary, if so agreed.

ARTICLE 17 CONSENT TO BE BOUND BY PART OF A TREATY AND CHOICE OF DIFFERING PROVISIONS

1. Without prejudice to articles 19 to 23, the consent of a State to be bound by part of a treaty is effective only if the treaty so permits or the other contracting States so agree.

2. The consent of a State to be bound by a treaty which permits a choice between differing provisions is effective only if it is made clear to which of the provisions the consent relates.

ARTICLE 18 OBLIGATION NOT TO DEFEAT THE OBJECT AND PURPOSE OF A TREATY PRIOR TO ITS ENTRY INTO FORCE

A State is obliged to refrain from acts which would defeat the object and purpose of a treaty when:

(a) it has signed the treaty or has exchanged instruments constituting the treaty subject to ratification, acceptance or approval, until it shall have made its intention clear not to become a party to the treaty; or

(b) it has expressed its consent to be bound by the treaty, pending the entry into force of the treaty and provided that such entry into force is not unduly delayed.

Section 2 Reservations

ARTICLE 19 FORMULATION OF RESERVATIONS

A State may, when signing, ratifying, accepting, approving or acceding to a treaty, formulate a reservation unless:

(a) the reservation is prohibited by the treaty;
(b) the treaty provides that only specified reservations, which do not include the reservation in question, may be made; or
(c) in cases not falling under sub-paragraphs *(a)* and *(b)*, the reservation is incompatible with the object and purpose of the treaty.

ARTICLE 20 ACCEPTANCE OF AND OBJECTION TO RESERVATIONS

1. A reservation expressly authorized by a treaty does not require any subsequent acceptance by the other contracting States unless the treaty so provides.
2. When it appears from the limited number of the negotiating States and the object and purpose of a treaty that the application of the treaty in its entirety between all the parties is an essential condition of the consent of each one to be bound by the treaty, a reservation requires acceptance by all the parties.
3. When a treaty is a constituent instrument of an international organization and unless it otherwise provides, a reservation requires the acceptance of the competent organ of that organization.
4. In cases not falling under the preceding paragraphs and unless the treaty otherwise provides:

(a) acceptance by another contracting State of a reservation constitutes the reserving State a party to the treaty in relation to that other State if or when the treaty is in force for those States;
(b) an objection by another contracting State to a reservation does not preclude the entry into force of the treaty as between the objecting and reserving States unless the contrary intention is definitely expressed by the objecting State;
(c) an act expressing a State's consent to be bound by the treaty and containing a reservation is effective as soon as at least one other contracting State has accepted the reservation.

5. For the purposes of paragraphs 2 and 4 and unless the treaty otherwise provides, a reservation is considered to have been accepted by a State if it shall have raised no objection to the reservation by the end of a period of twelve months after it was notified of the reservation or by the date on which it expressed its consent to be bound by the treaty, whichever is later.

ARTICLE 21 LEGAL EFFECTS OF RESERVATIONS AND OF OBJECTIONS TO
RESERVATIONS

1. A reservation established with regard to another party in accordance
with articles 19, 20 and 23:

>*(a)* modifies for the reserving State in its relations with that other party
>the provisions of the treaty to which the reservation relates to the extent
>of the reservation; and
>*(b)* modifies those provisions to the same extent for that other party in its
>relations with the reserving State.

2. The reservation does not modify the provisions of the treaty for the other
parties to the treaty *inter se.*
3. When a State objecting to a reservation has not opposed the entry into
force of the treaty between itself and the reserving State, the provisions to
which the reservation relates do not apply as between the two States to the
extent of the reservation.

ARTICLE 22 WITHDRAWAL OF RESERVATIONS AND OF OBJECTIONS TO
RESERVATIONS

1. Unless the treaty otherwise provides, a reservation may be withdrawn at
any time and the consent of a State which has accepted the reservation is not
required for its withdrawal.
2. Unless the treaty otherwise provides, an objection to a reservation may
be withdrawn at any time.
3. Unless the treaty otherwise provides, or it is otherwise agreed:

>*(a)* the withdrawal of a reservation becomes operative in relation to
>another contracting State only when notice of it has been received by that
>State;
>*(b)* the withdrawal of an objection to a reservation becomes operative
>only when notice of it has been received by the State which formulated
>the reservation.

ARTICLE 23 PROCEDURE REGARDING RESERVATIONS

1. A reservation, an express acceptance of a reservation and an objection to
a reservation must be formulated in writing and communicated to the
contracting States and other States entitled to become parties to the treaty.
2. If formulated when signing the treaty subject to ratification, acceptance
or approval, a reservation must be formally confirmed by the reserving State
when expressing its consent to be bound by the treaty. In such a case the

reservation shall be considered as having been made on the date of its confirmation.

3. An express acceptance of, or an objection to, a reservation made previously to confirmation of the reservation does not itself require confirmation.

4. The withdrawal of a reservation or of an objection to a reservation must be formulated in writing.

Section 3 Entry into force and provisional application of treaties

ARTICLE 24 ENTRY INTO FORCE

1. A treaty enters into force in such manner and upon such date as it may provide or as the negotiating States may agree.

2. Failing any such provision or agreement, a treaty enters into force as soon as consent to be bound by the treaty has been established for all the negotiating States.

3. When the consent of a State to be bound by a treaty is established on a date after the treaty has come into force, the treaty enters into force for that State on that date, unless the treaty otherwise provides.

4. The provisions of a treaty regulating the authentication of its text, the establishment of the consent of States to be bound by the treaty, the manner or date of its entry into force, reservations, the functions of the depositary and other matters arising necessarily before the entry into force of the treaty apply from the time of the adoption of its text.

ARTICLE 25 PROVISIONAL APPLICATION

1. A treaty or a part of a treaty is applied provisionally pending its entry into force if:

  (a) the treaty itself so provides; or
  (b) the negotiating States have in some other manner so agreed.

2. Unless the treaty otherwise provides or the negotiating States have otherwise agreed, the provisional application of a treaty or a part of a treaty with respect to a State shall be terminated if that State notifies the other States between which the treaty is being applied provisionally of its intention not to become a party to the treaty.

Part III Observance, application and interpretation of treaties

Section 1 Observance of treaties

ARTICLE 26 *PACTA SUNT SERVANDA*

Every treaty in force is binding upon the parties to it and must be performed by them in good faith.

ARTICLE 27 INTERNAL LAW AND OBSERVANCE OF TREATIES

A party may not invoke the provisions of its internal law as justification for its failure to perform a treaty. This rule is without prejudice to article 46.

Section 2 Application of treaties

ARTICLE 28 NON-RETROACTIVITY OF TREATIES

Unless a different intention appears from the treaty or is otherwise established, its provisions do not bind a party in relation to any act or fact which took place or any situation which ceased to exist before the date of the entry into force of the treaty with respect to that party.

ARTICLE 29 TERRITORIAL SCOPE OF TREATIES

Unless a different intention appears from the treaty or is otherwise established, a treaty is binding upon each party in respect of its entire territory.

ARTICLE 30 APPLICATION OF SUCCESSIVE TREATIES RELATING TO THE SAME SUBJECT-MATTER

1. Subject to Article 103 of the Charter of the United Nations, the rights and obligations of States parties to successive treaties relating to the same subject-matter shall be determined in accordance with the following paragraphs.
2. When a treaty specifies that it is subject to, or that it is not to be considered as incompatible with, an earlier or later treaty, the provisions of that other treaty prevail.
3. When all the parties to the earlier treaty are parties also to the later treaty but the earlier treaty is not terminated or suspended in operation under article 59, the earlier treaty applies only to the extent that its provisions are compatible with those of the later treaty.
4. When the parties to the later treaty do not include all the parties to the earlier one:

   (a) as between States parties to both treaties the same rule applies as in paragraph 3;
   (b) as between a State party to both treaties and a State party to only one of the treaties, the treaty to which both States are parties governs their mutual rights and obligations.

5. Paragraph 4 is without prejudice to article 41, or to any question of the termination or suspension of the operation of a treaty under article 60 or to

any question of responsibility which may arise for a State from the conclusion or application of a treaty the provisions of which are incompatible with its obligations towards another State under another treaty.

Section 3 Interpretation of treaties

ARTICLE 31 GENERAL RULE OF INTERPRETATION

1. A treaty shall be interpreted in good faith in accordance with the ordinary meaning to be given to the terms of the treaty in their context and in the light of its object and purpose.
2. The context for the purpose of the interpretation of a treaty shall comprise, in addition to the text, including its preamble and annexes:

   (a) any agreement relating to the treaty which was made between all the parties in connexion with the conclusion of the treaty;
   (b) any instrument which was made by one or more parties in connexion with the conclusion of the treaty and accepted by the other parties as an instrument related to the treaty.

3. There shall be taken into account, together with the context:

   (a) any subsequent agreement between the parties regarding the interpretation of the treaty or the application of its provisions;
   (b) any subsequent practice in the application of the treaty which establishes the agreement of the parties regarding its interpretation;
   (c) any relevant rules of international law applicable in the relations between the parties.

4. A special meaning shall be given to a term if it is established that the parties so intended.

ARTICLE 32 SUPPLEMENTARY MEANS OF INTERPRETATION

Recourse may be had to supplementary means of interpretation, including the preparatory work of the treaty and the circumstances of its conclusion, in order to confirm the meaning resulting from the application of article 31, or to determine the meaning when the interpretation according to article 31:

   (a) leaves the meaning ambiguous or obscure; or
   (b) leads to a result which is manifestly absurd or unreasonable.

ARTICLE 33 INTERPRETATION OF TREATIES AUTHENTICATED IN TWO OR MORE LANGUAGES

1. When a treaty has been authenticated in two or more languages, the text is equally authoritative in each language, unless the treaty provides or the parties agree that, in case of divergence, a particular text shall prevail.

2. A version of the treaty in a language other than one of those in which the text was authenticated shall be considered an authentic text only if the treaty so provides or the parties so agree.

3. The terms of the treaty are presumed to have the same meaning in each authentic text.

4. Except where a particular text prevails in accordance with paragraph 1, when a comparison of the authentic texts discloses a difference of meaning which the application of articles 31 and 32 does not remove, the meaning which best reconciles the texts, having regard to the object and purpose of the treaty, shall be adopted.

Section 4 Treaties and third States

ARTICLE 34 GENERAL RULE REGARDING THIRD STATES

A treaty does not create either obligations or rights for a third State without its consent.

ARTICLE 35 TREATIES PROVIDING FOR OBLIGATIONS FOR THIRD STATES

An obligation arises for a third State from a provision of a treaty if the parties to the treaty intend the provision to be the means of establishing the obligation and the third State expressly accepts that obligation in writing.

ARTICLE 36 TREATIES PROVIDING FOR RIGHTS FOR THIRD STATES

1. A right arises for a third State from a provision of a treaty if the parties to the treaty intend the provision to accord that right either to the third State, or to a group of States to which it belongs, or to all States, and the third State assents thereto. Its assent shall be presumed so long as the contrary is not indicated, unless the treaty otherwise provides.

2. A State exercising a right in accordance with paragraph 1 shall comply with the conditions for its exercise provided for in the treaty or established in conformity with the treaty.

ARTICLE 37 REVOCATION OR MODIFICATION OF OBLIGATIONS OR RIGHTS OF THIRD STATES

1. When an obligation has arisen for a third State in conformity with article 35, the obligation may be revoked or modified only with the consent of the parties to the treaty and of the third State, unless it is established that they had otherwise agreed.

2. When a right has arisen for a third State in conformity with article 36, the right may not be revoked or modified by the parties if it is established that

the right was intended not to be revocable or subject to modification without the consent of the third State.

ARTICLE 38 RULES IN A TREATY BECOMING BINDING ON THIRD STATES THROUGH INTERNATIONAL CUSTOM

Nothing in articles 34 to 37 precludes a rule set forth in a treaty from becoming binding upon a third State as a customary rule of international law, recognized as such.

Part IV Amendment and modification of treaties

ARTICLE 39 GENERAL RULE REGARDING THE AMENDMENT OF TREATIES

A treaty may be amended by agreement between the parties. The rules laid down in Part II apply to such an agreement except in so far as the treaty may otherwise provide.

ARTICLE 40 AMENDMENT OF MULTILATERAL TREATIES

1. Unless the treaty otherwise provides, the amendment of multilateral treaties shall be governed by the following paragraphs.
2. Any proposal to amend a multilateral treaty as between all the parties must be notified to all the contracting States, each one of which shall have the right to take part in:

   (a) the decision as to the action to be taken in regard to such proposal;
   (b) the negotiation and conclusion of any agreement for the amendment of the treaty.

3. Every State entitled to become a party to the treaty shall also be entitled to become a party to the treaty as amended.
4. The amending agreement does not bind any State already a party to the treaty which does not become a party to the amending agreement; article 30, paragraph 4*(b)*, applies in relation to such State.
5. Any State which becomes a party to the treaty after the entry into force of the amending agreement shall, failing an expression of a different intention by that State:

   (a) be considered as a party to the treaty as amended; and
   (b) be considered as a party to the unamended treaty in relation to any party to the treaty not bound by the amending agreement.

ARTICLE 41 AGREEMENTS TO MODIFY MULTILATERAL TREATIES BETWEEN CERTAIN OF THE PARTIES ONLY

1. Two or more of the parties to a multilateral treaty may conclude an agreement to modify the treaty as between themselves alone if:

(a) the possibility of such a modification is provided for by the treaty; or
(b) the modification in question is not prohibited by the treaty and:
  (i) does not affect the enjoyment by the other parties of their rights under the treaty or the performance of their obligations;
  (ii) does not relate to a provision, derogation from which is incompatible with the effective execution of the object and purpose of the treaty as a whole.

2. Unless in a case falling under paragraph 1*(a)* the treaty otherwise provides, the parties in question shall notify the other parties of their intention to conclude the agreement and of the modification to the treaty for which it provides.

Part V Invalidity, termination and suspension of the operation of treaties

Section 1 General provisions

ARTICLE 42 VALIDITY AND CONTINUANCE IN FORCE OF TREATIES

1. The validity of a treaty or of the consent of a State to be bound by a treaty may be impeached only through the application of the present Convention.
2. The termination of a treaty, its denunciation or the withdrawal of a party, may take place only as a result of the application of the provisions of the treaty or of the present Convention. The same rule applies to suspension of the operation of a treaty.

ARTICLE 43 OBLIGATIONS IMPOSED BY INTERNATIONAL LAW
INDEPENDENTLY OF A TREATY

The invalidity, termination or denunciation of a treaty, the withdrawal of a party from it, or the suspension of its operation, as a result of the application of the present Convention or of the provisions of the treaty, shall not in any way impair the duty of any State to fulfil any obligation embodied in the treaty to which it would be subject under international law independently of the treaty.

ARTICLE 44 SEPARABILITY OF TREATY PROVISIONS

1. A right of a party, provided for in a treaty or arising under article 56, to denounce, withdraw from or suspend the operation of the treaty may be exercised only with respect to the whole treaty unless the treaty otherwise provides or the parties otherwise agree.
2. A ground for invalidating, terminating, withdrawing from or suspending the operation of a treaty recognized in the present Convention may be

invoked only with respect to the whole treaty except as provided in the following paragraphs or in article 60.

3. If the ground relates solely to particular clauses, it may be invoked only with respect to those clauses where:

(a) the said clauses are separable from the remainder of the treaty with regard to their application;

(b) it appears from the treaty or is otherwise established that acceptance of those clauses was not an essential basis of the consent of the other party or parties to be bound by the treaty as a whole; and

(c) continued performance of the remainder of the treaty would not be unjust.

4. In cases falling under articles 49 and 50 the State entitled to invoke the fraud or corruption may do so with respect either to the whole treaty or, subject to paragraph 3, to the particular clauses alone.

5. In cases falling under articles 51, 52 and 53, no separation of the provisions of the treaty is permitted.

ARTICLE 45 LOSS OF A RIGHT TO INVOKE A GROUND FOR INVALIDATING, TERMINATING, WITHDRAWING FROM OR SUSPENDING THE OPERATION OF A TREATY

A State may no longer invoke a ground for invalidating, terminating, withdrawing from or suspending the operation of a treaty under articles 46 to 50 or articles 60 and 62 if, after becoming aware of the facts:

(a) it shall have expressly agreed that the treaty is valid or remains in force or continues in operation, as the case may be; or

(b) it must by reason of its conduct be considered as having acquiesced in the validity of the treaty or in its maintenance in force or in operation, as the case may be.

Section 2 Invalidity of treaties

ARTICLE 46 PROVISIONS OF INTERNAL LAW REGARDING COMPETENCE TO CONCLUDE TREATIES

1. A State may not invoke the fact that its consent to be bound by a treaty has been expressed in violation of a provision of its internal law regarding competence to conclude treaties as invalidating its consent unless that violation was manifest and concerned a rule of its internal law of fundamental importance.

2. A violation is manifest if it would be objectively evident to any State conducting itself in the matter in accordance with normal practice and in good faith.

ARTICLE 47 SPECIFIC RESTRICTIONS ON AUTHORITY TO EXPRESS THE CONSENT OF A STATE

If the authority of a representative to express the consent of a State to be bound by a particular treaty has been made subject to a specific restriction, his omission to observe that restriction may not be invoked as invalidating the consent expressed by him unless the restriction was notified to the other negotiating States prior to his expressing such consent.

ARTICLE 48 ERROR

1. A State may invoke an error in a treaty as invalidating its consent to be bound by the treaty if the error relates to a fact or situation which was assumed by that State to exist at the time when the treaty was concluded and formed an essential basis of its consent to be bound by the treaty.
2. Paragraph 1 shall not apply if the State in question contributed by its own conduct to the error or if the circumstances were such as to put that State on notice of a possible error.
3. An error relating only to the wording of the text of a treaty does not affect its validity; article 79 then applies.

ARTICLE 49 FRAUD

If a State has been induced to conclude a treaty by the fraudulent conduct of another negotiating State, the State may invoke the fraud as invalidating its consent to be bound by the treaty.

ARTICLE 50 CORRUPTION OF A REPRESENTATIVE OF A STATE

If the expression of a State's consent to be bound by a treaty has been procured through the corruption of its representative directly or indirectly by another negotiating State, the State may invoke such corruption as invalidating its consent to be bound by the treaty.

ARTICLE 51 COERCION OF A REPRESENTATIVE OF A STATE

The expression of a State's consent to be bound by a treaty which has been procured by the coercion of its representative through acts or threats directed against him shall be without any legal effect.

ARTICLE 52 COERCION OF A STATE BY THE THREAT OR USE OF FORCE

A treaty is void if its conclusion has been procured by the threat or use of force in violation of the principles of international law embodied in the Charter of the United Nations.

ARTICLE 53 TREATIES CONFLICTING WITH A PEREMPTORY NORM OF
GENERAL INTERNATIONAL LAW (*JUS COGENS*)

A treaty is void if, at the time of its conclusion, it conflicts with a peremptory
norm of general international law. For the purposes of the present
Convention, a peremptory norm of general international law is a norm
accepted and recognized by the international community of States as a
whole as a norm from which no derogation is permitted and which can be
modified only by a subsequent norm of general international law having the
same character.

Section 3 Termination and suspension of the operation of treaties

ARTICLE 54 TERMINATION OF OR WITHDRAWAL FROM A TREATY UNDER
ITS PROVISIONS OR BY CONSENT OF THE PARTIES

The termination of a treaty or the withdrawal of a party may take place:

(a) in conformity with the provisions of the treaty; or
(b) at any time by consent of all the parties after consultation with the
other contracting States.

ARTICLE 55 REDUCTION OF THE PARTIES TO A MULTILATERAL TREATY
BELOW THE NUMBER NECESSARY FOR ITS ENTRY INTO FORCE

Unless the treaty otherwise provides, a multilateral treaty does not
terminate by reason only of the fact that the number of the parties falls below
the number necessary for its entry into force.

ARTICLE 56 DENUNCIATION OF OR WITHDRAWAL FROM A TREATY
CONTAINING NO PROVISION REGARDING TERMINATION, DENUNCIATION
OR WITHDRAWAL

1. A treaty which contains no provision regarding its termination and which
does not provide for denunciation or withdrawal is not subject to denunciation or withdrawal unless:

(a) it is established that the parties intended to admit the possibility of
denunciation or withdrawal; or
(b) a right of denunciation or withdrawal may be implied by the nature of
the treaty.

2. A party shall give not less than twelve months' notice of its intention to
denounce or withdraw from a treaty under paragraph 1.

ARTICLE 57 SUSPENSION OF THE OPERATION OF A TREATY UNDER ITS
PROVISIONS OR BY CONSENT OF THE PARTIES

The operation of a treaty in regard to all the parties or to a particular party
may be suspended:

(a) in conformity with the provisions of the treaty; or
(b) at any time by consent of all the parties after consultation with the
other contracting States.

ARTICLE 58 SUSPENSION OF THE OPERATION OF A MULTILATERAL TREATY
BY AGREEMENT BETWEEN CERTAIN OF THE PARTIES ONLY

1. Two or more parties to a multilateral treaty may conclude an agreement
to suspend the operation of provisions of the treaty, temporarily and as
between themselves alone, if:

(a) the possibility of such a suspension is provided for by the treaty; or
(b) the suspension in question is not prohibited by the treaty and:
(i) does not affect the enjoyment by the other parties of their rights
under the treaty or the performance of their obligations;
(ii) is not incompatible with the object and purpose of the treaty.

2. Unless in a case falling under paragraph 1(a) the treaty otherwise
provides, the parties in question shall notify the other parties of their
intention to conclude the agreement and of those provisions of the treaty the
operation of which they intend to suspend.

ARTICLE 59 TERMINATION OR SUSPENSION OF THE OPERATION OF A
TREATY IMPLIED BY CONCLUSION OF A LATER TREATY

1. A treaty shall be considered as terminated if all the parties to it conclude a
later treaty relating to the same subject-matter and:

(a) it appears from the later treaty or is otherwise established that the
parties intended that the matter should be governed by that treaty; or
(b) the provisions of the later treaty are so far incompatible with those of
the earlier one that the two treaties are not capable of being applied at the
same time.

2. The earlier treaty shall be considered as only suspended in operation if it
appears from the later treaty or is otherwise established that such was the
intention of the parties.

ARTICLE 60 TERMINATION OR SUSPENSION OF THE OPERATION OF A
TREATY AS A CONSEQUENCE OF ITS BREACH

1. A material breach of a bilateral treaty by one of the parties entitles the
other to invoke the breach as a ground for terminating the treaty or
suspending its operation in whole or in part.

2. A material breach of a multilateral treaty by one of the parties entitles:

(a) the other parties by unanimous agreement to suspend the operation of the treaty in whole or in part or to terminate it either:
   (i) in relations between themselves and the defaulting State, or
   (ii) as between all the parties;
(b) a party specially affected by the breach to invoke it as a ground for suspending the operation of the treaty in whole or in part in the relations between itself and the defaulting State;
(c) any party other than the defaulting State to invoke the breach as a ground for suspending the operation of the treaty in whole or in part with respect to itself if the treaty is of such a character that a material breach of its provisions by one party radically changes the position of every party with respect to the further performance of its obligations under the treaty.

3. A material breach of a treaty, for the purposes of this article, consists in:

(a) a repudiation of the treaty not sanctioned by the present Convention; or
(b) the violation of a provision essential to the accomplishment of the object or purpose of the treaty.

4. The foregoing paragraphs are without prejudice to any provision in the treaty applicable in the event of a breach.
5. Paragraphs 1 to 3 do not apply to provisions relating to the protection of the human person contained in treaties of a humanitarian character, in particular to provisions prohibiting any form of reprisals against persons protected by such treaties.

ARTICLE 61 SUPERVENING IMPOSSIBILITY OF PERFORMANCE

1. A party may invoke the impossibility of performing a treaty as a ground for terminating or withdrawing from it if the impossibility results from the permanent disappearance or destruction of an object indispensable for the execution of the treaty. If the impossibility is temporary, it may be invoked only as a ground for suspending the operation of the treaty.
2. Impossibility of performance may not be invoked by a party as a ground for terminating, withdrawing from or suspending the operation of a treaty if the impossibility is the result of a breach by that party either of an obligation under the treaty or of any other international obligation owed to any other party to the treaty.

ARTICLE 62 FUNDAMENTAL CHANGE OF CIRCUMSTANCES

1. A fundamental change of circumstances which has occurred with regard to those existing at the time of the conclusion of a treaty, and which was not

foreseen by the parties, may not be invoked as a ground for terminating or withdrawing from the treaty unless:

(a) the existence of those circumstances constituted an essential basis of the consent of the parties to be bound by the treaty; and
(b) the effect of the change is radically to transform the extent of obligations still to be performed under the treaty.

2. A fundamental change of circumstances may not be invoked as a ground for terminating or withdrawing from a treaty:

(a) if the treaty establishes a boundary; or
(b) if the fundamental change is the result of a breach by the party invoking it either of an obligation under the treaty or of any other international obligation owed to any other party to the treaty.

3. If, under the foregoing paragraphs, a party may invoke a fundamental change of circumstances as a ground for terminating or withdrawing from a treaty it may also invoke the change as a ground for suspending the operation of the treaty.

ARTICLE 63 SEVERANCE OF DIPLOMATIC OR CONSULAR RELATIONS

The severance of diplomatic or consular relations between parties to a treaty does not affect the legal relations established between them by the treaty except in so far as the existence of diplomatic or consular relations is indispensable for the application of the treaty.

ARTICLE 64 EMERGENCE OF A NEW PEREMPTORY NORM OF GENERAL INTERNATIONAL LAW (*JUS COGENS*)

If a new peremptory norm of general international law emerges, any existing treaty which is in conflict with that norm becomes void and terminates.

Section 4 Procedure

ARTICLE 65 PROCEDURE TO BE FOLLOWED WITH RESPECT TO INVALIDITY, TERMINATION, WITHDRAWAL FROM OR SUSPENSION OF THE OPERATION OF A TREATY

1. A party which, under the provisions of the present Convention, invokes either a defect in its consent to be bound by a treaty or a ground for impeaching the validity of a treaty, terminating it, withdrawing from it or suspending its operation, must notify the other parties of its claim. The

notification shall indicate the measure proposed to be taken with respect to the treaty and the reasons therefor.

2. If, after the expiry of a period which, except in cases of special urgency, shall not be less than three months after the receipt of the notification, no party has raised any objection, the party making the notification may carry out in the manner provided in article 67 the measure which it has proposed.

3. If, however, objection has been raised by any other party, the parties shall seek a solution through the means indicated in Article 33 of the Charter of the United Nations.

4. Nothing in the foregoing paragraphs shall affect the rights or obligations of the parties under any provisions in force binding the parties with regard to the settlement of disputes.

5. Without prejudice to article 45, the fact that a State has not previously made the notification prescribed in paragraph 1 shall not prevent it from making such notification in answer to another party claiming performance of the treaty or alleging its violation.

ARTICLE 66 PROCEDURES FOR JUDICIAL SETTLEMENT, ARBITRATION AND CONCILIATION

If, under paragraph 3 of article 65, no solution has been reached within a period of twelve months following the date on which the objection was raised, the following procedures shall be followed:

(a) any one of the parties to a dispute concerning the application or the interpretation of article 53 or 64 may, by a written application, submit it to the International Court of Justice for a decision unless the parties by common consent agree to submit the dispute to arbitration;

(b) any one of the parties to a dispute concerning the application or the interpretation of any of the other articles in Part V of the present Convention may set in motion the procedure specified in the Annex to the Convention by submitting a request to that effect to the Secretary-General of the United Nations.

ARTICLE 67 INSTRUMENTS FOR DECLARING INVALID, TERMINATING, WITHDRAWING FROM OR SUSPENDING THE OPERATION OF A TREATY

1. The notification provided for under article 65, paragraph 1 must be made in writing.

2. Any act of declaring invalid, terminating, withdrawing from or suspending the operation of a treaty pursuant to the provisions of the treaty or of paragraphs 2 or 3 of article 65 shall be carried out through an instrument communicated to the other parties. If the instrument is not signed by the Head of State, Head of Government or Minister for Foreign Affairs, the

representative of the State communicating it may be called upon to produce full powers.

ARTICLE 68 REVOCATION OF NOTIFICATIONS AND INSTRUMENTS
PROVIDED FOR IN ARTICLES 65 AND 67

A notification or instrument provided for in articles 65 or 67 may be revoked at any time before it takes effect.

Section 5 Consequences of the invalidity, termination or suspension of the operation of a treaty

ARTICLE 69 CONSEQUENCES OF THE INVALIDITY OF A TREATY

1. A treaty the invalidity of which is established under the present Convention is void. The provisions of a void treaty have no legal force.
2. If acts have nevertheless been performed in reliance on such a treaty:

(a) each party may require any other party to establish as far as possible in their mutual relations the position that would have existed if the acts had not been performed;
(b) acts performed in good faith before the invalidity was invoked are not rendered unlawful by reason only of the invalidity of the treaty.

3. In cases falling under articles 49, 50, 51, or 52, paragraph 2 does not apply with respect to the party to which the fraud, the act of corruption or the coercion is imputable.
4. In the case of the invalidity of a particular State's consent to be bound by a multilateral treaty, the foregoing rules apply in the relations between that State and the parties to the treaty.

ARTICLE 70 CONSEQUENCES OF THE TERMINATION OF A TREATY

1. Unless the treaty otherwise provides or the parties otherwise agree, the termination of a treaty under its provisions or in accordance with the present Convention:

(a) releases the parties from any obligation further to perform the treaty;
(b) does not affect any right, obligation or legal situation of the parties created through the execution of the treaty prior to its termination.

2. If a State denounces or withdraws from a multilaterlal treaty, paragraph 1 applies in the relations between that State and each of the other parties to the treaty from the date when such denunciation or withdrawal takes effect.

ARTICLE 71 CONSEQUENCES OF THE INVALIDITY OF A TREATY WHICH
CONFLICTS WITH A PEREMPTORY NORM OF GENERAL INTERNATIONAL
LAW

1. In the case of a treaty which is void under article 53 the parties shall:

(a) eliminate as far as possible the consequences of any act performed in
reliance on any provision which conflicts with the peremptory norm of
general international law; and
(b) bring their mutual relations into conformity with the peremptory
norm of general international law.

2. In the case of a treaty which becomes void and terminates under article
64, the termination of the treaty:

(a) releases the parties from any obligation further to perform the treaty;
(b) does not affect any right, obligation or legal situation of the parties
created through the execution of the treaty prior to its termination;
provided that those rights, obligations or situations may thereafter be
maintained only to the extent that their maintenance is not in itself in
conflict with the new peremptory norm of general international law.

ARTICLE 72 CONSEQUENCES OF THE SUSPENSION OF THE OPERATION OF A
TREATY

1. Unless the treaty otherwise provides or the parties otherwise agree, the
suspension of the operation of a treaty under its provisions or in accordance
with the present Convention:

(a) releases the parties between which the operation of the treaty is
suspended from the obligation to perform the treaty in their mutual
relations during the period of the suspension;
(b) does not otherwise affect the legal relations between the parties
established by the treaty.

2. During the period of the suspension the parties shall refrain from acts
tending to obstruct the resumption of the operation of the treaty.

Part VI Miscellaneous provisions

ARTICLE 73 CASES OF STATE SUCCESSION, STATE RESPONSIBILITY AND
OUTBREAK OF HOSTILITIES

The provisions of the present Convention shall not prejudge any question
that may arise in regard to a treaty from a succession of States or from the

international responsibility of a State or from the outbreak of hostilities between States.

ARTICLE 74 DIPLOMATIC AND CONSULAR RELATIONS AND THE CONCLUSION OF TREATIES

The severence or absence of diplomatic or consular relations between two or more States does not prevent the conclusion of treaties between those States. The conclusion of a treaty does not in itself affect the situation in regard to diplomatic or consular relations.

ARTICLE 75 CASE OF AN AGGRESSOR STATE

The provisions of the present Convention are without prejudice to any obligation in relation to a treaty which may arise for an aggressor State in consequence of measures taken in conformity with the Charter of the United Nations with reference to that State's aggression.

Part VII Depositaries, notifications, corrections and registration

ARTICLE 76 DEPOSITARIES OF TREATIES

1. The designation of the depositary of a treaty may be made by the negotiating States, either in the treaty itself or in some other manner. The depositary may be one or more States, an international organization or the chief administrative officer of the organization.
2. The functions of the depositary of a treaty are international in character and the depositary is under an obligation to act impartially in their performance. In particular, the fact that a treaty has not entered into force between certain of the parties or that a difference has appeared between a State and a depositary with regard to the performance of the latter's functions shall not affect that obligation.

ARTICLE 77 FUNCTIONS OF DEPOSITARIES

1. The function of a depositary, unless otherwise provided in the treaty or agreed by the contracting States, comprise in particular:

   (a) keeping custody of the original text of the treaty and of any full powers delivered to the depositary;
   (b) preparing certified copies of the original text and preparing any further text of the treaty in such additional languages as may be required by the treaty and transmitting them to the parties and to the States entitled to become parties to the treaty;

(c) receiving any signatures to the treaty and receiving and keeping custody of any instruments, notifications and communications relating to it;

(d) examining whether the signature or any instrument, notification or communication relating to the treaty is in due and proper form and, if need be, bringing the matter to the attention of the State in question;

(e) informing the parties and the States entitled to become parties to the treaty of acts, notifications and communications relating to the treaty;

(f) informing the States entitled to become parties to the treaty when the number of signatures or of instruments of ratification, acceptance, approval or accession required for the entry into force of the treaty has been received or deposited;

(g) registering the treaty with the Secretariat of the United Nations;

(h) performing the functions specified in other provisions of the present Convention.

2. In the event of any difference appearing between a State and the depositary as to the performance of the latter's functions, the depositary shall bring the question to the attention of the signatory States and the contracting States or, where appropriate, of the competent organ of the international organization concerned.

ARTICLE 78 NOTIFICATIONS AND COMMUNICATIONS

Except as the treaty or the present Convention otherwise provide, any notification or communication to be made by any State under the present Convention shall:

(a) if there is no depositary, be transmitted direct to the States for which it is intended, or if there is a depositary, to the latter;

(b) be considered as having been made by the State in question only upon its receipt by the State to which it was transmitted or, as the case may be, upon its receipt by the depositary;

(c) if transmitted to a depositary, be considered as received by the State for which it was intended only when the latter State has been informed by the depositary in accordance with article 77, paragraph 1 *(e)*.

ARTICLE 79 CORRECTION OF ERRORS IN TEXTS OR IN CERTIFIED COPIES OF TREATIES

1. Where, after the authentication of the text of a treaty, the signatory States and the contracting States are agreed that it contains an error, the error shall, unless they decide upon some other means of correction, be corrected:

(a) by having the appropriate correction made in the text and causing the correction to be initialled by duly authorized representatives;

(b) by executing or exchanging an instrument or instruments setting out the correction which it has been agreed to make; or

(c) by executing a corrected text of the whole treaty by the same procedure as in the case of the original text.

2. Where the treaty is one for which there is a depositary, the latter shall notify the signatory States and the contracting States of the error and of the proposal to correct it and shall specify an appropriate time-limit within which objection to the proposed correction may be raised. If, on the expiry of the time-limit:

(a) no objection has been raised, the depositary shall make and initial the correction in the text and shall execute a *procès-verbal* of the rectification of the text and communicate a copy of it to the parties and to the States entitled to become parties to the treaty;

(b) an objection has been raised, the depositary shall communicate the objection to the signatory States and to the contracting States.

3. The rules in paragraphs 1 and 2 apply also where the text has been authenticated in two or more languages and it appears that there is a lack of concordance which the signatory States and the contracting States agree should be corrected.

4. The corrected text replaces the defective text *ab initio,* unless the signatory States and the contracting States otherwise decide.

5. The correction of the text of a treaty that has been registered shall be notified to the Secretariat of the United Nations.

6. Where an error is discovered in a certified copy of a treaty, the depositary shall execute a *procès-verbal* specifying the rectification and communicate a copy of it to the signatory States and to the contracting States.

ARTICLE 80 REGISTRATION AND PUBLICATION OF TREATIES

1. Treaties shall, after their entry into force, be transmitted to the Secretariat of the United Nations for registration or filing and recording, as the case may be, and for publication.

2. The designation of a depositary shall constitute authorization for it to perform the acts specified in the preceding paragraph.

Part VIII Final provisions

ARTICLE 81 SIGNATURE

The present Convention shall be open for signature by all States Members of the United Nations or of any of the specialized agencies or of the

International Atomic Energy Agency or parties to the Statute of the International Court of Justice, and by any other State invited by the General Assembly of the United Nations to become a party to the Convention, as follows: until 30 November 1969, at the Federal Ministry for Foreign Affairs of the Republic of Austria, and subsequently, until 30 April 1970, at United Nations Heaquarters, New York.

ARTICLE 82 RATIFICATION

The present Convention is subject to ratification. The instruments of ratification shall be deposited with the Secretary-General of the United Nations.

ARTICLE 83 ACCESSION

The present Convention shall remain open for accession by any State belonging to any of the categories mentioned in article 81. The instruments of accession shall be deposited with the Secretary-General of the United Nations.

ARTICLE 84 ENTRY INTO FORCE

1. The present Convention shall enter into force on the thirtieth day following the date of deposit of the thirty-fifth instrument of ratification or accession.
2. For each State ratifying or acceding to the Convention after the deposit of the thirty-fifth instrument of ratification or accession, the Convention shall enter into force on the thirtieth day after deposit by such State of its instrument of ratification or accession.

ARTICLE 85 AUTHENTIC TEXTS

The original of the present Convention, of which the Chinese, English, French, Russian and Spanish texts are equally authentic, shall be deposited with the Secretary-General of the United Nations. IN WITNESS WHEREOF the undersigned Plenipotentiaries, being duly authorized thereto by their respective Governments, have signed the present Convention.
DONE AT VIENNA, this twenty-third day of May, one thousand nine hundred and sixty-nine.

Annex

1. A list of conciliators consisting of qualified jurists shall be drawn up and maintained by the Secretary-General of the United Nations. To this end,

every State which is a Member of the United Nations or a party to the present Convention shall be invited to nominate two conciliators, and the names of the persons so nominated shall constitute the list. The term of a conciliator, including that of any conciliator nominated to fill a casual vacancy, shall be five years and may be renewed. A conciliator whose term expires shall continue to fulfil any function for which he shall have been chosen under the following paragraph.

2. When a request has been made to the Secretary-General under article 66, the Secretary-General shall bring the dispute before a conciliation commission constituted as follows:The State or States constituting one of the parties to the dispute shall appoint:

> (a) one conciliator of the nationality of that State or of one of those States, who may or may not be chosen from the list referred to in paragraph 1; and
> (b) one conciliator not of the nationality of that State or of any of those States, who shall be chosen from the list.

The State or States constituting the other party to the dispute shall appoint two conciliators in the same way. The four conciliators chosen by the parties shall be appointed within sixty days following the date on which the Secretary-General receives the request.

The four conciliators shall, within sixty days following the date of the last of their own appointments, appoint a fifth conciliator chosen from the list, who shall be chairman.

If the appointment of the chairman or of any of the other conciliators has not been made within the period prescribed above for such appointment, it shall be made by the Secretary-General within sixty days following the expiry of that period. The appointment of the chairman may be made by the Secretary-General either from the list or from the membership of the International Law Commission. Any of the periods within which appointments must be made may be extended by agreement between the parties to the dispute.

Any vacancy shall be filled in the manner prescribed for the initial appointment.

3. The Conciliation Commission shall decide its own procedure. The Commission, with the consent of the parties to the dispute, may invite any party to the treaty to submit to it its views orally or in writing. Decisions and recommendations of the Commission shall be made by a majority vote of the five members.

4. The Commission may draw the attention of the parties to the dispute to any measures which might facilitate an amicable settlement.

5. The Commission shall hear the parties, examine the claims and objections, and make proposals to the parties with a view to reaching an amicable settlement of the dispute.

6. The Commission shall report within twelve months of its constitution. Its report shall be deposited with the Secretary-General and transmitted to the

parties to the dispute. The report of the Commission, including any conclusions stated therein regarding the facts or questions of law, shall not be binding upon the parties and it shall have no other character than that of recommendations submitted for the consideration of the parties in order to facilitate an amicable settlement of the dispute.

7. The Secretary-General shall provide the Commission with such assistance and facilities as it may require. The expenses of the Commission shall be borne by the United Nations.

Appendix II

Vienna Convention on the Law of Treaties between States and International Organizations or between International Organizations (21 March 1986)

The Parties to the present Convention

Considering the fundamental role of treaties in the history of international relations,

Recognizing the consensual nature of treaties and their ever-increasing importance as a source of international law,

Noting that the principles of free consent and of good faith and the *pacta sunt servanda* rule are universally recognized,

Affirming the importance of enhancing the process of codification and progressive development of international law at a universal level,

Believing that the codification and progressive development of the rules relating to treaties between States and international organizations or between international organizations are means of enhancing legal order in international relations and of serving the purposes of the United Nations,

Having in mind the principles of international law embodied in the Charter of the United Nations, such as the principles of the equal rights and self-determination of peoples, of the sovereign equality and independence of all States, of non-interference in the domestic affairs of States, of the prohibition of the threat or use of force and of universal respect for, and observance of, human rights and fundamental freedoms for all,

Bearing in mind the provisions of the Vienna Convention on the Law of Treaties of 1969,

Recognizing the relationship between the law of treaties between States and the law of treaties between States and international organizations or between international organizations,

Considering the importance of treaties between States and international organizations or between international organizations as a useful means of developing international relations and ensuring conditions for peaceful co-operation among nations, whatever their constitutional and social systems,

Having in mind the specific features of treaties to which international organizations are parties as subjects of international law distinct from States,

Noting that international organizations possess the capacity to conclude treaties which is necessary for the exercise of their functions and the fulfilment of their purposes,

Recognizing that the practice of international organizations in concluding treaties with States or between themselves should be in accordance with their constituent instruments,

Affirming that nothing in the present Convention should be interpreted as affecting those relations between an international organization and its members which are regulated by the rules of the organization,

Affirming also that disputes concerning treaties, like other international disputes, should be settled, in conformity with the Charter of the United Nations, by peaceful means and in conformity with the principles of justice and international law,

Affirming also that the rules of customary international law will continue to govern questions not regulated by the provisions of the present Convention.

Have agreed as follow:

Part I Introduction

ARTICLE 1 SCOPE OF THE PRESENT CONVENTION

The present Convention applies to:

(a) treaties between one or more States and one or more international organizations, and

(b) treaties between international organizations.

ARTICLE 2 USE OF TERMS

1. For the purposes of the present Convention:

(a) 'treaty' means an international agreement governed by international law and concluded in written form:

(i) between one or more States and one or more international organizations; or

(ii) between international organizations,

whether that agreement is embodied in a single instrument or in two or more related instruments and whatever its particular designation;

(b) 'ratification' means the international act so named whereby a State establishes on the international plane its consent to be bound by a treaty;

(b *bis*) 'act of formal confirmation' means an international act corresponding to that of ratification by a State, whereby an international organization establishes on the international plane its consent to be bound by a treaty;

(b *ter*) 'acceptance', 'approval' and 'accession' mean in each case the international act so named whereby a State or an international organization establishes on the international plane its consent to be bound by a treaty;

(c) 'full powers' means a document emanating from the competent authority of a State or from the competent organ of an international organization designating a person or persons to represent the State or the organization for negotiating, adopting or authenticating the text of a treaty, for expressing the consent of the State or of the organization to be bound by a treaty, or for accomplishing any other act with respect to a treaty;

(d) 'reservation' means a unilateral statement, however phrased or named, made by a State or by an international organization when signing, ratifying, formally confirming, accepting, approving or acceding to a treaty, whereby it purports to exclude or to modify the legal effect of certain provisions of the treaty in their application to that State or to that organization;

(e) 'negotiating State' and 'negotiating organization' mean respectively:
  (i) a State, or
  (ii) an international organization, which took part in the drawing up and adoption of the text of the treaty;

(f) 'contracting State' and 'contracting organization' mean respectively:
  (i) a State, or
  (ii) an international organization, which has consented to be bound by the treaty, whether or not the treaty has entered into force;

(g) 'party' means a State or an international organization which has consented to be bound by the treaty and for which the treaty is in force;

(h) 'third State' and 'third organization' mean respectively:
  (i) a State, or
  (ii) an international organization, not a party to the treaty;

(i) 'international organization' means an intergovernmental organization;

(j) 'rules of the organization' means, in particular, the constituent instruments, decisions and resolutions adopted in accordance with them, and established practice of the organization.

2. The provisions of paragraph 1 regarding the use of terms in the present Convention are without prejudice to the use of those terms or to the meanings which may be given to them in the internal law of any State or in the rules of any international organization.

ARTICLE 3 INTERNATIONAL AGREEMENTS NOT WITHIN THE SCOPE OF THE PRESENT CONVENTION

The fact that the present Convention does not apply:

(i) to international agreements to which one or more States, one or more international organizations and one or more subjects of international law other than States or organizations are parties;

(ii) to international agreements to which one or more international organizations and one or more subjects of international law other than States or organizations are parties;

(iii) to international agreements not in written form between one or more States and one or more international organizations, or between international organizations; or

(iv) to international agreements between subjects of international law other than States or international organizations;

shall not affect:

(a) the legal force of such agreements;

(b) the application to them of any of the rules set forth in the present Convention to which they would be subject under international law independently of the Convention;

(c) the application of the Convention to the relations between States and international organizations or to the relations of organizations as between themselves, when those relations are governed by international agreements to which other subjects of international law are also parties.

ARTICLE 4 NON-RETROACTIVITY OF THE PRESENT CONVENTION

Without prejudice to the application of any rules set forth in the present Convention to which treaties between one or more States and one or more international organizations or between international organizations would be subject under international law independently of the Convention, the Convention applies only to such treaties concluded after the entry into force of the present Convention with regard to those States and those organizations.

ARTICLE 5 TREATIES CONSTITUTING INTERNATIONAL ORGANIZATIONS AND TREATIES ADOPTED WITHIN AN INTERNATIONAL ORGANIZATION

The present Convention applies to any treaty between one or more States and one or more international organizations which is the constituent instrument of an international organization and to any treaty adopted within an international organization, without prejudice to any relevant rules of the organization.

Part II Conclusion and entry into force of treaties

Section 1 Conclusion of treaties

ARTICLE 6 CAPACITY OF INTERNATIONAL ORGANIZATIONS TO CONCLUDE TREATIES

The capacity of an international organization to conclude treaties is governed by the rules of that organization.

ARTICLE 7 FULL POWERS

1. A person is considered as representing a State for the purpose of adopting or authenticating the text of a treaty or for the purpose of expressing the consent of the State to be bound by a treaty if:

(a) that person produces appropriate full powers; or
(b) it appears from practice or from other circumstances that it was the intention of the States and international organizations concerned to consider that person as representing the State for such purposes without having to produce full powers.

2. In virtue of their functions and without having to produce full powers, the following are considered as representing their State:

(a) Heads of State, Heads of Government and Ministers for Foreign Affairs, for the purpose or performing all acts relating to the conclusion of a treaty between one or more States and one or more international organizations;
(b) representatives accredited by States to an international conference, for the purpose of adopting the text of a treaty between States and international organizations;
(c) representatives accredited by States to an international organization or one of its organs, for the purpose of adopting the text of a treaty in that organization or organ;
(d) heads of permanent missions to an international organization, for the purpose of adopting the text of a treaty between the accrediting States and that organization.

3. A person is considered as representing an international organization for the purpose of adopting or authenticating the text of a treaty, or expressing the consent of that organization to be bound by a treaty if:

(a) that person produces appropriate full powers; or
(b) it appears from the circumstances that it was the intention of the States and international organizations concerned to consider that person as representing the organization for such purposes, in accordance with the rules of the organization, without having to produce full powers.

ARTICLE 8 SUBSEQUENT CONFIRMATION OF AN ACT PERFORMED WITHOUT AUTHORIZATION

An act relating to the conclusion of a treaty performed by a person who cannot be considered under article 7 as authorized to represent a State or an international organization for that purpose is without legal effect unless afterwards confirmed by that State or that organization.

ARTICLE 9 ADOPTION OF THE TEXT

1. The adoption of the text of a treaty takes place by the consent of all the States and international organizations or, as the case may be, all the organizations participating in its drawing up except as provided in paragraph 2.
2. The adoption of the text of a treaty at an international conference takes place in accordance with the procedure agreed upon by the participants in that conference. If, however, no agreement is reached on any such procedure, the adoption of the text shall take place by the vote of two-thirds of the participants present and voting unless by the same majority they shall decide to apply a different rule.

ARTICLE 10 AUTHENTICATION OF THE TEXT

1. The text of a treaty between one or more States and one or more international organizations is established as authentic and definitive:

(a) by such procedure as may be provided for in the text or agreed upon by the States and organizations participating in its drawing up; or
(b) failing such procedure, by the signature, signature *ad referendum* or initialling by the representatives of those States and those organizations of the text of the treaty or of the Final Act of a conference incorporating the text.

2. The text of a treaty between international organizations is established as authentic and definitive:

(a) by such procedure as may be provided for in the text or agreed upon by the organizations participating in its drawing up; or
(b) failing such procedure, by the signature, signature *ad referendum* or initialling by the representatives of those organizations of the text of the treaty or of the Final Act of a conference incorporating the text.

ARTICLE 11 MEANS OF EXPRESSING CONSENT TO BE BOUND BY A TREATY

1. The consent of a State to be bound by a treaty may be expressed by signature, exchange of instruments constituting a treaty, ratification, acceptance, approval or accession, or by any other means if so agreed.
2. The consent of an international organization to be bound by a treaty may be expressed by signature, exchange of instruments constituting a treaty, act of formal confirmation, acceptance, approval or accession, or by any other means if so agreed.

ARTICLE 12 CONSENT TO BE BOUND BY A TREATY EXPRESSED BY SIGNATURE

1. The consent of a State or of an international organization to be bound by a treaty is expressed by the signature of the representative of that State or of that organization when:

(a) the treaty provides that signature shall have that effect;

(b) it is otherwise established that the negotiating States and negotiating organizations or, as the case may be, the negotiating organizations were agreed that signature should have that effect; or

(c) the intention of the State or organization to give that effect to the signature appears from the full powers of its representative or was expressed during the negotiation.

2. For the purposes of paragraph 1:

(a) the initialling of a text constitutes a signature of the treaty when it is established that the negotiating States and negotiating organizations or, as the case may be, the negotiating organizations so agreed;

(b) the signature *ad referendum* of a treaty by the representative of a State or an international organization, if confirmed by his State or organization, constitutes a full signature of the treaty.

ARTICLE 13 CONSENT TO BE BOUND BY A TREATY EXPRESSED BY AN
EXCHANGE OF INSTRUMENTS CONSTITUTING A TREATY

The consent of States or of international organizations to be bound by a treaty constituted by instruments exchanged between them is expressed by that exchange when:

(a) the instruments provide that their exchange shall have that effect; or

(b) it is otherwise established that those States and those organizations or, as the case may be, those organizations were agreed that the exchange of instruments should have that effect.

ARTICLE 14 CONSENT TO BE BOUND BY A TREATY EXPRESSED BY
RATIFICATION, ACT OF FORMAL CONFIRMATION, ACCEPTANCE OR
APPROVAL

1. The consent of a State to be bound by a treaty is expressed by ratification when:

(a) the treaty provides for such consent to be expressed by means of ratification;

(b) it is otherwise established that the negotiating States and negotiating organizations were agreed that ratification should be required;

(c) the representative of the State has signed the treaty subject to ratification; or

(d) the intention of the State to sign the treaty subject to ratification appears from the full powers of its representative or was expressed during the negotiation.

2. The consent of an international organization to be bound by a treaty is expressed by an act of formal confirmation when:

(a) the treaty provides for such consent to be expressed by means of an act of formal confirmation;
(b) it is otherwise established that the negotiating States and negotiating organizations or, as the case may be, the negotiating organizations were agreed that an act of formal confirmation should be required;
(c) the representative of the organization has signed the treaty subject to an act of formal confirmation; or
(d) the intention of the organization to sign the treaty subject to an act of formal confirmation appears from the full powers of its representative or was expressed during the negotiation.

3. The consent of a State or of an international organization to be bound by a treaty is expressed by acceptance or approval under conditions similar to those which apply to ratification or, as the case may be, to an act of formal confirmation.

ARTICLE 15 CONSENT TO BE BOUND BY A TREATY EXPRESSED BY ACCESSION

The consent of a State or of an international organization to be bound by a treaty is expressed by accession when:

(a) the treaty provides that such consent may be expressed by that State or that organization by means of accession;
(b) it is otherwise established that the negotiating States and negotiating organizations or, as the case may be, the negotiating organizations were agreed that such consent may be expressed by that State or that organization by means of accession; or
(c) all the parties have subsequently agreed that such consent may be expressed by that State or that organization by means of accession.

ARTICLE 16 EXCHANGE OR DEPOSIT OF INSTRUMENTS OF RATIFICATION, FORMAL CONFIRMATION, ACCEPTANCE, APPROVAL OR ACCESSION

1. Unless the treaty otherwise provides, instruments of ratification, instruments relating to an act of formal confirmation or instruments of acceptance, approval or accession establish the consent of a State or of an international organization to be bound by a treaty between one or more States and one or more international organizations upon:

(a) their exchange between the contracting States and contracting organizations;

(b) their deposit with the depositary; or
(c) their notification to the contracting States and to the contracting organizations or to the depositary, if so agreed.

2. Unless the treaty otherwise provides, instruments relating to an act of formal confirmation or instruments of acceptance, approval or accession establish the consent of an international organization to be bound by a treaty between international organizations upon:

(a) their exchange between the contracting organizations;
(b) their deposit with the depositary; or
(c) their notification to the contracting organizations or to the depositary, if so agreed.

ARTICLE 17 CONSENT TO BE BOUND BY PART OF A TREATY AND CHOICE OF DIFFERING PROVISIONS

1. Without prejudice to articles 19 to 23, the consent of a State or of an international organization to be bound by part of a treaty is effective only if the treaty so permits, or if the contracting States and contracting organizations or, as the case may be, the contracting organizations so agree.
2. The consent of a State or of an international organization to be bound by a treaty which permits a choice between differing provisions is effective only if it is made clear to which of the provisions the consent relates.

ARTICLE 18 OBLIGATION NOT TO DEFEAT THE OBJECT AND PURPOSE OF A TREATY PRIOR TO ITS ENTRY INTO FORCE

A State or an international organization is obliged to refrain from acts which would defeat the object and purpose of a treaty when:

(a) that State or that organization has signed the treaty or has exchanged instruments constituting the treaty subject to ratification, act of formal confirmation, acceptance or approval, until that State or that organization shall have made its intention clear not to become a party to the treaty; or
(b) that State or that organization has expressed its consent to be bound by the treaty, pending the entry into force of the treaty and provided that such entry into force is not unduly delayed.

Section 2 Reservations

ARTICLE 19 FORMULATION OF RESERVATIONS

A State or an international organization may, when signing, ratifying, formally confirming, accepting, approving or acceding to a treaty, formulate a reservation unless:

(a) the reservation is prohibited by the treaty;

(b) the treaty provides that only specified reservations, which do not include the reservation in question, may be made; or

(c) in cases not falling under sub-paragraphs (a) and (b), the reservation is incompatible with the object and purpose of the treaty.

ARTICLE 20 ACCEPTANCE OF AND OBJECTION TO RESERVATIONS

1. A reservation expressly authorized by a treaty does not require any subsequent acceptance by the contracting States and contracting organizations or, as the case may be, by the contracting organizations unless the treaty so provides.

2. When it appears from the limited number of the negotiating States and negotiating organizations or, as the case may be, of the negotiating organizations and the object and purpose of a treaty that the application of the treaty in its entirety between all the parties is an essential condition of the consent of each one to be bound by the treaty, a reservation requires acceptance by all the parties.

3. When a treaty is a constituent instrument of an international organization and unless it otherwise provides, a reservation requires the acceptance of the competent organ of that organization.

4. In cases not falling under the preceding paragraphs and unless the treaty otherwise provides:

(a) acceptance of a reservation by a contracting State or by a contracting organization constitutes the reserving State or international organization a party to the treaty in relation to the accepting State or organization if or when the treaty is in force for the reserving State or organization and for the accepting State or organization;

(b) an objection by a contracting State or by a contracting organization to a reservation does not preclude the entry into force of the treaty as between the objecting State or international organization and the reserving State or organization unless a contrary intention is definitely expressed by the objecting State or organization;

(c) an act expressing the consent of a State or of an international organization to be bound by the treaty and containing a reservation is effective as soon as at least one contracting State or one contracting organization has accepted the reservation.

5. For the purposes of paragraphs 2 and 4 and unless the treaty otherwise provides, a reservation is considered to have been accepted by a State or an international organization if it shall have raised no objection to the reservation by the end of a period of twelve months after it was notified of the reservation or by the date on which it expressed its consent to be bound by the treaty, whichever is later.

ARTICLE 21 LEGAL EFFECTS OF RESERVATIONS AND OF OBJECTIONS TO RESERVATIONS

1. A reservation established with regard to another party in accordance with articles 19, 20 and 23:

(a) modifies for the reserving State or international organization in its relations with that other party the provisions of the treaty to which the reservation relates to the extent of the reservation; and
(b) modifies those provisions to the same extent for that other party in its relations with the reserving State or international organization.

2. The reservation does not modify the provisions of the treaty for the other parties to the treaty *inter se*.
3. When a State or an international organization objecting to a reservation has not opposed the entry into force of the treaty between itself and the reserving State or organization, the provisions to which the reservation relates do not apply as between the reserving State or organization and the objecting State or organization to the extent of the reservation.

ARTICLE 22 WITHDRAWAL OF RESERVATIONS AND OF OBJECTIONS TO RESERVATIONS

1. Unless the treaty otherwise provides, a reservation may be withdrawn at any time and the consent of a State or of an international organization which has accepted the reservation is not required for its withdrawal.
2. Unless the treaty otherwise provides, an objection to a reservation may be withdrawn at any time.
3. Unless the treaty otherwise provides, or it is otherwise agreed:

(a) the withdrawal of a reservation becomes operative in relation to a contracting State or a contracting organization only when notice of it has been received by that State or that organization;
(b) the withdrawal of an objection to a reservation becomes operative only when notice of it has been received by the State or international organization which formulated the reservation.

ARTICLE 23 PROCEDURE REGARDING RESERVATIONS

1. A reservation, an express acceptance of a reservation and an objection to a reservation must be formulated in writing and communicated to the contracting States and contracting organizations and other States and international organizations entitled to become parties to the treaty.
2. If formulated when signing the treaty subject to ratification, act of formal confirmation, acceptance or approval, a reservation must be formally

confirmed by the reserving State or international organization when expressing its consent to be bound by the treaty. In such a case the reservation shall be considered as having been made on the date of its confirmation.

3. An express acceptance of, or an objection to, a reservation made previously to confirmation of the reservation does not itself require confirmation.

4. The withdrawal of a reservation or of an objection to a reservation must be formulated in writing.

Section 3 Entry into force and provisional application of treaties

ARTICLE 24 ENTRY INTO FORCE

1. A treaty enters into force in such manner and upon such date as it may provide or as the negotiating States and negotiating organizations or, as the case may be, the negotiating organizations may agree.

2. Failing any such provision or agreement, a treaty enters into force as soon as consent to be bound by the treaty has been established for all the negotiating States and negotiating organizations or, as the case may be, all the negotiating organizations.

3. When the consent of a State or of an international organization to be bound by a treaty is established on a date after the treaty has come into force, the treaty enters into force for that State or that organization on that date, unless the treaty otherwise provides.

4. The provisions of a treaty regulating the authentication of its text, the establishment of consent to be bound by the treaty, the manner or date of its entry into force, reservations, the functions of the depositary and other matters arising necessarily before the entry into force of the treaty apply from the time of the adoption of its text.

ARTICLE 25 PROVISIONAL APPLICATION

1. A treaty or a part of a treaty is applied provisionally pending its entry into force if:

    (a) the treaty itself so provides; or
    (b) the negotiating States and negotiating organizations or, as the case may be, the negotiating organizations have in some other manner so agreed.

2. Unless the treaty otherwise provides or the negotiating States and negotiating organizations or, as the case may be, the negotiating organizations have otherwise agreed, the provisional application of a treaty or a part of a treaty with respect to a State or an international organization shall be

terminated if that State or that organization notifies the States and organizations with regard to which the treaty is being applied provisionally of its intention not to become a party to the treaty.

Part III Observance, application and interpretation of treaties

Section 1 Observance of treaties

ARTICLE 26 *PACTA SUNT SERVANDA*

Every treaty in force is binding upon the parties to it and must be performed by them in good faith.

ARTICLE 27 INTERNAL LAW OF STATES, RULES OF INTERNATIONAL ORGANIZATIONS AND OBSERVANCE OF TREATIES

1. A State party to a treaty may not invoke the provisions of its internal law as justification for its failure to perform the treaty.
2. An international organization party to a treaty may not invoke the rules of the organization as justification for its failure to perform the treaty.
3. The rules contained in the preceding paragraphs are without prejudice to article 46.

Section 2 Application of treaties

ARTICLE 28 NON-RETROACTIVITY OF TREATIES

Unless a different intention appears from the treaty or is otherwise established, its provisions do not bind a party in relation to any act or fact which took place or any situation which ceased to exist before the date of the entry into force of the treaty with respect to that party.

ARTICLE 29 TERRITORIAL SCOPE OF TREATIES

Unless a different intention appears from the treaty or is otherwise established, a treaty between one or more States and one or more international organizations is binding upon each State party in respect of its entire territory.

ARTICLE 30 APPLICATION OF SUCCESSIVE TREATIES RELATING TO THE SAME SUBJECT-MATTER

1. The rights and obligations of States and international organizations parties to successive treaties relating to the same subject-matter shall be determined in accordance with the following paragraphs.

2. When a treaty specifies that it is subject to, or that it is not to be considered as incompatible with, an earlier or later treaty, the provisions of that other treaty prevail.

3. When all the parties to the earlier treaty are parties also to the later treaty but the earlier treaty is not terminated or suspended in operation under article 59, the earlier treaty applies only to the extent that its provisions are compatible with those of the later treaty.

4. When the parties to the later treaty do not include all the parties to the earlier one:

(a) as between two parties, each of which is a party to both treaties, the same rule applies as in paragraph 3;
(b) as between a party to both treaties and a party to only one of the treaties, the treaty to which both are parties governs their mutual rights and obligations.

5. Paragraph 4 is without prejudice to article 41, or to any question of the termination or suspension of the operation of a treaty under article 60 or to any question of responsibility which may arise for a State or for an international organization from the conclusion or application of a treaty the provisions of which are incompatible with its obligations towards a State or an organization under another treaty.

6. The preceding paragraphs are without prejudice to the fact that, in the event of a conflict between obligations under the Charter of the United Nations and obligations under a treaty, the obligations under the Charter shall prevail.

Section 3 Interpretation of treaties

ARTICLE 31 GENERAL RULE OF INTERPRETATION

1. A treaty shall be interpreted in good faith in accordance with the ordinary meaning to be given to the terms of the treaty in their context and in the light of its object and purpose.

2. The context for the purpose of the interpretation of a treaty shall comprise, in addition to the text, including its preamble and annexes:

(a) any agreement relating to the treaty which was made between all the parties in connection with the conclusion of the treaty;
(b) any instrument which was made by one or more parties in connection with the conclusion of the treaty and accepted by the other parties as an instrument related to the treaty.

3. There shall be taken into account, together with the context:

(a) any subsequent agreement between the parties regarding the interpretation of the treaty or the application of its provisions;

(b) any subsequent practice in the application of the treaty which establishes the agreement of the parties regarding its interpretation;
(c) any relevant rules of international law applicable in the relations between the parties.

4. A special meaning shall be given to a term if it is established that the parties so intended.

ARTICLE 32 SUPPLEMENTARY MEANS OF INTERPRETATION

Recourse may be had to supplementary means of interpretation, including the preparatory work of the treaty and the circumstances of its conclusion, in order to confirm the meaning resulting from the application of article 31, or to determine the meaning when the interpretation according to article 31:

(a) leaves the meaning ambiguous or obscure; or
(b) leads to a result which is manifestly absurd or unreasonable.

ARTICLE 33 INTERPRETATION OF TREATIES AUTHENTICATED IN TWO OR MORE LANGUAGES

1. When a treaty has been authenticated in two or more languages, the text is equally authoritative in each language, unless the treaty provides or the parties agree that, in case of divergence, a particular text shall prevail.
2. A version of the treaty in a language other than one of those in which the text was authenticated shall be considered an authentic text only if the treaty so provides or the parties so agree.
3. The terms of a treaty are presumed to have the same meaning in each authentic text.
4. Except where a particular text prevails in accordance with paragraph 1, when a comparison of the authentic texts discloses a difference of meaning which the application of articles 31 and 32 does not remove, the meaning which best reconciles the texts, having regard to the object and purpose of the treaty, shall be adopted.

Section 4 Treaties and third States or third organizations

ARTICLE 34 GENERAL RULE REGARDING THIRD STATES AND THIRD ORGANIZATIONS

A treaty does not create either obligations or rights for a third State or a third organization without the consent of that State or that organization.

ARTICLE 35 TREATIES PROVIDING FOR OBLIGATIONS FOR THIRD STATES OR THIRD ORGANIZATIONS

An obligation arises for a third State or a third organization from a provision of a treaty if the parties to the treaty intend the provision to be the means of establishing the obligation and the third State or the third organization expressly accepts that obligation in writing. Acceptance by the third organization of such an obligation shall be governed by the rules of that organization.

ARTICLE 36 TREATIES PROVIDING FOR RIGHTS FOR THIRD STATES OR THIRD ORGANIZATIONS

1. A right arises for a third State from a provision of a treaty if the parties to the treaty intend the provision to accord that right either to the third State, or to a group of States to which it belongs, or to all States, and the third State assents thereto. Its assent shall be presumed so long as the contrary is not indicated, unless the treaty otherwise provides.
2. A right arises for a third organization from a provision of a treaty if the parties to the treaty intend the provision to accord that right either to the third organization, or to a group of international organizations to which it belongs, or to all organizations, and the third organization assents thereto. Its assent shall be governed by the rules of the organization.
3. A State or an international organization exercising a right in accordance with paragraph 1 or 2 shall comply with the conditions for its exercise provided for in the treaty or established in conformity with the treaty.

ARTICLE 37 REVOCATION OR MODIFICATION OF OBLIGATIONS OR RIGHTS OF THIRD STATES OR THIRD ORGANIZATIONS

1. When an obligation has arisen for a third State or a third organization in conformity with article 35, the obligation may be revoked or modified only with the consent of the parties to the treaty and of the third State or the third organization, unless it is established that they had otherwise agreed.
2. When a right has arisen for a third State or a third organization in conformity with article 36, the right may not be revoked or modified by the parties if it is established that the right was intended not to be revocable or subject to modification without the consent of the third State or the third organization.
3. The consent of an international organization party to the treaty or of a third organization, as provided for in the foregoing paragraphs, shall be governed by the rules of that organization.

ARTICLE 38 RULES IN A TREATY BECOMING BINDING ON THIRD STATES OR THIRD ORGANIZATIONS THROUGH INTERNATIONAL CUSTOM

Nothing in articles 34 to 37 precludes a rule set forth in a treaty from becoming binding upon a third State or a third organization as a customary rule of international law, recognized as such.

Part IV Amendment and modification of treaties

ARTICLE 39 GENERAL RULE REGARDING THE AMENDMENT OF TREATIES

1. A treaty may be amended by agreement between the parties. The rules laid down in Part II apply to such an agreement except in so far as the treaty may otherwise provide.
2. The consent of an international organization to an agreement provided for in paragraph 1 shall be governed by the rules of that organization.

ARTICLE 40 AMENDMENT OF MULTILATERAL TREATIES

1. Unless the treaty otherwise provides, the amendment of multilateral treaties shall be governed by the following paragraphs.
2. Any proposal to amend a multilateral treaty as between all the parties must be notified to all the contracting States and all the contracting organizations, each one of which shall have the right to take part in:

(a) the decision as to the action to be taken in regard to such proposal;
(b) the negotiation and conclusion of any agreement for the amendment of the treaty.

3. Every State or international organization entitled to become a party to the treaty shall also be entitled to become a party to the treaty as amended.
4. The amending agreement does not bind any State or international organization already a party to the treaty which does not become a party to the amending agreement; article 30, paragraph 4(b), applies in relation to such State or organization.
5. Any State or international organization which becomes a party to the treaty after the entry into force of the amending agreement shall, failing an expression of a different intention by that State or that organization:

(a) be considered as a party to the treaty as amended; and
(b) be considered as a party to the unamended treaty in relation to any party to the treaty not bound by the amending agreement.

ARTICLE 41 AGREEMENTS TO MODIFY MULTILATERAL TREATIES BETWEEN CERTAIN OF THE PARTIES ONLY

1. Two or more of the parties to a multilateral treaty may conclude an agreement to modify the treaty as between themselves alone if:

(a) the possibility of such a modification is provided for by the treaty; or
(b) the modification in question is not prohibited by the treaty

and:

   (i) does not affect the enjoyment by the other parties of their rights under
the treaty or the performance of their obligations;
   (ii) does not relate to a provision, derogation from which is incompatible
with the effective execution of the object and purpose of the treaty as a
whole.

2. Unless in a case falling under paragraph 1 (a) the treaty otherwise
provides, the parties in question shall notify the other parties of their
intention to conclude the agreement and of the modification to the treaty for
which it provides.

Part V Invalidity, termination and suspension of the operation of treaties

Section 1 General provisions

ARTICLE 42 VALIDITY AND CONTINUANCE IN FORCE OF TREATIES

1. The validity of a treaty or of the consent of a State or an international
organization to be bound by a treaty may be impeached only through the
application of the present Convention.
2. The termination of a treaty, its denunciation or the withdrawal of a party,
may take place only as a result of the application of the provisions of the
treaty or of the present Convention. The same rule applies to suspension of
the operation of a treaty.

ARTICLE 43 OBLIGATIONS IMPOSED BY INTERNATIONAL LAW
INDEPENDENTLY OF A TREATY

The invalidity, termination or denunciation of a treaty, the withdrawal of a
party from it, or the suspension of its operation, as a result of the application
of the present Convention or of the provisions of the treaty, shall not in any
way impair the duty of any State or of any international organization to fulfil
any obligation embodied in the treaty to which that State or that
organization would be subject under international law independently of the
treaty.

ARTICLE 44 SEPARABILITY OF TREATY PROVISIONS

1. A right of a party, provided for in a treaty or arising under article 56, to
denounce, withdraw from or suspend the operation of the treaty may be
exercised only with respect to the whole treaty unless the treaty otherwise
provides or the parties otherwise agree.

2. A ground for invalidating, terminating, withdrawing from or suspending the operation of a treaty recognized in the present Convention may be invoked only with respect to the whole treaty except as provided in the following paragraphs or in article 60.

3. If the ground relates solely to particular clauses, it may be invoked only with respect to those clauses where:

(a) the said clauses are separable from the remainder of the treaty with regard to their application;

(b) it appears from the treaty or is otherwise established that acceptance of those clauses was not an essential basis of the consent of the other party or parties to be bound by the treaty as a whole; and

(c) continued performance of the remainder of the treaty would not be unjust.

4. In cases falling under articles 49 and 50, the State or international organization entitled to invoke the fraud or corruption may do so with respect either to the whole treaty or, subject to paragraph 3, to the particular clauses alone.

5. In cases falling under articles 51, 52 and 53, no separation of the provisions of the treaty is permitted.

ARTICLE 45 LOSS OF A RIGHT TO INVOKE A GROUND FOR INVALIDATING, TERMINATING, WITHDRAWING FROM OR SUSPENDING THE OPERATION OF A TREATY

1. A State may no longer invoke a ground for invalidating, terminating, withdrawing from or suspending the operation of a treaty under articles 46 to 50 or articles 60 and 62 if, after becoming aware of the facts:

(a) it shall have expressly agreed that the treaty is valid or remains in force or continues in operation, as the case may be; or

(b) it must by reason of its conduct be considered as having acquiesced in the validity of the treaty or in its maintenance in force or in operation, as the case may be.

2. An international organization may no longer invoke a ground for invalidating, terminating, withdrawing from or suspending the operation of a treaty under articles 46 to 50 or articles 60 and 62 if, after becoming aware of the facts:

(a) it shall have expressly agreed that the treaty is valid or remains in force or continues in operation, as the case may be; or

(b) it must by reason of the conduct of the competent organ be considered as having renounced the right to invoke that ground.

Section 2 Invalidity of treaties

ARTICLE 46 PROVISIONS OF INTERNAL LAW OF A STATE AND RULES OF AN
INTERNATIONAL ORGANIZATION REGARDING COMPETENCE TO
CONCLUDE TREATIES

1. A State may not invoke the fact that its consent to be bound by a treaty
has been expressed in violation of a provision of its internal law regarding
competence to conclude treaties as invalidating its consent unless that
violation was manifest and concerned a rule of its internal law of
fundamental importance.
2. An international organization may not invoke the fact that its consent to
be bound by a treaty has been expressed in violation of the rules of the
organization regarding competence to conclude treaties as invalidating its
consent unless that violation was manifest and concerned a rule of
fundamental importance.
3. A violation is manifest if it would be objectively evident to any State or
any international organization conducting itself in the matter in accordance
with the normal practice of States and, where appropriate, of international
organizations and in good faith.

ARTICLE 47 SPECIFIC RESTRICTIONS ON AUTHORITY TO EXPRESS THE
CONSENT OF A STATE OR AN INTERNATIONAL ORGANIZATION

If the authority of a representative to express the consent of a State or of an
international organization to be bound by a particular treaty has been made
subject to a specific restriction, his omission to observe that restriction may
not be invoked as invalidating the consent expressed by him unless the
restriction was notified to the negotiating States and negotiating organizations prior to his expressing such consent.

ARTICLE 48 ERROR

1. A State or an international organization may invoke an error in a treaty
as invalidating its consent to be bound by the treaty if the error relates to a
fact or situation which was assumed by that State or that organization to exist
at the time when the treaty was concluded and formed an essential basis of
the consent of that State or that organization to be bound by the treaty.
2. Paragraph 1 shall not apply if the State or international organization in
question contributed by its own conduct to the error or if the circumstances
were such as to put that State or that organization on notice of a possible
error.
3. An error relating only to the wording of the text of a treaty does not affect
its validity; article 80 then applies.

ARTICLE 49 FRAUD

A State or an international organization induced to conclude a treaty by the fraudulent conduct of a negotiating State or a negotiating organization may invoke the fraud as invalidating its consent to be bound by the treaty.

ARTICLE 50 CORRUPTION OF A REPRESENTATIVE OF A STATE OR OF AN INTERNATIONAL ORGANIZATION

A State or an international organization the expression of whose consent to be bound by a treaty has been procured through the corruption of its representative directly or indirectly by a negotiating State or a negotiating organization may invoke such corruption as invalidating its consent to be bound by the treaty.

ARTICLE 51 COERCION OF A REPRESENTATIVE OF A STATE OR OF AN INTERNATIONAL ORGANIZATION

The expression by a State or an international organization of consent to be bound by a treaty which has been procured by the coercion of the representative of that State or that organization through acts or threats directed against him shall be without any legal effect.

ARTICLE 52 COERCION OF A STATE OR OF AN INTERNATIONAL ORGANIZATION BY THE THREAT OR USE OF FORCE

A treaty is void if its conclusion has been procured by the threat or use of force in violation of the principles of international law embodied in the Charter of the United Nations.

ARTICLE 53 TREATIES CONFLICTING WITH A PEREMPTORY NORM OF GENERAL INTERNATIONAL LAW (*JUS COGENS*)

A treaty is void if, at the time of its conclusion, it conflicts with a peremptory norm of general international law. For the purposes of the present Convention, a peremptory norm of general international law is a norm accepted and recognized by the international community of States as a whole as a norm from which no derogation is permitted and which can be modified only by a subsequent norm of general international law having the same character.

Section 3 Termination and suspension of the operation of treaties

ARTICLE 54 TERMINATION OF OR WITHDRAWAL FROM A TREATY UNDER ITS PROVISIONS OR BY CONSENT OF THE PARTIES

The termination of a treaty or the withdrawal of a party may take place:

(a) in conformity with the provisions of the treaty; or
(b) at any time by consent of all the parties after consultation with the contracting States and contracting organizations.

ARTICLE 55 REDUCTION OF THE PARTIES TO A MULTILATERAL TREATY BELOW THE NUMBER NECESSARY FOR ITS ENTRY INTO FORCE

Unless the treaty otherwise provides, a multilateral treaty does not terminate by reason only of the fact that the number of the parties falls below the number necessary for its entry into force.

ARTICLE 56 DENUNCIATION OF OR WITHDRAWAL FROM A TREATY CONTAINING NO PROVISION REGARDING TERMINATION, DENUNCIATION OR WITHDRAWAL

1. A treaty which contains no provision regarding its termination and which does not provide for denunciation or withdrawal is not subject to denunciation or withdrawal unless:

(a) it is established that the parties intended to admit the possibility of denunciation or withdrawal; or
(b) a right of denunciation or withdrawal may be implied by the nature of the treaty.

2. A party shall give not less than twelve months' notice of its intention to denounce or withdraw from a treaty under paragraph 1.

ARTICLE 57 SUSPENSION OF THE OPERATION OF A TREATY UNDER ITS PROVISIONS OR BY CONSENT OF THE PARTIES

The operation of a treaty in regard to all the parties or to a particular party may be suspended:

(a) in conformity with the provisions of the treaty; or
(b) at any time by consent of all the parties after consultation with the contracting States and contracting organizations.

ARTICLE 58 SUSPENSION OF THE OPERATION OF A MULTILATERAL TREATY BY AGREEMENT BETWEEN CERTAIN OF THE PARTIES ONLY

1. Two or more parties to a multilateral treaty may conclude an agreement to suspend the operation of provisions of the treaty, temporarily and as between themselves alone, if:

(a) the possibility of such a suspension is provided for by the treaty; or
(b) the suspension in question is not prohibited by the treaty and:
    (i) does not affect the enjoyment by the other parties of their rights under the treaty or the performance of their obligations;
    (ii) is not incompatible with the object and purpose of the treaty.

2. Unless in a case falling under paragraph 1(a) the treaty otherwise provides, the parties in question shall notify the other parties of their intention to conclude the agreement and of those provisions of the treaty the operation of which they intend to suspend.

ARTICLE 59 TERMINATION OR SUSPENSION OF THE OPERATION OF A
TREATY IMPLIED BY CONCLUSION OF A LATER TREATY

1. A treaty shall be considered as terminated if all the parties to it conclude a later treaty relating to the same subject-matter and:

(a) it appears from the later treaty or is otherwise established that the parties intended that the matter should be governed by that treaty; or
(b) the provisions of the later treaty are so far incompatible with those of the earlier one that the two treaties are not capable of being applied at the same time.

2. The earlier treaty shall be considered as only suspended in operation if it appears from the later treaty or is otherwise established that such was the intention of the parties.

ARTICLE 60 TERMINATION OR SUSPENSION OF THE OPERATION OF A
TREATY AS A CONSEQUENCE OF ITS BREACH

1. A material breach of a bilateral treaty by one of the parties entitles the other to invoke the breach as a ground for terminating the treaty or suspending its operation in whole or in part.
2. A material breach of a multilateral treaty by one of the parties entitles:

(a) the other parties by unanimous agreement to suspend the operation of the treaty in whole or in part or to terminate it either:
    (i) in the relations between themselves and the defaulting State or international organization, or
    (ii) as between all the parties;
(b) a party specially affected by the breach to invoke it as a ground for suspending the operation of the treaty in whole or in part in the relations between itself and the defaulting State or international organization;
(c) any party other than the defaulting State or international organization to invoke the breach as a ground for suspending the operation of the

treaty in whole or in part with respect to itself if the treaty is of such a character that a material breach of its provisions by one party radically changes the position of every party with respect to the further performance of its obligations under the treaty.

3. A material breach of a treaty, for the purposes of this article, consists in:

(a) a repudiation of the treaty not sanctioned by the present Convention; or
(b) the violation of a provision essential to the accomplishment of the object or purpose of the treaty.

4. The foregoing paragraphs are without prejudice to any provision in the treaty applicable in the event of a breach.
5. Paragraphs 1 to 3 do not apply to provisions relating to the protection of the human person contained in treaties of a humanitarian character, in particular to provisions prohibiting any form of reprisals against persons protected by such treaties.

ARTICLE 61 SUPERVENING IMPOSSIBILITY OF PERFORMANCE

1. A party may invoke the impossibility of performing a treaty as a ground for terminating or withdrawing from it if the impossibility results from the permanent disappearance or destruction of an object indispensable for the execution of the treaty. If the impossibility is temporary, it may be invoked only as a ground for suspending the operation of the treaty.
2. Impossibility of performance may not be invoked by a party as a ground for terminating, withdrawing from or suspending the operation of a treaty if the impossibility is the result of a breach by that party either of an obligation under the treaty or of any other international obligation owed to any other party to the treaty.

ARTICLE 62 FUNDAMENTAL CHANGE OF CIRCUMSTANCES

1. A fundamental change of circumstances which has occurred with regard to those existing at the time of the conclusion of a treaty, and which was not foreseen by the parties, may not be invoked as a ground for terminating or withdrawing from the treaty unless:

(a) the existence of those circumstances constituted an essential basis of the consent of the parties to be bound by the treaty; and
(b) the effect of the change is radically to transform the extent of obligations still to be performed under the treaty.

2. A fundamental change of circumstances may not be invoked as a ground for terminating or withdrawing from a treaty between two or more States

and one or more international organizations if the treaty establishes a boundary.

3. A fundamental change of circumstances may not be invoked as a ground for terminating or withdrawing from a treaty if the fundamental change is the result of a breach by the party invoking it either of an obligation under the treaty or of any other international obligation owed to any other party to the treaty.

4. If, under the foregoing paragraphs, a party may invoke a fundamental change of circumstances as a ground for terminating or withdrawing from a treaty it may also invoke the change as a ground for suspending the operation of the treaty.

ARTICLE 63 SEVERANCE OF DIPLOMATIC OR CONSULAR RELATIONS

The severance of diplomatic or consular relations between States parties to a treaty between two or more States and one or more international organizations does not affect the legal relations established between those States by the treaty except in so far as the existence of diplomatic or consular relations is indispensable for the application of the treaty.

ARTICLE 64 EMERGENCE OF A NEW PEREMPTORY NORM OF GENERAL INTERNATIONAL LAW (*JUS COGENS*)

If a new peremptory norm of general international law emerges, any existing treaty which is in conflict with that norm becomes void and terminates.

Section 4 Procedure

ARTICLE 65 PROCEDURE TO BE FOLLOWED WITH RESPECT TO INVALIDITY, TERMINATION, WITHDRAWAL FROM OR SUSPENSION OF THE OPERATION OF A TREATY

1. A party which, under the provisions of the present Convention, invokes either a defect in its consent to be bound by a treaty or a ground for impeaching the validity of a treaty, terminating it, withdrawing from it or suspending its operation, must notify the other parties of its claim. The notification shall indicate the measure proposed to be taken with respect to the treaty and the reasons therefor.

2. If, after the expiry of a period which, except in cases of special urgency, shall not be less than three months after the receipt of the notification, no party has raised any objection, the party making the notification may carry out in the manner provided in article 67 the measure which it has proposed.

3. If, however, objection has been raised by any other party, the parties shall seek a solution through the means indicated in Article 33 of the Charter of the United Nations.

4. The notification or objection made by an international organization shall be governed by the rules of that organization.

5. Nothing in the foregoing paragraphs shall affect the rights or obligations of the parties under any provisions in force binding the parties with regard to the settlement of disputes.

6. Without prejudice to article 45, the fact that a State or an international organization has not previously made the notification prescribed in paragraph 1 shall not prevent it from making such notification in answer to another party claiming performance of the treaty or alleging its violation.

ARTICLE 66 PROCEDURES FOR JUDICIAL SETTLEMENT, ARBITRATION AND CONCILIATION

1. If, under paragraph 3 of article 65, no solution has been reached within a period of twelve months following the date on which the objection was raised, the procedures specified in the following paragraphs shall be followed.

2. With respect to a dispute concerning the application or the interpretation of article 53 or 64;

(a) if a State is a party to the dispute with one or more States, it may, by a written application, submit the dispute to the International Court of Justice for a decision;

(b) if a State is a party to the dispute to which one or more international organizations are parties, the State may, through a Member State of the United Nations if necessary, request the General Assembly or the Security Council or, where appropriate, the competent organ of an international organization which is a party to the dispute and is authorized in accordance with Article 96 of the Charter of the United Nations, to request an advisory opinion of the International Court of Justice in accordance with article 65 of the Statute of the Court;

(c) if the United Nations or an international organization that is authorized in accordance with Article 96 of the Charter of the United Nations is a party to the dispute, it may request an advisory opinion of the International Court of Justice in accordance with article 65 of the Statute of the Court;

(d) if an international organization other than those referred to in sub-paragraph (c) is a party to the dispute, it may, through a Member State of the United Nations, follow the procedure specified in sub-paragraph (b);

(e) the advisory opinion given pursuant to sub-paragraph (b), (c) or (d) shall be accepted as decisive by all the parties to the dispute concerned;

(f) if the request under sub-paragraph (b), (c) or (d) for an advisory opinion of the Court is not granted, any one of the parties to the dispute may, by written notification to the other party or parties, submit it to arbitration in accordance with the provisions of the Annex to the present Convention.

3. The provisions of paragraph 2 apply unless all the parties to a dispute referred to in that paragraph by common consent agree to submit the dispute to an arbitration procedure, including the one specified in the Annex to the present Convention.

4. With respect to a dispute concerning the application or the interpretation of any of the articles in Part V, other than articles 53 and 64, of the present Convention, any one of the parties to the dispute may set in motion the conciliation procedure specified in the Annex to the Conventon by submitting a request to that effect to the Secretary-General of the United Nations.

ARTICLE 67 INSTRUMENTS FOR DECLARING INVALID, TERMINATING, WITHDRAWING FROM OR SUSPENDING THE OPERATION OF A TREATY

1. The notification provided for under article 65, paragraph 1 must be made in writing.

2. Any act declaring invalid, terminating, withdrawing from or suspending the operation of a treaty pursuant to the provisions of the treaty or of paragraphs 2 or 3 of article 65 shall be carried out through an instrument communicated to the other parties. If the instrument emanating from a State is not signed by the Head of State, Head of Government or Minister for Foreign Affairs, the representative of the State communicating it may be called upon to produce full powers. If the instrument emanates from an international organization, the representative of the organization communicating it may be called upon to produce full powers.

ARTICLE 68 REVOCATION OF NOTIFICATIONS AND INSTRUMENTS PROVIDED FOR IN ARTICLES 65 AND 67

A notification or instrument provided for in articles 65 or 67 may be revoked at any time before it takes effect.

Section 5 Consequences of the invalidity, termination or suspension of the operation of a treaty

ARTICLE 69 CONSEQUENCES OF THE INVALIDITY OF A TREATY

1. A treaty the invalidity of which is established under the present Convention is void. The provisions of a void treaty have no legal force.

2. If acts have nevertheless been performed in reliance on such a treaty:

(a) each party may require any other party to establish as far as possible in their mutual relations the position that would have existed if the acts had not been performed;

(b) acts performed in good faith before the invalidity was invoked are not rendered unlawful by reason only of the invalidity of the treaty.

3. In cases falling under articles 49, 50, 51 or 52, paragraph 2 does not apply with respect to the party to which the fraud, the act of corruption or the coercion is imputable.

4. In the case of the invalidity of the consent of a particular State or a particular international organization to be bound by a multilateral treaty, the foregoing rules apply in the relations between that State or that organization and the parties to the treaty.

ARTICLE 70 CONSEQUENCES OF THE TERMINATION OF A TREATY

1. Unless the treaty otherwise provides or the parties otherwise agree, the termination of a treaty under its provisions or in accordance with the present Convention:

(a) releases the parties from any obligation further to perform the treaty;
(b) does not affect any right, obligation or legal situation of the parties created through the execution of the treaty prior to its termination.

2. If a State or an international organization denounces or withdraws from a multilateral treaty, paragraph 1 applies in the relations between that State or that organization and each of the other parties to the treaty from the date when such denunciation or withdrawal takes effect.

ARTICLE 71 CONSEQUENCES OF THE INVALIDITY OF A TREATY WHICH CONFLICTS WITH A PEREMPTORY NORM OF GENERAL INTERNATIONAL LAW

1. In the case of a treaty which is void under article 53 the parties shall:

(a) eliminate as far as possible the consequences of any act performed in reliance on any provision which conflicts with the peremptory norm of general international law; and
(b) bring their mutual relations into conformity with the peremptory norm of general international law.

2. In the case of a treaty which becomes void and terminates under article 64, the termination of the treaty:

(a) releases the parties from any obligation further to perform the treaty;
(b) does not affect any right, obligation or legal situation of the parties created through the execution of the treaty prior to its termination; provided that those rights, obligations or situations may thereafter be

maintained only to the extent that their maintenance is not in itself in conflict with the new peremptory norm of general international law.

ARTICLE 72 CONSEQUENCES OF THE SUSPENSION OF THE OPERATION OF A TREATY

1. Unless the treaty otherwise provides or the parties otherwise agree, the suspension of the operation of a treaty under its provisions or in accordance with the present Convention:

(a) releases the parties between which the operation of the treaty is suspended from the obligation to perform the treaty in their mutual relations during the period of the suspension;
(b) does not otherwise affect the legal relations between the parties established by the treaty.

2. During the period of the suspension the parties shall refrain from acts tending to obstruct the resumption of the operation of the treaty.

Part VI Miscellaneous provisions

ARTICLE 73 RELATIONSHIP TO THE VIENNA CONVENTION ON THE LAW OF TREATIES

As between States parties to the Vienna Convention on the Law of Treaties of 1969, the relations of those States under a treaty between two or more States and one or more international organizations shall be governed by that Convention.

ARTICLE 74 QUESTIONS NOT PREJUDGED BY THE PRESENT CONVENTION

1. The provisions of the present Convention shall not prejudge any question that may arise in regard to a treaty between one or more States and one or more international organizations from a succession of States or from the international responsibility of a State or from the outbreak of hostilities between States.
2. The provisions of the present Convention shall not prejudge any question that may arise in regard to a treaty from the international responsibility of an international organization, from the termination of the existence of the organization or from the termination of participation by a State in the membership of the organization.
3. The provision of the present Convention shall not prejudge any question that may arise in regard to the establishment of obligations and rights for

States members of an international organization under a treaty to which that
organization is a party.

ARTICLE 75 DIPLOMATIC AND CONSULAR RELATIONS AND THE
CONCLUSION OF TREATIES

The severance or absence of diplomatic or consular relations between two or
more States does not prevent the conclusion of treaties between two or more
of those States and one or more international organizations. The conclusion
of such a treaty does not in itself affect the situation in regard to diplomatic
or consular relations.

ARTICLE 76 CASE OF AN AGGRESSOR STATE

The provisions of the present Convention are without prejudice to any
obligation in relation to a treaty between one or more States and one or
more international organizations which may arise for an aggressor State in
consequence of measures taken in conformity with the Charter of the United
Nations with reference to that State's aggression.

Part VII Depositaries, notifications, corrections and registration

ARTICLE 77 DEPOSITARIES OF TREATIES

1. The designation of the depositary of a treaty may be made by the
negotiating States and negotiating organizations or, as the case may be, the
negotiating organizations, either in the treaty itself or in some other manner.
The depositary may be one or more States, an international organization or
the chief administrative officer of the organization.
2. The functions of the depositary of a treaty are international in character
and the depositary is under an obligation to act impartially in their
performance. In particular, the fact that a treaty has not entered into force
between certain of the parties or that a difference has appeared between a
State or an international organization and a depositary with regard to the
performance of the latter's functions shall not affect that obligation.

ARTICLE 78 FUNCTIONS OF DEPOSITARIES

1. The functions of a depositary, unless otherwise provided in the treaty or
agreed by the contracting States and contracting organizations or, as the
case may be, by the contracting organizations, comprise in particular:

  (a) keeping custody of the original text of the treaty and of any full
  powers delivered to the depositary;

(b) preparing certified copies of the original text and preparing any further text of the treaty in such additional languages as may be required by the treaty and transmitting them to the parties and to the States and international organizations entitled to become parties to the treaty;

(c) receiving any signatures to the treaty and receiving and keeping custody of any instruments, notifications and communications relating to it;

(d) examining whether the signature or any instrument, notification or communication relating to the treaty is in due and proper form and, if need be, bringing the matter to the attention of the State or international organization in question;

(e) informing the parties and the States and international organizations entitled to become parties to the treaty of acts, notifications and communications relating to the treaty;

(f) informing the States and international organizations entitled to become parties to the treaty when the number of signatures or of instruments of ratification, instruments relating to an act of formal confirmation, or of instruments of acceptance, approval or accession required for the entry into force of the treaty has been received or deposited;

(g) registering the treaty with the Secretariat of the United Nations;

(h) performing the functions specified in other provisions of the present Convention.

2. In the event of any difference appearing between a State or an international organization and the depositary as to the performance of the latter's functions, the depositary shall bring the question to the attention of:

(a) the signatory States and organizations and the contracting States and contracting organizations; or

(b) where appropriate, the competent organ of the international organization concerned.

ARTICLE 79 NOTIFICATION AND COMMUNICATIONS

Except as the treaty or the present Convention otherwise provide, any notification or communication to be made by any State or any international organization under the present Convention shall:

(a) if there is no depositary, be transmitted direct to the States and organizations for which it is intended, or if there is a depositary, to the latter;

(b) be considered as having been made by the State or organization in question only upon its receipt by the State or organization to which it was transmitted or, as the case may be, upon its receipt by the depositary;

(c) if transmitted to a depositary, be considered as received by the State or organization for which it was intended only when the latter State or organization has been informed by the depositary in accordance with article 78, paragraph 1(e).

ARTICLE 80 CORRECTION OF ERRORS IN TEXTS OR IN CERTIFIED COPIES OF TREATIES

1. Where, after the authentication of the text of a treaty, the signatory States and international organizations and the contracting States and contracting organizations are agreed that it contains an error, the error shall, unless those States and organizations decide upon some other means of correction, be corrected:

(a) by having the appropriate correction made in the text and causing the correction to be initialled by duly authorized representatives;
(b) by executing or exchanging an instrument or instruments setting out the correction which it has been agreed to make; or
(c) by executing a corrected text of the whole treaty by the same procedure as in the case of the original text.

2. Where the treaty is one for which there is a depositary, the latter shall notify the signatory States and international organizations and the contracting States and contracting organizations of the error and of the proposal to correct it and shall specify an appropriate time-limit within which objection to the proposed correction may be raised. If, on the expiry of the time-limit:

(a) no objection has been raised, the depositary shall make and initial the correction in the text and shall execute a *procès-verbal* of the rectification of the text and communicate a copy of it to the parties and to the States and organizations entitled to become parties to the treaty;
(b) an objection has been raised, the depositary shall communicate the objection to the signatory States and organizations and to the contracting States and contracting organizations.

3. The rules in paragraphs 1 and 2 apply also where the text has been authenticated in two or more languages and it appears that there is a lack of concordance which the signatory States and international organizations and the contracting States and contracting organizations agree should be corrected.
4. The corrected text replaces the defective text *ab initio,* unless the signatory States and international organizations and the contracting States and contracting organizations otherwise decide.
5. The correction of the text of a treaty that has been registered shall be notified to the Secretariat of the United Nations.

6. Where an error is discovered in a certified copy of a treaty, the depositary shall execute a *procès-verbal* specifying the rectification and communicate a copy of it to the signatory States and international organizations and to the contracting States and contracting organizations.

ARTICLE 81 REGISTRATION AND PUBLICATION OF TREATIES

1. Treaties shall, after their entry into force, be transmitted to the Secretariat of the United Nations for registration or filing and recording, as the case may be, and for publication.
2. The designation of a depositary shall constitute authorization for it to perform the acts specified in the preceding paragraph.

Part VIII Final provisions

ARTICLE 82 SIGNATURE

The present Convention shall be open for signature until 31 December 1986 at the Federal Ministry for Foreign Affairs of the Republic of Austria, and subsequently, until 30 June 1987, at United Nations Headquarters, New York by:

(a) all States;
(b) Namibia, represented by the United Nations Council for Namibia;
(c) international organizations invited to participate in the United Nations Conference on the Law of Treaties between States and International Organizations or between International Organizations.

ARTICLE 83 RATIFICATION OR ACT OF FORMAL CONFIRMATION

The present Convention is subject to ratification by States and by Namibia, represented by the United Nations Council for Namibia, and to acts of formal confirmation by international organizations. The instruments of ratification and those relating to acts of formal confirmation shall be deposited with the Secretary-General of the United Nations.

ARTICLE 84 ACCESSION

1. The present Convention shall remain open for accession by any State, by Namibia, represented by the United Nations Council for Namibia, and by any international organization which has the capacity to conclude treaties.
2. An instrument of accession of an international organization shall contain a declaration that it has the capacity to conclude treaties.

3. The instruments of accession shall be deposited with the Secretary-General of the United Nations.

ARTICLE 85 ENTRY INTO FORCE

1. The present Convention shall enter into force on the thirtieth day following the date of deposit of the thirty-fifth instrument of ratification or accession by States or by Namibia, represented by the United Nations Council for Namibia.
2. For each State or for Namibia, represented by the United Nations Council for Namibia, ratifying or acceding to the Convention after the condition specified in paragraph 1 has been fulfilled, the Convention shall enter into force on the thirtieth day after deposit by such State or by Namibia of its instrument of ratification or accession.
3. For each international organization depositing an instrument relating to an act of formal confirmation or an instrument of accession, the Convention shall enter into force on the thirtieth day after such deposit, or at the date the Convention enters into force pursuant to paragraph 1, whichever is later.

ARTICLE 86 AUTHENTIC TEXTS

The original of the present Convention, of which the Arabic, Chinese, English, French, Russian and Spanish texts are equally authentic, shall be deposited with the Secretary-General of the United Nations.
   IN WITNESS WHEREOF the undersigned Plenipotentiaries, being duly authorized by their respective Governments, and duly authorized representatives of the United Nations Council for Namibia and of international organizations have signed the present Convention.
   DONE AT VIENNA this twenty-first day of March one thousand nine hundred and eighty-six.

Annex
Arbitration and conciliation procedures established in application of article 66

I Establishment of the Arbitral Tribunal or Conciliation Commission

1. A list consisting of qualified jurists, from which the parties to a dispute may choose the persons who are to constitute an arbitral tribunal or, as the case may be, a conciliation commission, shall be drawn up and maintained by the Secretary-General of the United Nations. To this end, every State which is a Member of the United Nations and every party to the present Convention shall be invited to nominate two persons, and the names of the persons so nominated shall constitute the list, a copy of which shall be transmitted to the President of the International Court of Justice. The term

of office of a person on the list, including that of any person nominated to fill a casual vacancy, shall be five years and may be renewed. A person whose term expires shall continue to fulfil any function for which he shall have been chosen under the following paragraphs.

2. When notification has been made under article 66, paragraph 2, subparagraph (f), or agreement on the procedure in the present Annex has been reached under paragraph 3, the dispute shall be brought before an arbitral tribunal. When a request has been made to the Secretary-General under article 66, paragraph 4, the Secretary-General shall bring the dispute before a conciliation commission. Both the arbitral tribunal and the conciliation commission shall be constituted as follows:

The States, international organizations or, as the case may be, the States and organizations which constitute one of the parties to the dispute shall appoint by common consent:

(a) one arbitrator or, as the case may be, one conciliator, who may or may not be chosen from the list referred to in paragraph 1; and

(b) one arbitrator or, as the case may be, one conciliator, who shall be chosen from among those included in the list and shall not be of the nationality of any of the States or nominated by any of the organizations which constitute that party to the dispute, provided that a dispute between two international organizations is not considered by nationals of one and the same State.

The States, international organizations or, as the case may be, the States and organizations which constitute the other party to the dispute shall appoint two arbitrators or, as the case may be, two conciliators, in the same way. The four persons chosen by the parties shall be appointed within sixty days following the date on which the other party to the dispute receives notification under article 66, paragraph 2, sub-paragraph (f), or on which the agreement on the procedure in the present Annex under paragraph 3 is reached, or on which the Secretary-General receives the request for conciliation.

The four persons so chosen shall, within sixty days following the date of the last of their own appointments, appoint from the list a fifth arbitrator or, as the case may be, conciliator, who shall be chairman.

If the appointment of the chairman, or any of the arbitrators or, as the case may be, conciliators, has not been made within the period prescribed above for such appointment, it shall be made by the Secretary-General of the United Nations within sixty days following the expiry of that period. The appointment of the chairman may be made by the Secretary-General either from the list or from the membership of the International Law Commission. Any of the periods within which appointments must be made may be extended by agreement between the parties to the dispute. If the United Nations is a party or is included in one of the parties to the dispute, the Secretary-General shall transmit the above-mentioned request to the President of the International Court of Justice, who shall perform the functions conferred upon the Secretary-General under this sub-paragraph.

Any vacancy shall be filled in the manner prescribed for the initial appointment.

The appointment of arbitrators or conciliators by an international organization provided for in paragraphs 1 and 2 shall be governed by the rules of that organization.

II Functioning of the Arbitral Tribunal

3. Unless the parties to the dispute otherwise agree, the Arbitral Tribunal shall decide its own procedure, assuring to each party to the dispute a full opportunity to be heard and to present its case.
4. The Arbitral Tribunal, with the consent of the parties to the dispute, may invite any interested State or international organization to submit to it its views orally or in writing.
5. Decisions of the Arbitral Tribunal shall be adopted by a majority vote of the members. In the event of an equality of votes, the vote of the Chairman shall be decisive.
6. When one of the parties to the dispute does not appear before the Tribunal or fails to defend its case, the other party may request the Tribunal to continue the proceedings and to make its award. Before making its award, the Tribunal must satisfy itself not only that it has jurisdiction over the dispute but also that the claim is well founded in fact and law.
7. The award of the Arbitral Tribunal shall be confined to the subject-matter of the dispute and state the reasons on which it is based. Any member of the Tribunal may attach a separate or dissenting opinion to the award.
8. The award shall be final and without appeal. It shall be complied with by all parties to the dispute.
9. The Secretary-General shall provide the Tribunal with such assistance and facilities as it may require. The expenses of the Tribunal shall be borne by the United Nations.

III Functioning of the Conciliation Commission

10. The Conciliation Commission shall decide its own procedure. The Commission, with the consent of the parties to the dispute, may invite any party to the treaty to submit to it its views orally or in writing. Decisions and recommendations of the Commission shall be made by a majority vote of the five members.
11. The Commission may draw the attention of the parties to the dispute to any measures which might facilitate an amicable settlement.
12. The Commission shall hear the parties, examine the claims and objections, and make proposals to the parties with a view to reaching an amicable settlement of the dispute.

13. The Commission shall report within twelve months of its constitution. Its report shall be deposited with the Secretary-General and transmitted to the parties to the dispute. The report of the Commission, including any conclusions stated therein regarding the facts or questions of law, shall not be binding upon the parties and it shall have no other character than that of recommendations submitted for the consideration of the parties in order to facilitate an amicable settlement of the dispute.

14. The Secretary-General shall provide the Commission with such assistance and facilities as it may require. The expenses of the Commission shall be borne by the United Nations.

Index

Note: All references are to paragraph numbers. References in **bold** relate to a detailed discussion of a topic. References followed by an asterisk relate to notes.